Rebel!

REBEL!

A Biography of
Thomas Paine

SAMUEL EDWARDS

NEW ENGLISH LIBRARY
TIMES MIRROR

First published in the United States of America
by Praeger Publishers, Inc. of New York.

First published in Great Britain by New English Library,
Barnard's Inn, Holborn, London, E.C.1. in 1974.

Reproduced and printed by photolithography and bound in
Great Britain at The Pitman Press, Bath

45002185 8

For Milton S. Mayer

Contents

*It is dangerous in any government to say to a nation,
Thou shalt not read.* – THOMAS PAINE

Rebel!

1

Corset-Maker
Extraordinary

The eighteenth-century England in which Thomas Paine was born and grew to manhood was a land of contrasts, contradictions, and ironies. There was a tradition of personal freedom, but the poor, who were everywhere, were less free than the few who were wealthy and powerful; and a judiciary that was less than perfect made certain that the lower classes remembered where they belonged and did not try to reach too high. Politically, socially and economically Great Britain was an oligarchy. Foreigners from Germany, the Hanoverian Georges, sat on the throne, but they cooperated with the wealthy nobles who were the nation's largest landowners, and it was an unwritten agreement that nothing would be allowed to disturb the *status quo*.

Britain was going through a time of dynamic expansion that brought large sections of the earth's surface, both populated and unpopulated, under her flag, and through trade added to her wealth. She acquired large portions of North America and through the East India Company gained domination of the sub-continent of India. Her fleet, which became larger and larger to protect her merchantmen, was already the most powerful in the world. She demonstrated, in a series of wars with France, that she was the strongest nation on the globe.

Her politics, both in the House of Lords and the House of Commons, was dominated by members of the all-powerful Whig party. Their few opponents, although articulate, lacked muscle, but in times of crisis they were no less chauvinistic.

The eighteenth century was the Age of Enlightenment, the Age of Reason, but few men were reasonable and fewer were en-lightened. A handful of intellectuals, most of them philosophers, authors, and scientists, hacked new paths through the morass of superstition and rigid mores. As yet, however, few people en-joyed the benefits of their efforts. England was a nation of farmers, tradesmen, and laborers, ruled by men of enormous power and great wealth. The caste system had existed for centuries, and it was difficult, usually impossible, for a man to rise above the class into which he had been born.

The rural yeomanry into which Thomas Paine was born made up the solid base on which English society was built. There were few who were lower on the ladder, and his chance of moving upward, like that of other members of his class, was virtually nonexistent. Yet he became one of the most influential and re-nowned men of his time. In his own day he left an indelible mark on America, Great Britain, and France, and since then his ideas have spread and have been accepted throughout the civilized world.

This is the story of that extraordinary man.

Even in his own time Thomas Paine was regarded throughout the Western world as unique, and so complex that neither friend nor foe could classify him. Was he a true humanist, dedicated to the cause of freedom; or was he merely an iconoclast who advocated revolution for its own sake? Was he a deist or an atheist? Was he a philosopher whose thought was a natural extension of the work of John Locke, or was he an intellectual charlatan? Men could agree only that his pen was mighty beyond compare and that his eccentricities fascinated, amused, and repelled them.

Certainly he was well acquainted with the great men of the age in three nations. In the new United States, eternally in his debt, he was a friend of Benjamin Franklin and Thomas Jefferson, of John and Samuel Adams and the Lees of Virginia, of George Washington, James Monroe, and Benjamin Rush. In England he was the friend of Edmund Burke, Oliver Goldsmith, Thomas Erskine, and Richard Brinsley Sheridan, and the enemy of William Pitt the Younger. In Paris, where he joined the party of the Girondists during the French Revolution, he came to know men of every political and philosophical persuasion, from the marquis de Lafayette, Condorcet, and Vergennes to Robespierre, Danton, and Marat. At one time or another many admired him, some loved him, others loathed him, and all were astonished by him. His contemporaries, no matter what their own persuasions, were in agreement: Alternately stunned and bewildered by him, they swore that he defied description.

Nothing in Thomas Paine's background made it likely that he would become what the eighteenth century liked to call an 'Original Man'. His parents, Joseph and Frances Cocke Paine (who sometimes spelled their name Pain) were poor, obscure gentlefolk who lived in the little English town of Thetford, not far from Norwich in Norfolk County. A diligent search for distinguished ancestors reveals only a handful. One Sir Joseph Paine was mayor of Norwich in the seventeenth century, and his statue still stands in Saint Thomas Church there. One Francis Cocke, who also lived in the seventeenth century, was chief justice of the county.

Joseph Paine was a farmer and, as a young man, a member of the Society of Friends. According to a story that cannot be verified, the Quakers expelled him in 1734 because a priest of the Church of England performed the ceremony that united him and his wife in that year. Little is known about Joseph Paine other than that his neighbors considered him 'a reputable citizen, and though poor, an honest man'. In 1737 he was made a freeman of Thetford, which gave him the right to use the town common for pasturage.

His wife, Frances Cocke Paine, 'a woman of sour temper and an eccentric character', was avoided by all who knew her well, and no one was more assiduous in this regard than her husband. She was homely as well as a scold, and it can only be assumed that Joseph Paine married her because her father offered him a handsome dowry. He maintained a discreet and gentlemanly silence on the matter.

Their renowned son's attitude toward them speaks for itself. In his many published works Thomas Paine makes a number of references to his father, all of them indicating affection and filial respect, but he says nothing about his mother. Only in his personal correspondence does he write about her at all, and always with a humorous sense of irony. In a letter to Benjamin Franklin he called her 'a virago who, had she lived two hundred years ago, might have served as the model for Shakespeare's *Shrew*'. And when commenting to James Monroe about a woman whom he found both unpleasant and objectionable, he wrote, 'It is my misfortune that she reminds me of my mother'.

The early years of Joseph Paine's marriage were difficult. His farm, which had earned him only a marginal living, still did not prosper, so he rented it to a tenant and moved into Thetford, buying a little house on Bridge Street. In 1736 he found employment as a corset-maker, which remained his occupation for most of his life. The couple's first child, a son, was born on January 29, 1737, and was called Thomas.

An early writer on Thomas Paine, writing in 1791 while his subject was still very much alive, went to great lengths to illustrate his thesis that Paine had been a religious nonconformist from infancy. He wrote:

> It arose probably from the tenets of the father, and from the eccentricity of the mother, that our author was never baptized, though he was privately named; and never received, like true Christians, into the bosom of any church, though he was indeed confirmed by the bishop of Norwich. This last circumstance was owing to the orthodox zeal of Mistress Cocke, his aunt, a woman of such goodness, that though she lived on a small annuity, she imparted much of this little to his mother.

Reason, which became Paine's private god, indicates that this stretched the truth. Elizabeth Paine, a year and a half younger than her brother, was duly baptized, and it is unlikely that the ceremony would have been performed on her behalf but omitted in her brother's earliest days. Even more important, the boy could not have been confirmed had he not been baptized; the Church of England is firm and permits no exceptions. That the adult Thomas Paine elected to abandon the religious tenets he had been taught as a child is another matter.

Thetford, with a population in 1740 of about 1,500 persons, was a sleepy market town with a few small cottage industries, a tranquil community in which a boy could grow. The residents enjoyed few cultural advantages, and, from all accounts, they didn't miss what they didn't know. Aside from the Anglican church and the large homes of a few wealthy people, there were no buildings of consequence in the town. A child could wander through the fields and nearby woods, pick berries, apples, and pears, set traps for small animals, fish in any of several small streams, and wrestle with his peers in dusty High Street. He could also enjoy the benefits of a good education. The Thetford Grammar School, founded in 1566, was one of the largest in the county. It boasted a library of several hundred volumes, and its teachers were men of talent rather than the usual social misfits of the period. The town was proud of the fact that a number of prominent authors had attended the school, among them Sir Joseph Williamson, who in 1666 had founded London's first newspaper, the *Gazette*, and essayist John Brame, whom posterity has forgotten. Through happenstance the school may have been one of the best in England in the middle of the eighteenth century, owing, at least in part, to its own traditions. Parents were required to pay a small fee each year for the education of their sons, and ambitious teachers accepted positions there because such posts might lead to future employment at more prestigious institutions. Paine, who attended the school from the age of about seven until the age of thirteen, followed the usual curriculum: English, Latin, Greek, and mathematics were studied, and classical literature was stressed. Most important, the school authorities had long enjoyed a tradition of encouraging learning for its own sake, which was unusual at a time when most English schools taught small boys by rote.

The most important influence in the molding of the boy's mind was his father. Joseph Paine was not allowed to attend meetings of the Society of Friends, but he remained a Quaker until he died in 1786 at the age of 78. He sent his son to the meetinghouse in Thetford from the age of six, and in his writings Thomas Paine repeatedly mentions the impact of Quaker teachings on his young mind.

His mother's influence was negative. She sometimes imagined insults and refused to speak to him for days at a time; when in a talkative mood, she was even more unpleasant, criticizing him endlessly. She was undemonstrative, too, rarely showing affection for her children, and they soon learned to have little to do with

15

her. But it was impossible for them to avoid her sister, their 'good aunt', and Miss Cocke, who visited the house daily, delivered long, gloomy sermons warning the youngsters that the world and its inhabitants were evil.

Perhaps the most significant fact to be culled from Thomas Paine's childhood is that it was joyless. No anecdotes illuminate his early years. He applied himself to his studies, spending at least eight hours each week at the Quaker meetinghouse and listening dutifully to his aunt's lectures. His mother ignored him, and his only playmate was his conscientious but less talented sister.

His earliest known work, an epitaph written at the age of eight when he buried a pet crow in a backyard garden plot, illustrates his attitude as well as his facility with a pen:

> Here lies the body of John Crow,
> Who once was high, but now is low;
> Ye brother Crows, take warning all,
> For as you rise, so must you fall.

Paine struggled all his life to overcome the burdens imposed on him in his boyhood, and at no time could he be called light-hearted. He did manage to gain a better perspective, however, and in his middle age he was able to write, 'Though I reverence their philosophy, I cannot help smiling at the conceit, that if the taste of a Quaker had been consulted at the creation, what a silent and drab-colored creation it would have been! Not a flower would have blossomed its gaieties, nor a bird been permitted to sing'.

Paine's education was supervised by the headmaster of the school, the Reverend William Knowler, who found him an exceptional student in both mathematics and poetry, and who was perceptive enough to find this combination unusual. Unlike his classmates, however, the boy avoided Latin, giving his reasons many years later in his one detailed reference to his early education:

My parents were not able to give me a shilling, beyond what they gave me in education; and to do even this they distressed themselves.

My father being of the Quaker profession, it was my good fortune to have an exceedingly good moral education, and a tolerable stock of useful learning. Though I went to grammar school . . . , I did not learn Latin, not only because I had no inclination to learn languages, but because of the objection the Quakers have against the books in which the language is taught. But this did not prevent me from being acquainted with the subjects of all the Latin books used in the school. The natural bent of my mind was to science. I had some turn, and I believe some talent, for poetry; but this I rather repressed than encouraged, as leading too much into the field of imagination.

I happened, when a schoolboy, to pick up a pleasing natural history of Virginia, and my inclination from that day of seeing the western side of the Atlantic never left me.

It was impossible for the ungainly, poverty-stricken child to conceal his lively imagination from his teacher, and Reverend Knowler, who realized that the boy's mind was unusual, quietly encouraged him. The clergyman frequently invited Thomas to his home for dinner, and on these occasions Knowler regaled his young guest with tales of his own adventures as a chaplain stationed on board a Royal Navy man-of-war. These tales left the boy with a thirst for romantic adventures of his own.

It appeared likely, however, that this thirst would be satisfied only in his daydreams. His family could not afford to continue his education after he completed his studies at the grammar school, and at the age of thirteen he became an apprentice in his father's little corset-making business. He accepted his fate, probably because it did not occur to him that there might be any alternative, and by the time he was fifteen, in 1752, he was promoted to journeyman status. In all, Thomas spent almost five years, first as an apprentice and then as a journeyman, in his father's business; he said later that they were the five most miserable years of his life.

It seemed to young Paine that he would spend his entire life as a stay-maker. But his family's poverty could not curb his imagination, and he continued to read constantly, borrowing books by the armload from the obliging Reverend Knowler. The clergyman, convinced that the youth's future lay in some field more esoteric than the manufacture of corsets, saw to it that he received the equivalent of secondary school education and more. Paine could not read the classics in the original, it was true, but eighteenth-century scholars were writing first-rate translations, and he became thoroughly familiar with Homer, Aristotle, Plato, and Seneca.

The boy's restlessness increased, and when he was sixteen he went for a visit to London, where he impulsively signed as an apprentice seaman on board a privateer, the *Terrible*, that was

17

being sent by her owners to prey on French trade ships in the New World. Fortunately for Thomas, however, his father followed him to London and dragged him home before the ship sailed. Less than two weeks later, the *Terrible* sank in an Atlantic storm and all hands perished.

Young Paine's yearning for an active life went unrequited. In 1756, however, Britain, in competition with France for domination of the New World, declared war on her rival, thus giving the youth the opportunity he sought. Again he went off to London, and this time his quest was successful. He joined the crew of another privateer, the *King of Prussia*, as an apprentice seaman, and a few days later sailed off to adventure.

Little is known about the year that Paine spent at sea other than that he soon had his fill of life as a sailor, as he himself would later write. The *King of Prussia* sailed for a year, and he was compelled to serve until she returned to England. During the voyage a number of French merchant vessels were captured and their cargoes confiscated, as was the custom, and on three occasions Captain William Mendez noted in his log that apprentice seaman Paine took an active part in the fighting that preceded the surrender of the French. Twice he was a member of boarding parties and distinguished himself by being reckless to the point of foolhardiness. Presumably he forgot his Quaker precepts when, cutlass in hand, he climbed onto the deck of a French brig.

The privateer spent a part of her year at sea in the Caribbean, on the lookout for enemy vessels sailing between the French West Indies and Europe. On occasion Captain Mendez put into British or neutral ports for supplies and to give his crew shore leave. It was on one of these occasions, in Port Royal, Jamaica, that Paine was initiated into the mysteries of sex by a blonde prostitute. Thereafter he frequently accompanied other sailors on similar expeditions, but he quickly established his own standards and would not deviate from them. His shipmates teased him because he would bed only blondes, who were difficult to find in Caribbean brothels, and when none were available, he avoided sex. It may be worthy of note that his mother was a brunette.

The *King of Prussia* returned to England in 1757, when Paine was twenty, and he did not sign on for another voyage. Instead he sought employment in London in the one trade he knew, corset-making. Certainly he had no intention of returning to semi-rural life in Norfolk. He soon found a position with a stay-maker named Morris, in Hanover Street, and worked in the Morris shop for almost two years.

Paine was exceptionally tall, towering above most of his contemporaries. His shoulders were broad, and, although he walked with a sloping gait that made him appear as though he would lose his balance at any moment, his hands were strong and his arms sinewy, as befitted a man who bent and shaped whalebone into stays. His hair was sandy; his face, long and lean; and the expression in his pale eyes was somber.

There had been ample time for him to think about his future during his year at sea, and he knew he wanted to become something more than a corset-maker. 'As soon as I was able,' Paine wrote many years later, 'I purchased a pair of globes, and attended the philosophical lectures of Martin and Ferguson, and became afterwards acquainted with Dr Bevis, of the society called the Royal Society, then living in the Temple, and an excellent astronomer.' In this laconic statement he reveals that he was continuing his education on his own initiative, and his choice of teachers indicates the direction in which he was moving. Adam Ferguson, the Scottish philosopher and historian, who was a friend and disciple of David Hume's, was spending a few months in London before returning to Edinburgh, where he became a professor of moral philosophy. Influenced by Montesquieu as well as Hume, Ferguson was an impassioned advocate of civil liberty and was regarded as something of a radical because he believed that Great Britain's colonial subjects in North America were endowed with the same 'natural rights' enjoyed by all Englishmen. James Hale Martin was a lawyer who, far ahead of his time, urged the abolition of child labor. He was particularly incensed by the execution of minors – including children as young as nine and ten years – for stealing bread, and he campaigned vigorously against such practices. John Bevis, although known principally as an astronomer, became active in Whig politics and during the American Revolution was an advocate of the colonists' cause. Although nothing specific is known of his attitudes during the years he and Paine were acquainted, it may be presumed that he had already developed his stand in favor of humanism and civil liberty.

For more than two years in London Paine pursued a higher education under the influence of teachers who shaped the principles that he would advocate in his maturity. Although he did not yet know what profession he wanted to enter, he was one of very few craftsmen attending lectures at the Royal Society. But he still had a living to earn, and in February, 1759, for reasons unknown, his employment with Morris was terminated. Paine went off to Dover, perhaps because he had learned that a position was open there, and found work with a corset-maker named Grace. That place did not suit him, however, and in April he went to the town of Sandwich, in Kent, where he opened his own shop as a master corset-maker. He was now twenty-two years old and as yet had done nothing to distinguish himself.

2

In the King's Service, More or Less

Some of Thomas Paine's early biographers were inclined to believe that during his sojourn in Sandwich he developed a desire to become a clergyman. They further claim, without offering substantiation, that he gathered a small congregation in his living quarters and there delivered a series of sermons, either as an independent or as a Methodist. It is far more certain that he met and fell in love with Mary Lambert, who was a year his junior. She had blonde hair, and, although no portraits were ever made of her, Paine himself has written of her that she was beautiful. An orphan, she worked as a servingmaid in the home of Mrs Richard Solly, the wife of a draper. Mary returned the earnest young man's affection, and they were married in an Anglican ceremony on September 27, 1759, by the Reverend William Bunce, rector of Saint Peter's Church in Sandwich.

The good ladies of Sandwich were slow to buy the wares of the young corset-maker, and after a short time Paine and his bride moved to Margate. There, although business was still slow and their financial position precarious, they lived for the next year and were ecstatically happy, as he indicated many years later to Thomas Jefferson.

Late in 1760 Mary Paine fell ill and died; no details of her ailment are known. The tragedy left her husband shattered, and for the rest of his life he grieved for her, claiming that their relationship had been perfect. It is impossible to determine whether their marriage was truly idyllic, but Paine convinced himself that Mary had been a paragon, and that belief was all-important to his future. His dissatisfaction with the women he met throughout the rest of his long life can be traced in part to his idealization of Mary.

The stunned young widower, compelled to reorganize his life, decided to emulate Mary's late father, who had been an exciseman, a minor government official whose duties combined the functions of both a tax collector and an internal revenue field investigator. What impelled Paine to seek such work can only be guessed, as the hours were long, the work arduous, and the personal, physical risks great. It may be that he regarded the vocation as romantic. No other logical explanation suggests itself.

In any event, Paine corresponded with his father, who liked the idea and promised to exert what influence he could in Thetford to obtain a position for his son. At the end of 1760 young Paine returned to London, and for the next six months he went to a special government-owned school to learn the duties of an exciseman. It is not known whether he continued to attend the philosophy lectures of Martin and Ferguson.

In July, 1761, he returned to Thetford, where his father had obtained a position for him as a probationary excise officer, and for the first time since he had gone off to sea he resumed life under his parents' roof. In January, 1762, he received his appointment as a full-fledged exciseman and made his headquarters at Thetford, although his responsibilities extended to a number of neighboring towns. The job often placed him in dangerous situations, and the wages of £50 per year were woefully inadequate. As Paine himself said, 'After tax, charity and fitting expenses are deducted, there remains very little more than forty-six pounds; and the expenses of housekeeping in many places cannot be bought for under fourteen pounds a year, besides the purchase at first, and the hazard of life, which reduces it to thirty-two pounds per annum, or one shilling and ninepence farthing per day.' The government had set a low pay scale deliberately because substantial bonuses were offered to excisemen who caught smugglers, but it was not unusual for a collector to suffer severe physical injury or even death at the hands of those who operated outside the law.

No records of Paine's immediately subsequent activities exist, but, as far as is known, he performed his simple duties in a manner that satisfied his superiors, and in August, 1764, he was given a minor promotion and transferred to the Norfolk seacoast, where smugglers were more active. For another year he performed routine duties and soon fell into a habit practiced by many of his colleagues, that of certifying the merchandise in a warehouse without actually inspecting it. A supervisor discovered his negligence and in late August, 1765, he was suspended. He was a failure at the age of twenty-eight. Returning to the only other vocation he knew, that of a corset-maker, he drifted through Norfolk and Lincolnshire as a journeyman for the next year, rarely staying in one place for any length of time. Troubled by his lack of accomplishment, perhaps, he developed a vile temper reminiscent of his mother's and frequently quarreled with his fellow workers. He moved so often that it is impossible to trace his travels during that year.

In the summer of 1766 he demeaned himself by writing a groveling letter to the Board of Excise asking for reinstatement. Repeatedly stressing his humility, he said he had learned a lesson and would not fall into the same errors again; he also emphasized that, unlike many of his colleagues, he had never been dishonest or accepted bribes. The appeal must have shattered what little was left of his pride, but his letter was effective, and he was restored to the active list of excisemen. At that time, however, there were no openings in the service, and he was forced to wait until a place opened for him. Suddenly, late in July, 1766, he reappeared in London and quickly found a temporary position somewhat more suited to his proclivities. Even though his own formal education was woefully inadequate, he obtained a post as an English teacher in an academy in Goodman's Fields owned by a Mr Noble, and for six months' work was paid the less than princely sum of £25, the same wages he had earned as an exciseman. In January, 1767, his contract expired, and he found another teaching position with a Mr Gardiner at a boys' school in

Kensington. Precisely how long he remained there is difficult to determine, but one of Paine's biographers claimed that the employment lasted for no more than three months.

During this time Paine suddenly and inexplicably felt the urge to become a clergyman, and applied to the Anglican bishop of London for ordination as a priest. He had no Church of England background; his claims as an English scholar were superficial, at best; and the bishop firmly rejected the request. Refusing to accept defeat, he became an itinerant preacher and spent the rest of the year traveling from one small town to another, preaching and holding highly irregular church services. Now thirty years old, he was dependent for food, lodging, and small contributions of cash on the people who attended his sermons. In May the Board of Excise offered him a post in Cornwall, but he turned it down, preferring to wait for another opening, so it must be presumed that he was earning enough as an itinerant minister to support himself.

Finally, in February, 1768, he returned to the excise service as an inspector for the town of Lewes and the little fishing village of Brighton. Lewes, with a population of about five thousand, had acquired notoriety as a smugglers' haven; contraband goods were imported and exported at will in fleets of fishing boats. Virtually every merchant in town was engaged in smuggling, and Paine was unpopular with his fellow citizens from the day of his arrival. His expression became even gloomier, his scowl deepened, and his hair began to turn gray. Lewes had made life thoroughly uncomfortable for his predecessors, and it seemed likely that Paine would not last long or, if he persisted, would be incapacitated by an accident on a dark night. But, to the astonishment of all who predicted that dire things would happen to him, Paine soon became acclimated to the life of Lewes. There is no proof that he accepted bribes, although the excise service was badly crippled by corruption at that time. It may be that he did not take his official duties too seriously, and that would have satisfied the people of Lewes. He began to frequent a tavern called the White Hart, whose patrons sometimes interrupted their drinking to discuss politics and philosophy, and there he acquired a reputation as a man who refused to accept defeat in a debate.

There was nothing of the crusader in the thirty-one-year-old Paine, no indication that he found weaknesses in the Crown's method of governing citizens or that he was aware of the issues causing Samuel Adams and others in Great Britain's North American colonies to demand a greater share of self-government. In winter the exciseman for Lewes became an expert ice skater, and in summer he became such an energetic boating enthusiast that his many friends gave him the nickname 'Commodore'.

He also became the town's poet-in-residence, often entertaining the regulars at the White Hart with his compositions. He seems to have become fairly active as a Whig, and a man named Rumbold, the party's candidate for a seat in the House of Commons, paid him three guineas for a campaign song he composed. Rumbold lost the election, and the literary effort has been lost to posterity. As mildly patriotic as others of the working and lower middle classes, he also wrote the lyrics for a song that commemorated the tragic death, in the autumn of 1759, of General James Wolfe on the Plains of Abraham while storming Quebec. These words were later set to music, and the piece was popular for many years in musical societies. Viewed charitably, Paine's effort was uninspired. Britain was described as a 'disconsolate dame', and Wolfe had not died but had been 'summoned to lead the armies above' against the forces of evil sent to conquer heaven. The ballad, the first literary effort by Paine ever to reach an audience of consequence, contained no hint of the thinking that would make him the age's demonic reformer.

Paine was living in lodgings provided by Samuel Ollive, a Quaker who earned his living as a tobacconist, and the two became sufficiently friendly for the landlord to teach his guest how to operate the tobacco mill in the cellar of the house. Ollive died in July, 1769, leaving his widow and children in poverty. According to Paine's Victorian biographers he immediately moved elsewhere, but the pre-Victorians mention no such change of address. Be that as it may, he had become involved in the family's affairs: In 1770 he and Ollive's son, Thomas, became partners, opening a tobacco shop together, and on March 26, 1771, Paine was married to Thomas's sister, Elizabeth, by the Reverend Robert Austen, rector of Saint Michael's Church in Lewes. Elizabeth Ollive was ten years younger than her husband and had fallen in love with him when he had first come to Lewes. She was blonde and very pretty, and, because the Quakers believed their daughters should be educated, she knew how to read and write. But the bride and groom were badly mismated. Quick-tempered and vociferous,

Paine was just beginning to find himself after years of aimless drifting, while Elizabeth was lethargic, slow, disinterested in the outside world, and as sensitive as her husband.

There are hints in Paine's later works that he never loved his second wife and married her only because he felt sorry for her, but he may have used hindsight as an attempt to excuse himself. Attractive blondes were a weakness of his, and Elizabeth's hero worship was so blatant that he may have imagined himself in love with her. No matter how the couple felt at first, their mutual illusions were soon destroyed. When Elizabeth became irritable, Paine lost his temper, and they quarreled frequently. Within a few weeks of the wedding he was spending most of his evenings at the White Hart again, and Elizabeth, seeking revenge, began to flirt with other men in the hope that she would arouse her husband's jealousy.

But Thomas Paine, now thirty-five years old, was beginning to come into his own and had little time for domesticity. He and his fellow excisemen were disgruntled because they earned so little money, and by the late spring of 1771 he began to travel throughout England, organizing his colleagues so they could speak to Parliament with one voice. They appealed to friends for funds to help their cause, and many merchants contributed, realizing they could stop handing out bribes if the taxmen were paid a living wage. More than £5,000 was raised, and the excisemen named Paine as the custodian of the money.

Of far greater significance was his leadership in another phase of the campaign. He took it upon himself to write an appeal to Parliament; this pamphlet, *The Case of the Officers of Excise*, was the first that he ever wrote. Cogent, blunt, and crisp, it reveals talents that neither he nor anyone else had suspected he possessed. In 1772 it was sent to all members of both houses of Parliament, but it had little effect. Paine himself commented that 'a rebellion of the excisemen, who seldom have the populace on their side, was not much feared by their superiors'. Undaunted by the refusal of either house to take the appeal seriously, he wrote two more pamphlets with which he bombarded Parliament. The only result was a totally unexpected one. A leading poet and playwright of the day, Oliver Goldsmith, happened to read the new pamphlets, admired them, and sought out the author. Paine, flattered, sent him a copy of *The Case of the Officers of Excise*, and the two men met in London and became close friends. Their relationship was Paine's first association on an equal footing with a man of stature.

Paine, ignoring the tobacco mill, his work as an exciseman, and his wife, began to spend much of his time in London, where he acted as a lobbyist for his colleagues. His superiors became increasingly annoyed, particularly when he obtained the sympathetic ears of such prominent antiadministration members of the Commons as Edmund Burke and Charles James Fox. On April 8, 1774, the Board of Excise discharged him. It has been commonly supposed that Paine lost his position because he had been dealing in smuggled tobacco. This charge, promulgated by many of Paine's biographers, is untrue. The board would have been delighted had it possessed documentary evidence proving that he had been dishonest; the only charge made against him in the dismissal order, however, was that he had absented himself from his post without obtaining the permission of his superiors.

The news that Paine had been discharged created chaos. He owed money to a number of prominent citizens of Lewes, and they threatened to send him to debtors' prison unless they were repaid without delay. He was forced to leave the town for a few weeks and go into hiding until he could rearrange his affairs. In desperation he sold all of the contents of his tobacco shop at auction, including mills for 'horse' or pipe tobacco and for snuff, as well as several unopened crates of tobacco recently imported from Virginia. He used the proceeds to pay off his creditors and late in May returned to Lewes, safe but penniless. On June 4, the thirty-seven-year-old Paine and his second wife formally separated. Many of Paine's early biographers claimed that the couple had never lived together, but they offered no proof of this assertion. Neither at the time nor afterward did either of the principals discuss the matter, and Paine silenced a good friend who dared to question him, saying, 'It is nobody's business but my own; I had cause for it, but I will name it to no one.'

Various documents in the town records of Lewes indicate that Paine turned over his house and all other personal property to Elizabeth, keeping only what he was wearing, plus an extra suit, a spare pair of boots, some shirts, and his underclothes. Again he petitioned the Board of Excise for reinstatement, but he could not really have believed that the appeal would be accepted. A day or two after Paine's separation from his wife, he set out for London. The excisemen, disappointed because their campaign for higher wages had failed, turned on him in anger. They declared that he alone was responsible; one group even claimed that he had absconded with funds entrusted to his care, a charge later proved false. The truth notwithstanding, he was a convenient scapegoat.

Some historians have claimed that Elizabeth left her husband because of his neglect, his temper, and his drinking, although there is no evidence to indicate that the immoderate consumption of alcohol had as yet caused him any problems. Others have said, admittedly without proof, that it was Paine who became disillusioned and sought the separation because of his wife's affairs with other men. Only tenuous evidence can be offered to uphold this second thesis: Many of the good citizens of Lewes called Elizabeth a flirt, but they might have been responding to unsubstantiated gossip. In the eighteenth century, as in later times, an attractive woman who left her husband caused talk.

When the separation became final, Elizabeth went to live with her brother Thomas, a watchmaker. She resided with him and his family for many years, and in 1800 she signed a deposition in which she stated that 'the said Thomas Pain had many years quitted this kingdom and resided (if living) in parts beyond the seas, but had not since been heard of by the said Elizabeth Pain, nor was it known for certain whether he was living or dead.' In view of the furor Paine created on two continents and in Great Britain during the quarter of a century that elapsed after his separation from his wife, Elizabeth's assertion is astonishing. One might assume that she lived in seclusion and had no knowledge whatever of political, social, and military upheavals that shook and almost destroyed the very foundations of the society she knew. Several of Paine's friends claimed, without proof, that he always spoke solicitously of his wife and, when he could, sent anonymous donations of cash to Elizabeth, always taking care that others prepare the envelopes so that she would not recognize his handwriting. If he actually did so, he never wrote about it.

On July 27, 1774 Paine's mother wrote a letter to her daughter-in-law:

Dear Daughter,–
I must beg leave to trouble you with my inquiries concerning my unhappy son and your husband: various are the reports, which I find come originally from the Excise-office. Such as his vile treatment to you, his secreting upwards of £30 intrusted with him to manage the petition for advancement of salary; and that since his discharge he

have petitioned to be restored, which was rejected with scorn. Since which I am told he have left England. To all which I beg you'll be kind enough to answer me by due course of post.

You'll not be a little surprised at my so strongly desiring to know what's become of him after I repeat to you his undutiful behavior to the tenderness of parents; he never asked of us anything, but what was granted, that were in our poor abilities to do; nay, even distressed ourselves, whose works are given over by old age, to let him have £20 on bond, and every other tender mark a parent could possibly shew a child; his ingratitude, or rather want of duty, has been such, that he have not wrote to me upwards of two years.

If the above account be true, I am heartily sorry, that a woman whose character and amiableness deserves the greatest respect, love, and esteem, as I have always on enquiry been informed that yours did, should be tied for life to the worst of husbands.

I am, dear daughter, your affectionate mother,
F. Pain.

For God's sake, let me have your answer, as I am almost distracted.

3

The Immigrant Editor

In the last decades of the eighteenth century, London had over a million inhabitants and boasted that it was the fastest-growing city on earth. It would have been easy for a man to lose or conceal himself in the overcrowded metropolis. How the penniless Thomas Paine managed to support himself during his sojourn there in the late spring and early summer of 1774 is not known. Presumably he borrowed small sums from various friends.

In the two years he had been lobbying on behalf of the excisemen, he had developed a deep interest in politics. He probably came to share the contempt that Fox and other Whigs felt for the indelicate and dictatorial George III, the Hanoverian monarch who, as Paine was to write, 'treats Members of Parliament like naughty nephews, and subjects who will not bow to his every whim like wayward stepchildren'. Although they disagreed with the King's policies, most Whigs were loyal to the institution of the Crown, but Paine was already showing signs of the contempt for monarchy everywhere that would be a foundation stone of his political thought for the rest of his life.

Through Oliver Goldsmith he had become acquainted with the man whom most Englishmen and Europeans regarded as the most distinguished of the American colonials: Benjamin Franklin, who simultaneously served as assistant postmaster general and London political agent for the Pennsylvania and Massachusetts Bay colonies, was an author, editor, scientist, philosopher, publisher, diplomat, and politician. The ideal Englightenment man was proficient in many fields, and certainly no man of that time was more versatile than Dr Franklin.

To Franklin belongs the credit for first recognizing the potential of Thomas Paine. Paine, then thirty-seven years old, was bankrupt and separated from his wife – a total failure. He shared, however, Franklin's enthusiastic interest in all things scientific and was remarkably quick to grasp political principles. Above all, as his three little pamphlets on behalf of the excisemen demonstrated, he was endowed with a rare ability to state his arguments on paper pungently and with clarity. There was a need for such a man in the colonies, Franklin told him, thereby re-awakening the dream that Paine had nurtured since early childhood of visiting the North American continent. Impoverished and with no future in England, Paine had little trouble convincing himself that a comfortable living awaited him in America. During his frequent dinners with Franklin, Paine learned something about the colonial situation.

Until 1768 or thereabouts the colonists had been apathetic, content to allow the Crown and Parliament to direct their external affairs and establish policies of taxation as long as they were allowed to govern themselves in the domestic sphere. The arrangement had been profitable for both the mother country and her colonies: Britain obtained raw materials from the colonies and, in turn, provided the colonists with manufactured goods that they could not produce themselves.

But vast changes had taken place in recent years, and no one understood these changes more thoroughly than the sophisticated Franklin. The colonies were suffering growing pains and wanted to establish their own factories although this was forbidden by law. They also wanted to trade with France, Holland, Prussia, Sweden, and other Continental nations, but this, too, was prohibited. Until a year or two earlier, the vast majority of Americans had remained undeviatingly loyal to the Crown, but that situation was fast changing, partly because of the shortsighted policies of King George and his Tory ministers. The Crown insisted that the colonists accept the principle that they could be taxed at will by King and Parliament, and even some of America's Whig friends agreed with that stand. But a small band of colonials – among them Boston's great propagandist Samuel Adams and Virginia's Patrick Henry – were arguing that taxation without representation in the Commons was untenable.

Both sides stood adamant, and the possibility of achieving a compromise began to disappear. Tempers were rising on both sides of the Atlantic: Armed men had deliberately destroyed Crown property during the Boston Tea Party of 1773, and the Crown and Parliament instituted measures to punish the Massachusetts Bay Colony for its temerity. The radicals in the colonies had formed what they called Committees of Correspondence and in recent months had initiated agitation for the establishment of an independent nation. A call had already been issued for an intercolonial conference or congress, to be held in 1775, and Franklin expressed the conviction that, if moderates in the mother country and the colonies alike did not establish firm controls in the immediate future, a war between Great Britain and her North American colonies was a virtual certainty.

Paine not only grasped the intricacies of the complex situation but expressed a willingness to cast his lot with the colonials. Discharged from his poorly paid government post with no hope of reinstatement, permanently separated from his wife and with no future in England other than that of once again becoming a journeyman corset-maker, he had nothing to lose.

The nineteenth-century biographers who portrayed Thomas Paine as a blazing idealist who went off to America to help the colonists fight for liberty were as hopelessly romantic as Paine himself. He had not, up to this time, written of any deep convictions that he may have held on the rights of man, freedom of conscience, and the prerogatives guaranteed every Englishman under the Magna Carta. One might suspect that Paine went off to the New World for strictly opportunistic reasons, but he cannot be blamed for wanting to improve his miserable lot in life. Certainly it was opportunistic of Franklin to encourage his migration.

By late summer he had determined to go to America, but no ship was available until mid-October. The boycott of British manufactures was increasingly widespread in the colonies, and most merchantmen rode idly at anchor in English harbors, awaiting a better climate for trade. The threat to British ships was growing; owners shuddered when they thought of American mobs destroying their vessels.

At last a brig bound for New York was found, and Franklin quietly lent Paine the money for his passage. He also gave him a letter of introduction to his son-in-law, Richard Bache:

> The bearer Mr Thomas Paine is very well recommended to me an ingenious worthy young man. He goes to Pennsylvania with a view of settling there. I request you to give him your best advice and countenance, as he is quite a stranger there. If you can put him in a way of obtaining employment as a clerk, or assistant tutor in a school, or assistant surveyor, of all of which I think him very capable, so that he may procure a subsistence at least, till he can make acquaintance and obtain a knowledge of the country, you will do well, and much oblige your affectionate father.

The brig sailed from London on October 17, 1774, passed Gravesend the next day, and soon ran afoul of a fierce autumn gale. For two weeks she fought storms so severe that the captain was tempted to turn back, and Paine, his experiences as a sailor far behind him, became seasick and remained in his bunk. Then the weather cleared, Paine regained his sea legs, and the rest of the voyage was uneventful.

The America to which Paine was migrating was a quiet land, its peace disturbed only by conflicts with the Indians, who were losing their territory to the settlers, and by intermittent wars with the French. In 1774 the thirteen English-speaking colonies had a total population of fewer than 2 million. Roman Catholic French Canada had been ceded to Great Britain in 1763, at the conclusion of the last, most vicious of the French and Indian Wars. The colonial subjects of King George III governed themselves domestically through their legislatures and local town governments but had almost no voice in matters relating to foreign affairs, defense, taxation, or trade. Inheritors of the tradition of personal liberty that had been established under the Magna Carta, they nevertheless had no representation in Parliament and consequently were reduced to the status of second-class citizens.

British law prevented the establishment of factories in the New World, so the colonists remained basically an agricultural people who supplied raw materials to the mother country and received manufactured goods in return, thus providing Britain with a substantial, guaranteed market. Only a few, such as planters George Washington and Richard Henry Lee of Virginia and merchant John Hancock of Boston, were truly wealthy. Owing, however, to the availability of free land to all who wanted to settle it, few people starved.

Most men were either farmers or 'mechanics', that is, carpenters, masons, and other kinds of artisans. The educated class was small, education being limited to sons of the wealthy and of professional men. These privileged few attended such colleges as Harvard, Yale, the College of New Jersey (soon to become Princeton), and King's College (the future Columbia) in New York.

In 1774 most Americans, regardless of their class, were still loyal to the British Crown, at least nominally, because it had not yet occurred to them to be otherwise. The so-called radicals who agitated for the establishment of an independent nation were a small band of intellectuals – men like Samuel Adams of Massachusetts and Patrick Henry of Virginia. They had a following of mechanics and farmers, but until recently those who demanded liberty had made up only a very small minority of the population.

Now, however, that situation was changing rapidly. King George and his ministers, who completely misunderstood the love of freedom that the New World wilderness instilled in the self-reliant colonials, had been trying in vain for four years to force the Americans to submit to the will of the Crown and Parliament. Increasingly severe and often unreasonable repressive measures had swollen the ranks of the followers of Adams and Henry, and respectable and law-abiding men of prominence in every colony were giving serious consideration to the possibility of establishing an independent nation if they were refused justice. A spirit of rebellion was definitely in the air.

On November 29, 1774, Thomas Paine landed in New York, but he did not linger longer than overnight in America's third-largest city, which tried to maintain an austerity that its citizens imagined made it resemble London. The following day Paine arrived in Philadelphia, whose population of about 30,000 was almost as large as that of Boston. Philadelphia was the most culturally advanced and, at the same time, rowdiest city in the New World. Philadelphians were proud of their newspapers, magazines, lectures, and musicales. They grinned when they learned that sailors had rioted again in Market Street taverns, and, like Bostonians, they were rapidly approaching the point of no return in their thinking about the colonies' relations with the mother country. Respectable upper-class Philadelphians, like equally respectable Bostonians, spoke openly, freely, and forcefully when they advocated independence for America, a view that few of their compatriots yet shared.

Paine was warmly received by Bache, who helped him find an inexpensive lodginghouse off Market Street and took him home for dinner. Soon thereafter he introduced the newcomer to one of Philadelphia's more distinguished citizens, Robert Aitkin, proprietor of the city's largest bookstore and a printer who had published some of Franklin's works. Aitkin was struggling to put out a new periodical, the *Pennsylvania Magazine*, sometimes known by its subtitle, *American Museum*. He already had six hundred subscribers, and he offered the newcomer £5 to write an article for the first issue.

Paine agreed, and his choice of a subject was inspired. He chose to write an essay condemning the practice of slavery, little known in England but common in the colonies. Skeptics have claimed that he was strictly opportunistic, having known that most influential Philadelphians were opposed to the institution of slavery, but this is unlikely, if for no other reason than that the new arrival could have had no idea of what Philadelphians thought or believed. Very simply, he had observed on the brig an African slave accompanying a fellow passenger as manservant, and on the streets of Philadelphia he saw more such slaves; the Englishman was horrified. Although slavery was legal in England, Paine had never before seen a slave.

His indignation was explosive, and his essay guaranteed the success of the *Pennsylvania Magazine*. Aitken promptly offered the author the post of editor-in-chief and agreed to pay him a salary of £50 per year, which, prices being much lower in the colonies, was equal to a sum four times that amount in England. Paine happily accepted, and in March, 1775, he was able to write to Franklin that the publication had achieved a circulation of more than 1,500 and was still growing rapidly.

At the age of thirty-eight Thomas Paine had stumbled into his true vocation. His success as an author and editor was phenomenal and swift; he was the right man in the right place at the right time. The subject matter that was of vital interest to him also preoccupied his readers, but his standing as a literary figure and one of the most compelling propagandists in history depended even more on his hitherto unknown and virtually unused talents as a writer. Most educated eighteenth-century gentlemen wrote in a flowery, convoluted style, whereas Paine wrote simply, forcefully, and directly. He had had no real apprenticeship, no extended period of learning or of trial and error; his endowments were natural. His essays were incisive, clear, and timely and flowed from his pen without apparent effort.

He became the editor of the *Pennsylvania Magazine* in time to take responsibility for the second issue, and for the next year and a half he was in sole charge of the publication. Its circulation of five thousand then made it by far the most influential periodical in America.

Any account of Paine's early days in Philadelphia must deal with a myth that persists from that period. Benjamin Rush, the distinguished physician and patriot, has long been given full credit for sponsoring Paine and obtaining a position for him. But Rush himself said this credit was unjustified. When they met by accident in Aitkin's bookshop, Rush merely congratulated the author on his antislavery essay.

For his first issue as editor, Paine wrote a highly laudatory critical essay on the works of Oliver Goldsmith and, with a bow to Benjamin Franklin, an illustrated article on a new electrical storage battery. He also wrote an editorial in which he predicted that the native Indian would be absorbed into the mainstream of American culture. His interest in science was manifested in a series of illustrated articles on recent inventions, most of them English, including a spinning machine and a threshing machine. He also published a number of the short poems he had written for the entertainment of his friends at the White Hart in Lewes, and, for the first time, his song – complete with music – on the death of General Wolfe. Paine wrote so much that, precisely as Samuel Adams was doing in Boston newspapers, he used a number of pseudonyms. Among the most frequent were 'Vox Populi', 'Aesop', and 'Atlanticus'. More often than not, however, his shorter pieces were unsigned.

From the beginning he did not hesitate to deal with controversial subjects. Learning that Americans took the custom of duelling for granted and that none of the cultured gentlemen he met in Philadelphia objected to the practice, he wrote for his May,

1775, issue an essay in which he indignantly called duelling an outrage. For the same issue he wrote another piece strongly protesting cruelty to animals, and so probably became the first author on the western side of the Atlantic ever to write on this subject.

By the spring of 1775 he had become sufficiently acclimated to the New World to feel contempt for the institution of the British nobility; his essay on the subject said in part:

> The reasonable freeman sees through the magic of a title, and examines the man before he approves him. To him the honours of the worthless seem to write their masters' vices in capitals, and their Stars shine to no other end than to read them by. Modesty forbids men separately, or collectively, to assume titles. But as all honours, even that of kings, originated from the public, the public may justly be called the true fountain of honour. And it is with much pleasure I have heard the title 'Honourable' applied to a body of men, who nobly disregarding public ease and interest for public welfare, have justly merited the address of

> *The Honourable Continental Congress.*

The Continental Congress had been meeting in Philadelphia, and its deliberations, as well as the very fact that such a meeting of colonial leaders had been called, excited Paine's imagination. Although a number of wealthy and prominent Americans were delegates, most men of substance were still unwilling to commit themselves prematurely to a cause that was likely to require an ultimate formal rupture of relations with Great Britain.

But Paine, who had spent only six months in colonial America, had already thrown himself headlong into the camp of the radicals. He agreed with Samuel Adams, unreservedly and enthusiastically, that American subjects of the Crown were entitled to every right enjoyed by Englishmen. Having achieved respectability and stature for the first time in his life, Paine swiftly and effortlessly shifted his loyalties and became an American. It must be stressed, however, that there was neither hypocrisy nor opportunism in his change of allegiance, and he was completely sincere in his espousal of the American cause. His own experience had taught him that, had he remained in England, he would have been condemned to spend his entire life in the lower middle class, and he had learned that no matter what his talents he could climb no higher in a caste-bound system. In the colonies, however, a man could rise as high as his ambition and energies could drive him. Within a few months Paine had become a leader, respected by all, a man who molded public opinion.

Certainly his stand required courage. He knew, as did every other literate man in America, that the Tories in Parliament were demanding the imprisonment of such radical leaders as Samuel Adams and the wealthy shipowner and merchant John Hancock. An editor who expressed anti-British feelings freely would almost certainly find his name added to the proscribed list. Paine's advocacy of the radical cause – soon to become known as the Patriot cause – was solemn and deliberate. Like every other man who came to believe in the establishment of a free and independent nation, he had to be willing and prepared to take grave risks and make heavy sacrifices. Great Britain was the most powerful nation on earth, and the handful of Americans who opposed the mother country in the spring of 1775 knew the full weight of an empire would be brought to bear against them. No man who dreamed of American independence, and there were only a few at that early time, took his position lightly. By the late spring of 1775 Thomas Paine was universally regarded as a spokesman for the radicals.

Perhaps Paine had harbored firm opinions for many years on subjects ranging from slavery to the cruel treatment of animals but had found no outlet for his views. Certainly he did not hold back now that he had found a forum for his opinions. He was the first in the New World to raise a voice in protest against the inferior position of women. A very small number of pioneers in England had begun to agitate in Paine's time on behalf of feminism and women's rights, but none of their works had as yet been published. Mary Wollstonecraft Godwin, generally considered the founder of the women's right movement in Britain, was not yet of age in the mid-1770's, and most of her more important writing would be done two decades later, after she had become Paine's disciple and friend. So an essay he published in the August, 1775, issue of the *Pennsylvania Magazine* must be accepted as an expression of his own original thinking. He wrote:

Affronted in one country by polygamy, which gives them their rivals for inseparable companions; inslaved in another by indissoluble ties, which often join the gentle to the rude, and sensibility to brutality: Even in countries where they may be esteemed most happy, constrained in their desires in the disposal of their goods, robbed of freedom of will by the laws, the slaves of opinion, which rules them with absolute sway, and construes the slightest appearances into guilt, surrounded on all sides by judges who are at once their tyrants and seducers, and who after having prepared their faults, punish every lapse with dishonour – may usurp the right of degrading them on suspicion! – who does not feel for the tender sex? Yet such I am sorry to say is the lot of woman over the whole earth. Man with regard to them, in all climates and in all ages, has been either an insensible husband or an oppressor; but they have sometimes experienced the cold and deliberate oppression of pride, and sometimes the violent and terrible tyranny of jealousy. When they are not beloved they are nothing; and when they are they are tormented. They have almost equal cause to be afraid of indifference and love. Over three quarters of the globe Nature has placed them between contempt and misery.

Even among people where beauty receives the highest homage we find men who would deprive the sex of every kind of reputation. 'The most virtuous woman,' says a celebrated Greek, 'is she who is least talked of.' That morose man, while he imposes duties on women, would deprive them of the sweets of public esteem, and in exacting virtues from them would make it a crime to aspire to honour.

The astonishing record of the former corset-maker, exciseman, and tobacconist, an immigrant who had lived in at least partial ignorance of the forces that had shaped the principles and philosophy of the New World, speaks for itself. Paine was one of the first to advocate American independence, freedom for all under a republican form of government, and the abolition of all hereditary, royal, and ecclesiastical privileges. He was also the first to demand:

- The emancipation of slaves
- The primacy of national interests in the new United States
- The establishment of safeguards to prevent a President from acquiring the powers of a King
- The abolition of duelling
- The extension of equal rights to women
- The prevention of cruelty to animals
- The establishment of national and international copyright laws
- The establishment of rational, equitable divorce laws, which would be administered without prejudice to parties of either sex

The list is all the more remarkable because, aside from *The Case of the Officers of Excise*, Paine was not known to have expressed any opinions publicly in all of his previous thirty-eight years. He seems to have been reborn when he arrived in America;

the penniless refugee was transformed into the champion of liberty and equality, justice and fraternity. Whether he was familiar with the works of John Locke and David Hume before his arrival in America or was subsequently introduced to their philosophies by Thomas Jefferson and others is unknown. All that can be said with certainty is that he was under no direct outside influence during the eighteen months he edited the *Pennsylvania Magazine*. He became friendly with Jefferson, Samuel and John Adams, Richard Henry Lee, and others during this time, and he renewed his acquaintance with Franklin, too, after the great Philadelphian returned home from England. But he knew none of them well enough, as yet, to call upon any ideas other than his own.

Making up for lost years and working with furious intensity, Paine lived something of a hermit's life. He spent most of his waking hours at his desk in his tiny rented room, emerging only to eat frugal meals in the sailors' taverns on Market Street. By his own account he subsisted mainly on 'bread and inferior joints of beef'; his one luxury was clams, either raw or in a chowder, such delicacies being unknown in England. He dressed in a shabby black suit, did not bother to wear a wig, and only because he needed to protect himself from rowdy seamen at night did he carry a walking stick. Most of the time he could afford no drink other than ale, although he developed a fondness for rum, the common American beverage. He received many dinner invitations but was too busy and too shy to accept most of them. Although many ladies were anxious to meet him, he eschewed their company and apparently lived a celibate existence.

It was enough for the moment that thousands heeded his words, that he exerted an influence beyond his dreams. The colonies were hurtling toward a direct confrontation with Great Britain, and Paine, anticipating this, directed all of his energies toward a preparation for that struggle.

4

Common Sense

Several years after the outbreak of the American Revolution in
1775, Thomas Paine wrote that he had abhorred the institution
of monarchy all his life, regarding it as 'too debasing to the
dignity of man'. But, he added, 'I never troubled others with my
notions till lately.' This statement directly contradicts the ex-
pressions of respect for the Crown found in *The Case of the
Officers of Excise*, and he has been accused of inconsistency. But
his critics have missed the significance of his words. Paine
believed he had always been a republican, and his passion for the
cause of American independence and the establishment of a
democratic form of government made it impossible for him to
remember ever having felt any other way.

After the Battle of Lexington in April, 1775, when British
troops openly clashed with American regulars in Massachusetts,
Paine was one of the first to realize that war was inevitable and,
after Samuel Adams, may have been the first to advocate inde-

pendence. In an issue of the *Pennsylvania Magazine* published late in that same month, Paine quoted from a speech in which the elder Pitt, Earl of Chatham, said that 'the Crown would lose its lustre if robbed of so principal a jewel as America', to which the editor added a wry comment of his own, saying, 'The principal jewel of the Crown actually dropt out at the coronation.' The sentiment was evidently his own, as he had not yet met Adams, and it is unlikely that he had read any of the Bostonian's fiery articles and editorials in the Massachusetts newspapers, which frequently did not arrive in other colonies until months after their publication.

A few weeks before musket fire was exchanged at Lexington, Franklin assured Pitt that there was virtually no sentiment in favor of independence in the colonies. Even in the month after the battle, when George Washington of Virginia was traveling to Philadelphia to attend the Second Continental Congress, he still favored moderation. But a blaze of sentiment in favor of a complete break, fanned by the radicals, soon changed the feelings of thousands of colonials.

Paine, showing a newly developed sense of humor, wrote to Franklin, 'I thought it very hard to have the country set on fire about my ears almost the moment I got into it.' He neglected to add that he was one of the principal arsonists and, although he abhorred war, he agreed with Patrick Henry that America was compelled to fight for her honor and her freedom. Both sides had gone to such extremes that there was no longer a viable alternative.

The editor of the *Pennsylvania Magazine* made his feelings on the subject clear in the October, 1775, issue. Writting under the pseudonym of 'Humanus', he entitled his editorial *A Serious Thought* and said:

When I reflect on the horrid cruelties exercised by Britain in [India] – How thousands perished by artificial famine – how religion and every manly principle of honor and honesty were sacrificed to luxury and and pride – When I read of the wretched natives being blown away, for no other crime than because, sickened with the miserable scene, they refused to fight – When I reflect on these and a thousand instances of similar barbarity, I firmly believe that the Almighty, in compassion to mankind, will curtail the power of Britain.

And when I reflect on the use she hath made of the discovery of this new world – that the little paltry dignity of earthly kings hath been set up in preference to the great cause of the King of kings – that instead of Christian examples to the Indians, she hath basely tampered with their passions, imposed on their ignorance, and made them the tools of treachery and murder – And when to these and many other melancholy reflections I add this sad remark, that ever since the discovery of America she hath employed herself in the most horrid of all traffics, that of human flesh, unknown to the most savage nations, hath yearly (without provocation and in cold blood) ravaged the hapless shores of Africa, robbing it of its unoffending inhabitants to cultivate her stolen dominions in the West – When I reflect on these, I hesitate not for a moment to believe that the Almighty will finally separate America from Britain. Call it Independancy or what you will, if it is the cause of God and humanity it will go on.

And when the Almighty shall have blest us, and made us a people *dependent only upon Him*, then may our first gratitude be shown by an act of continental legislation, which shall put a stop to the importation of Negroes for sale, soften the hard fate of those already here, and in time procure their freedom.

This piece, in a sense, was Paine's own declaration of independence, and he joined the ranks of the still small but rapidly growing minority who felt it was too late for the colonies to effect a reconciliation with Great Britain. In the autumn of 1775, after the publication of *A Serious Thought*, he devoted virtually all of his spare time to the preparation of a pamphlet that he called *Common Sense*. That document would become the single most important work exhorting the American people to choose independence and would make Paine famous in both the New World and Europe. Apparently he had no idea, as he wrote, revised, and polished it, that, in the words of Benjamin Rush, it would 'burst from the press with an effect which has rarely been produced by types and paper in any age or country.'

Paine's timing was perfect. In June, 1775, the Battle of Bunker Hill had been fought in Boston, proving that the poorly trained colonials could stand up to the Redcoats. Shortly thereafter George Washington, appointed as major general and commander in chief by the Continental Congress, arrived in Massachusetts and began to train his troops in Cambridge. General Sir Thomas Gage and his successor, Sir William Howe, took no effective steps to oust the Americans, and by early March, 1776, the threat of American artillery made the British position untenable and Howe was forced to evacuate Boston.

In May, 1775, an expedition of irregulars jointly led by Benedict Arnold of Connecticut and Ethan Allen of Vermont captured Fort Ticonderoga on the road to the Saint Lawrence River. Late in the year, Brigadier General Richard Montgomery captured Montreal, then a small trading post, and in a joint venture with Arnold he attacked Quebec on December 31. Montgomery lost his life in that effort, and Arnold was unable to take Canada's most important city.

These campaigns had been minor, and the principal focus of attention remained on political matters. The Continental Congress had made a conciliatory gesture to the Crown and Parliament, but King George and his first minister, Lord North, had been stunned by the Battle of Bunker Hill and were in no mood for compromise. Calling the Americans rebels, they forbade commercial intercourse with the colonies, and the Tory majorities in both Houses of Parliament passed a bill establishing a blockade of American ports. By the end of 1775 there was no longer any hope of reconciliation: The authority of the Crown in the colonies had become even weaker, leaving actual control of the various colonial governments more or less in the hands of the radicals, who were demanding a total break in relations with the mother country.

America desperately needed new trading partners if her young, fragile economy hoped to survive. Moreover, with war virtually inevitable now, she required cannon, munitions, and the help of a powerful fleet of warships. There was little choice among the European powers: Spain was friendly but cautious, Austria was England's ally, and Prussia was maintaining strict neutrality. That left only Britain's traditional enemy France as a potential friend, and finally, in March, 1776, the Continental Congress issued an appeal to that nation for aid.

Although by the end of 1775 the radicals were boldly demanding independence, most Americans were still reluctant to take the plunge. The majority of the colonials were moderates who had respected the institution of the Crown since early childhood; the mere thought of establishing a new nation terrified them.

Common Sense, the little pamphlet published by Paine on January 10, 1776, changed the situation almost overnight. This bold essay, which marshaled the arguments for independence in a reasonable, forceful manner, turned the tide in favor of the radical movement and is rightly regarded as one of the principal immediate causes of the American Revolution. Initially it sold for two shillings per copy, but Paine made no money from his efforts, instead turning over all royalties to the Congress. The demand was so great that attempts to sell *Common Sense* were abandoned, and, with the Congress paying for the printing costs, more than three-quarters of a million copies were printed. It has been estimated that one copy was disseminated for every three men, women, and children in the American colonies, and it is no exaggeration to say that the work was read by virtually every literate person in what would become, in July, the independent nation of the United States of America.

Edmund Randolph of Virginia, a member of Washington's staff and destined to become, in 1789, the first attorney-general of the United States, said that King George's stand was the primary cause of the independence movement, and that after it came *Common Sense*. General Washington himself agreed, and Franklin, Rush, and a score of others gave Paine full credit for his achievement while the pamphlet was still being distributed. Its impact is difficult to grasp today, in an age when the public is inundated by the written word. In its own time *Common Sense* was absorbed by people who hardly ever looked at a newspaper, magazine, or book; it impressed tens of thousands who never read any work other than the Bible.

Paine had already grasped the spirit and the essence of the New World, as he clearly demonstrated in his very first editorial for the *Pennsylvania Magazine*, in December, 1774. Having taken eventual independence for granted, he had spoken of America as a nation:

America has now outgrown the state of infancy. Her strength and commerce make large advances to mankind, and science in all its branches has not only blossomed, but even ripened upon the soil. The cottages as it were of yesterday have grown to villages, and the villages to cities; and while proud antiquity, like a skeleton in rags, parades the streets of other nations, their genius, as if sickened and disgusted with the phantom, comes hither for recovery.

One of the most remarkable qualities of *Common Sense* is its clarity of style. Paine's earlier writing had been somewhat pedestrian and labored, but in the fifty-page pamphlet his natural gifts flourished, and some of his words still endure as a fundamental part of the American heritage:

liation is . . . a fallacious dream. . . . Everything that is right
al pleads for separation. The blood of the slain, the weeping
nature cries, ' 'Tis time to part.' Even the distance at which
the Almighty hath placed England and America is a strong and
natural proof that the authority of the one over the other was never
the design of Heaven. . . .

Freedom hath been hunted round the globe. Asia and Africa have
long expelled her. Europe regards her like a stranger, and England
hath given her warning to depart. . . . To talk of friendship with those
in whom our reason forbids us to have faith, and our affections
wounded through a thousand pores instruct us to detest, is madness
and folly. . . .

Ye that tell us of harmony and reconciliation, can ye restore to us
the time that is past? Can ye give to prostitution its former innocence? neither can ye reconcile Britain and America. The last cord
now is broken, the people of England are presenting addresses against
us. There are injuries which nature cannot forgive; she would cease
to be nature if she did. As well can the lover forgive the ravisher of
his mistress, as the continent forgive the murders of Britain. The
Almighty hath implanted in us these unextinguishable feelings for
good and wise purposes. They are the guardians of his image in our
hearts. They distinguish us from the herd of common animals. The
social compact would dissolve, and justice be extirpated from the
earth, or have only a casual existence were we callous to the touches
of affection. The robber and the murderer would often escape un-
punished, did not the injuries which our tempers sustain, provoke us
into justice. . . .

'Tis not in numbers but in unity that our great strength lies; yet our
present numbers are sufficient to repel the force of all the world. . . .
Debts we have none: and whatever we may contract on this account
will serve as a glorious memento of our virtue. Can we but leave
posterity with a settled form of government, an independent constitution of its own, the purchase at any price will be cheap. . . .

Some perhaps will say, that after we have made it up with Britain,
she will protect us. Can they be so unwise as to mean, that she will
anchor a navy in our harbors for that purpose? Common sense will
tell us, that a power which hath endeavored to subdue us, is of all
others, the most improper to defend us. Conquest may be effected
under the pretense of friendship; and ourselves, after a long and
brave resistance, be at last cheated into slavery. And if her ships are
not to be admitted into our harbors, I would ask, how is she to
protect us? A navy three or four thousand miles off can be of little
use, and on sudden emergencies, none at all. Wherefore if we must
hereafter protect ourselves, why not do it for ourselves? . . . From
Britain we can expect nothing but ruin. If she is once admitted to the

government of America again, this continent will not be worth living in. Jealousies will be always arising; insurrections will be constantly happening; and who will go forth to quell them? Who will venture his life to reduce his own countrymen to a foreign obedience?

America was overwhelmed by *Common Sense*. Members of the New York Assembly, who had been wavering, found the will and the strength to vote in favor of independence after they read the pamphlet. General Washington wrote that its effect on the people of Virginia was so great that it could not be calculated. Everywhere the results were the same, even within the ranks of the Continental Congress, which late in the spring appointed a committee to prepare a declaration of independence.

For a time the identity of the author was kept secret. Paine was so recently arrived in America that his arguments might have been weakened had people known he was an immigrant who had spent only a year on the western shores of the Atlantic. A great many people suspected that Franklin had written the pamphlet, but he publicly disclaimed any responsibility for it when he accepted the chairmanship of the committee that would write the Declaration of Independence.

Until recently, it was believed that Paine showed his work to no one while it was in progress, but there is evidence to suggest that Rush saw portions of the manuscript and approved of what he read. More important, he put Paine in touch with Robert Bell, a bookseller and printer of Scottish descent who had strong radical leanings. Because it would be seditious to print the pamphlet, most respectable printers would not have touched it, but Bell did not hesitate, and his presses worked day and night.

The first to guess Paine's identity as the author was the Reverend William Smith, the Loyalist president of the University of Philadelphia, who attacked him as a 'stranger intermeddling in our affairs' and called the pamphlet 'foul'. Virtually no one agreed with him, and by the beginning of summer in 1776, when the passage of the Declaration of Independence by the Continental Congress was regarded as a certainty, Paine found himself famous. He remained modest and retiring, however, and, having sworn members of the Congress to secrecy, did not reveal that he had donated his royalties from *Common Sense* to the cause of American liberty. In fact, the author purchased his own copies of the work and owed the printer the sum of twenty-nine pounds, twelve shillings, and a penny for a large stack that he bought and distributed.

When the identity of the author became public knowledge, first leaking into print in American newspapers, then appearing in the London press, Great Britain was bewildered. Few of the English had ever heard of Thomas Paine. Goldsmith announced that he was the pamphleteer's friend, and Edmund Burke, who believed that the Crown and the ministry were pursuing the wrong approach to the American problem, praised Paine in a speech in the House of Commons. Lord North responded by adding Paine's name to the proscribed list of traitors who would be granted no amnesty when the rebellion in the colonies was crushed, as the Tories so confidently expected it would be.

The most important personal result of the publication of *Common Sense* was Paine's immediate acceptance into the inner circle of the leaders of the Continental Congress. He renewed his acquaintance with Franklin, who was delighted that his protégé was doing so well; he became friendly with John and Samuel Adams and Richard Henry Lee of Virginia; and he was soon one of the few intimates of young Thomas Jefferson, the Virginia lawyer who was the principal author of the Declaration of Independence. One man with whom Paine's relations remained distant was John Hancock, the president of the Congress, whose manner was somewhat haughty and who regarded himself as a great patrician. Certainly he was one of the wealthiest men in the New World, and this in itself was enough to turn Paine against him, even though the immigrant admired him for risking his fortune for the sake of American liberty.

Paine dined with his new friends two or three days each week but apparently did not feel completely at ease in their company. In spite of his renown and the effect of *Common Sense* on the American people, he had been on close terms with very few men during his thirty-nine years, and he still regarded himself as an outsider as well as a newcomer. He continued to live in his tiny room off Market Street and, except when invited to dine with various members of the Congress, ate his meals alone. He seems to have been living in self-enforced celibacy, and, although it was later rumored that he sometimes availed himself of the services of the streetwalkers who congregated on the waterfront, no concrete evidence exists to substantiate this claim.

It has also been said that he began drinking to excess during this period, but the charge is absurd. Paine was working at least eighteen hours each day, churning out new pamphlets as well as writing and editing the *Pennsylvania Magazine;* he had no time for heavy drinking. He could not have maintained such a demanding schedule had he allowed himself to indulge in a drinking habit. There was plainly no reason for him to turn to alcohol. Although there was little improvement in his financial situation, he had finally achieved the renown that he had secretly desired. He had been accepted by the most prominent and prestigious men in the community, and he had proved that his was the most potent and influential voice in the New World. He had become a man of stature. According to his own later account, he was tasting the fruits of success and finding them ambrosial.

5

The Times That Tried Men's Souls

Late in the spring of 1776, while *Common Sense* was still winning converts by the thousands to the cause of independence, Thomas Paine struck yet another telling blow on behalf of his newly adopted country. The separation of America from the mother country was far from ensured during the month of June, though a special committee appointed by the Continental Congress was writing the Declaration of Independence. Six of the thirteen colonies were demonstrating a reluctance to cut their ties with Great Britain. Admiral Lord Howe, Sir William's older brother, was crossing the Atlantic with a large fleet of warships and, it was reported, was bringing with him a series of conciliatory proposals to the colonial leaders. No American could fail to understand the significance of Lord Howe's mission. If the government's offer, whatever it might contain, were accepted, the crisis would end, but, if the Americans rejected it, the powerful fleet would help to subdue the rebels.

Prominent men in every colony – among them, many leading merchants in Philadelphia, Boston, and New York – were reluctant to establish an independent nation. The radicals were able to ignore the protests of the Boston merchants, partly because the British occupation of the city had hardened public resistance to the Crown there, but principally because Samuel Adams and his followers had gained complete control of the Massachusetts legislature. The continuing opposition of the Philadelphia and New York business communities to the cause of independence, however, remained a major stumbling block.

Thomas Paine tried to persuade them to see the light of liberty in a new pamphlet, which he called *A Dialogue Between the Ghost of General Montgomery, Just Arrived from the Elysian Fields, and an American Delegate, in a Wood Near Philadelphia*. In spite of its cumbersome title by present-day standards, the work was cogent. Paine speaks his arguments through the mouth of America's first war hero, General Richard Montgomery, who had fallen at Quebec. 'Your dependancy upon the Crown is no advantage,' his Montgomery tells the wavering delegate, 'but rather an injury to the people of Great Britain, as it increases the power and influence of the King. The people are benefitted only by your trade, and this they may have after you are independent of the Crown.' Appealing to the latent patriotism of the delegate, the ghost sorrowfully reproaches him for even contemplating the acceptance of a 'pardon' from a 'royal criminal', and points out that Americans who seek liberty are defending 'the rights of humanity'. Paine cleverly uses every argument that can strengthen his case. France, the omniscient ghost insists, will come to the aid of America the moment independence is declared and not only will provide fighting men, munitions, and warships but also will become America's most active trading partner. Britain, Paine shrewdly points out, needs the raw materials of the New World and will be compelled to maintain a business relationship with America regardless of the political situation. Therefore, the merchants of Philadelphia and New York will double their business. America, he adds, in an appeal to the vanity and emotions of the merchants, 'teems with patriots, heroes, and legislators who are impatient to burst forth into light and importance.' He ends the diatribe by saying that 'monarchy and aristocracy have in all ages been the vehicles of slavery.'

It is difficult to gauge the influence of this pamphlet. But Paine and his friends saw to it that every delegate to the Continental Congress was furnished with a copy, and other copies were sent as gifts to the merchants of the principal cities. At the very least he contributed substantially to the pressures being exerted on the businessmen of America and on the delegates who represented them in the Congress.

Paine's propaganda was unique in its day because of its subtlety. Of all those writing and speaking on behalf of independence in America he alone gave the appearance of relying on a hard core of facts, and even his most outrageous claims seemed to be based on logic. The appeals of such men as Adams and Patrick Henry were blatant and crude in comparison. They sought to sway the feelings of the public: Their Americans were honorable, liberty-loving freemen, and their Britons were villainous, loutish oppressors. In essence, of course, Paine actually followed their example, but he clothed his arguments in intellectual finery, flattering his readers into believing he was directing his appeal to their minds. His conclusions were predetermined, as were those of his colleagues, but he stood apart because he gave his readers the impression that he worked his way, step by step, to these ends.

Numerous attempts were made in the nineteenth century to link Paine with the writing of the Declaration of Independence. But it has not been proved that he had a hand in its preparation. He dined with Jefferson a number of times during June of 1776, but that, in itself, has no significance. Similarly, a number of paragraphs that were deleted from the final version of the Declaration are similar to thoughts that Paine had already expressed in print. But it must be remembered that America's Founding Fathers thought alike on fundamental issues, and it was inevitable that they should paraphrase or even parrot each other from time to time.

Regardless of what his direct contribution may have been, Paine was not content to serve only as a propagandist, and early in July, 1776, while the Continental Congress was approving and publishing the Declaration of Independence, resigned his position as editor of the *Pennsylvania Magazine* and enlisted in the Pennsylvania militia as a private. He had no military experience, and at the age of thirty-nine he was too old for life in the field. Furthermore, he had never fired a musket in his life. But he persisted, and, when his sixty days of service expired, he re-enlisted.

The would-be soldier was assigned to the corps commanded by a fellow Quaker, General Nathanael Green of Rhode Island, who promptly gave him an appointment as a volunteer aide-de-camp. As a member of the general's official family, Paine slept under a roof, ate palatable food, and was relieved of the need to take part in such routine procedures as drilling. He enjoyed his position and made himself useful by writing most of General Greene's letters and reports. But he almost drove his superior to distraction by engaging in long arguments, usually during meals, with other members of the staff. It was his contention that mathematics was the only perfect science, and he supported his position volubly.

Life was neither easy nor pleasant for any American soldier in the months that followed the publication of the Declaration of Independence. General Howe, whose forces outnumbered the rebels by four to one, routed George Washington's raw troops in the Battle of Long Island and forced them to begin a slow retreat through New Jersey. But Howe, because of his dilatory tactics, lost the opportunity to win the war in the late summer and early autumn of 1776.

Paine described the march of Washington and his troops in an article he wrote for the *Pennsylvania Magazine*, published the following year. The American forces, plagued by expiring terms of enlistment and by rising desertions, never numbered more than four thousand men, and at times there were as few as one thousand effectives in the field. Howe, who had left a large garrison in occupied New York and had assigned other troops to guard his supply lines, was nevertheless able to follow with eight thousand fighting men. By November 22 the entire American army had retreated to Newark, where Washington's plan to make a stand was thwarted because men continued to disappear by the hundreds. Whole companies, even battalions, vanished overnight. Those who remained had no cause for cheer: Food was scarce and munitions nonexistent, there were no replacements for worn-out uniforms, and the men were paid in worthless paper money issued by the Continental Congress. The weather was foul, sickness decimated the ranks of the already weakened Americans, and by December the cause of American independence appeared virtually lost.

It was during these dark days that Paine wrote what was to become his most celebrated work, the first of his *Crisis* pamphlets. Most of his time during daylight hours was spent trying to determine how many additional men had deserted as the army continued its retreat into Pennsylvania. So he had to write at night, sitting close to a campfire for illumination and warmth. By the middle of the month, his self-appointed task was finished. The essay appeared originally on December 19 in the *Pennsylvania Journal* and then, four days later, in the form of a pamphlet, printed by Aitkin. This remarkable document was the first of sixteen pamphlets written between 1776 and 1783 that together have become known as *The American Crisis*. The author refused to accept a penny of payment for them and not only had them printed at his own expense but eventually went into debt because of them.

The first pamphlet revealed a Paine whose style and approach had matured. He no longer dealt with the abstract questions of democracy versus monarchy and freedom versus oppression. Personal suffering for a cause in which he believed had tempered him, and his labor under the most difficult conditions produced a work whose opening lines are familiar to every American:

These are the times that try men's souls. The summer soldier and the sunshine patriot will, in this crisis, shrink from the service of their country; but he that stands it *now*, deserves the love and thanks of man and woman. Tyranny, like hell, is not easily conquered; yet we have this consolation with us, that the harder the conflict, the more glorious the triumph. What we obtain too cheap, we esteem too lightly; it is dearness only that gives every thing its value. Heaven knows how to put a proper price upon its goods; and it would be strange indeed if so celestial an article as FREEDOM should not be highly rated. Britain, with an army to enforce her tyranny, has declared that she has a right (not only to tax) but 'to bind us in all cases whatsoever', and if being bound in that manner, is not slavery, then is there not such a thing as slavery upon earth. Even the expression is impious; for so unlimited a power can belong only to God.

Whether the independence of the continent was declared too soon, or delayed too long, I will not now enter into as argument; my own simple opinion is, that had it been eight months earlier, it would have been much better. We did not make a proper use of last winter, neither could we, while we were in a dependent state. However, the fault, if it were one, was all our own; we have none to blame but ourselves. But no great deal is lost yet. All that Howe has been doing for this month past, is rather a ravage than a conquest, which the spirit of the Jerseys, a year ago, would have quickly repulsed, and which time and a little resolution will soon recover.

I have as little superstition in me as any man living, but my secret opinion has ever been, and still is, that God Almighty will not give up a people to military destruction, or leave them unsupportedly to perish, who have so earnestly and so repeatedly sought to avoid the calamities of war, by every decent method which wisdom could invent. Neither have I so much of the infidel in me, as to suppose that He has relinquished the government of the world, and given us up to the care of devils; and as I do not, I cannot see on what ground the king of Britain can look up to heaven for help against us; a common murderer, a highwayman, or a house-breaker has as good a pretense as he.

'Tis surprising to see how rapidly a panic will sometimes run through a country. All nations and ages have been subject to them. Britain has trembled like an ague at the report of a French fleet of flat-bottomed boats; and in the fourteenth century the whole English army, after ravaging the kingdom of France, was driven back like men petrified with fear; and this brave exploit was performed by a few broken forces collected and headed by a woman, Joan of Arc. Would that heaven might inspire some Jersey maid to spirit up her countrymen, and save her fair fellow sufferers from ravage and ravishment! Yet panics, in some cases, have their uses; they produce as much good as hurt. Their duration is always short; the mind soon grows through them, and acquires a firmer habit than before. But their peculiar advantage is, that they are the touchstones of sincerity and hypocrisy, and bring things and men to light, which might otherwise have lain forever undiscovered. In fact, they have the same effect on secret traitors, which an imaginary apparition would have upon a private murderer. They sift out the hidden thoughts of man, and hold them up in public in the world.

Paine's approach was calm and reasonable – no mean feat when we consider that he was undergoing personal hardships and privations. After describing the military situation in detail, he allowed his tone to become warmer. The British, he said, were concentrating their military efforts in the mid-Atlantic states because of their mistaken belief that the public there supported the Crown. New England saw no redcoats because there were no Tories in that portion of the country. Then he appealed to the faint-hearted and the fence-sitters in words calculated to arouse their latent patriotism:

Before the line of irrevocable separation be drawn between us, let us reason the matter together: Your conduct is an invitation to the enemy, yet not one in a thousand of you has heart enough to join him. Howe is as much deceived by you as the American cause is injured by you. He expects you will all take up arms, and flock to his standard, with muskets on your shoulders. Your opinions are of no use to him, unless you support him personally, for 'tis soldiers, and not Tories, that he wants.

I once felt all that kind of anger, which a man ought to feel, against the mean principles that are held by the Tories; a noted one, who kept a tavern at Amboy, was standing at his door, with as pretty a child in his hand, about eight or nine years old, as I ever saw, and after speaking his mind as freely as he thought was prudent, finished with this unfatherly expression, 'Well! Give me peace in my day!' Not a man lives on the continent but fully believes that a separation must some time or other finally take place, and a generous parent should have said, '*If there must be trouble, let it be in my day, that my child might have peace,*' and this single reflection, well applied, is sufficient to awaken every man to duty. Not a place upon earth might be so happy as America. Her situation is remote from all the wrangling world, and she has nothing to do but to trade with them. A man can distinguish himself between temper and principle, and I am confident, as I am that God governs the world, that America will never be happy till she gets clear of foreign dominion. Wars, without ceasing, will break out till that period arrives, and the continent must in the end be conqueror; for though the flame of liberty may sometimes cease to shine, the coal can never expire.

Having presented his case concisely, Paine doubled back and repeated his arguments in different words, by which he weakened his presentation. But it is wrong to judge him by late-twentieth-century standards. His readers expected him to handle his material as he did, and even in a time of grave crisis the Enlightenment man had ample time to read, re-read, and ponder. The thesis of the pamphleteer-soldier was basically simple: All who failed to follow the American colors, or at the very least actively support the cause as civilians, were thereby giving aid and comfort to an enemy who was determined to make slaves of the people of the former colonies. No halfway measures were possible; the time had come for all men to make their principles known and to take a strong stand on behalf of them.

Always at his best when summarizing, Paine closed on a rousing note:

I thank God, that I fear not. I see no real cause for fear. I know our situation well, and can see the way out of it. While our army was collected, Howe dared not risk a battle; and it is no credit to him that he decamped from the White Plains, and waited a mean opportunity to ravage the defenseless Jerseys; but it is great credit to us that, with a handful of men, we sustained an orderly retreat for near an hundred miles, brought off our ammunition, all our field pieces, the greatest part of our stores, and had four rivers to pass. None can say that our retreat was precipitate, for we were near three weeks in performing it, that the country might have time to come in. Twice we marched back to meet the enemy, and remained out till dark. The sign of fear was not seen in our camp, and had not some of the cowardly, disaffected inhabitants spread false alarms through the country, the Jerseys had never been ravaged. Once more we are again collected and collecting; our new army at both ends of the continent is recruiting fast, and we shall be able to open the next campaign with sixty thousand men, well armed and clothed. This is our situation, and who will may know it. By perseverance and fortitude we have the prospect of a glorious issue; by cowardice and submission, the sad choice of a variety of evils – a ravaged country – a depopulated city – habitations without safety, and slavery without hope – our homes turned into barracks and bawdy-houses for Hessians, and a future race to provide for, whose fathers we shall doubt of.

Look on this picture, and weep over it! and if there yet remains one thoughtless wretch who believes it not, let him suffer it unlamented.

Following the custom of the period, Paine signed the pamphlet 'Common Sense', which was a signal to hundreds of thousands of Americans that the author of *The American Crisis* was the same man who had written the work with which the entire nation was familiar.

Only two days after the leaflet made its appearance General Washington recrossed the Delaware River and, to improve his troops' morale, conducted his Christmas raid on the British and their German mercenary allies at Trenton.

A self-taught propagandist, Paine thoroughly understood the principles of his profession. The cause of the infant United States was almost hopeless. The Continental Congress was bankrupt, and the states, themselves poor, were reluctant to provide funds for the embryo national government. Men thought of themselves as New Yorkers or Pennsylvanians or Virginians, not citizens of the United States, and those who volunteered for army duty preferred to serve for short periods in their own militia rather than in the Continental Line, where they would have to enlist for a year or two at a time.

It was inconceivable that sixty thousand men would volunteer for any American armed force, and there were no funds either in the Congress's treasury or in those of the states with which to pay for food, munitions and uniforms, much less provide medical treatment and other care. The American Navy consisted only of a few privateers, privately owned ships whose crews were more interested in prize money than in destroying British warships. Any intelligent man familiar with the over-all situation was certain to conclude that the Americans could not win the war.

Paine knew the facts, but, having made the cause of American independence his own, he took a bold stand. Washington's attack on Trenton gave Paine's words seeming validity, convincing the American people that the portrait of the military situation drawn in his pamphlet was accurate. Between them, the commander in chief and the writer-soldier saved the day. The results of their combined offensive were spectacular: Desertions, which had been bleeding Washington's forces, ceased abruptly, and several thousand newcomers – the precise number has never been accurately determined – rallied to the colors. At least for the moment, the armed forces of the new United States were saved from the threat of disintegration.

It has been said that Paine wrote his pamphlet because he knew of Washington's forthcoming surprise attack, but such advance knowledge would have been impossible. General Greene's volunteer aide could not have been privy to a closely held secret known only to a small handful of the commander in chief's immediate subordinates. But, even supposing that General Green had confided in Paine, the pamphlet had been written before Washington had made his bold plan to recross the Delaware River. The fact that the publication of Paine's words was simultaneous with Washington's assault was a happy coincidence, one of the few accidents that benefited the American cause in the early days of the war. Had the publication and the attack been intentionally synchronized, the effect could not have been greater.

The first *Crisis* reached an audience only a trifle smaller than the readership of *Common Sense* and was an effective instrument in bolstering the resolve of the American people to prosecute the war to a successful conclusion. Franklin, who, at the time of the new pamphlet's publication, sailed for France in order to join Arthur Lee and Silas Deane in attempts to persuade the French Government to support the war, called his protégé 'the most renowned and convincing author in the United States'.

By the time the first *Crisis* pamphlet was published Paine was already at work on a second. In all, he wrote eighteen pamphlets before the war ended, each of them contributing enormously to the spirit of the beleaguered people. The second *Crisis* is of special interest because, for the first time, the author allowed his own personality to enter into his writing. It was addressed to Admiral Lord Howe, and the corset-maker from Thetford showed his pride when he wrote, 'Your lordship, I find, has now commenced author, and published a proclamation; I have published a *Crisis*.'

At the conclusion of the second pamphlet, which appeared about a month after the publication of the first *Crisis*, Paine wrote at some length about himself. He was motivated not by vanity but by his changed and still rapidly changing situation. It was inevitable that his increased prominence should have caused envy, and a number of unpleasant rumors were being circulated about him. According to one of them, the recent immigrant was an imported hired hand, a professional writer who had no patriotic principles of his own and had been brought to America for the purpose of churning out propaganda documents for pay. A second story insisted that he was writing pamphlets strictly for his own gain and that his labors on behalf of independence were making him wealthy. He would leave the country, this account stated, as soon as he acquired his fortune. In the second pamphlet, his reply to the gossip-mongers was succinct:

What I write is pure nature, and my pen and my soul have ever gone together. My writings I have always given away, receiving only the expense of printing and paper, and sometimes not even that. I never counted either fame or interest, and my manner of life, to those who know it, will justify what I say. My study is to be useful.

Paine's brief comments about himself called the attention of his military superiors to his personal situation. He was forty in January, 1777, and was totally unsuited for life as a soldier. Nathanael Greene appreciated his assistance in handling correspondence and other documents, but it was apparent that his talents were being wasted. General Washington, who was well aware of the influence that had been exerted by *Common Sense* and the first *Crisis* pamphlet, felt the same way.

But Paine had developed a fierce sense of pride, and under no circumstances did his superiors want to crush his spirit or even hurt his feelings. Therefore, his transfer from military life to the role of a civilian had to be accomplished with tact. Greene conferred privately in Philadelphia with Aitkin and Rush. They, in turn, talked at some length with the man who was then emerging as the most powerful politician in Pennsylvania, Joseph Reed, the state's chairman of public safety. And it was Reed who found a graceful way out for Paine. On January 20, 1777, acting with the secret connivance of Samuel Adams, the first of the great American propagandists and by now an enthusiastic admirer of Paine's work, the Philadelphia Council of Safety offered Paine a post as secretary of a commission that would be sent jointly by the council and the Continental Congress to negotiate a treaty with the Indians of Pennsylvania. Paine had already expressed in print his passionate concern for the Indians, and he found it difficult, too, to resist the lump sum offered him for the work – £300 in cash. He later revealed that, at the time, he had had less than three shillings to his name, and it is doubtful that he had ever seen as much as £100 on any single occasion.

General Greene urged his aide-de-camp to accept the offer, saying that Paine could accomplish far more good for the people of America by negotiating with the Indians than he could as an army private holding a courtesy rank. So Paine agreed, and on January 21 he became a civilian again. He had no idea his friends were making certain that other employment would be found for him as soon as dealings with the Indians ended.

6

The Peripatetic Patriot

Thomas Paine's military service ended on the day he was appointed as secretary of the commission to treat with the Indians. Although General Greene wrote him a glowing letter of thanks for his efforts as a soldier, Paine later wrote that he was 'suffused with shame' because he had never fired a musket at the enemy.

He owned one threadbare suit and a single pair of shoes, so he had to replenish his wardrobe. First-rate material that had been stored in Philadelphia warehouses for several years was still available, but he chose a new suit of inexpensive cloth and elected to buy utilitarian boots rather than shoes. He could afford better, but after living in penury for so many years he had developed an indifference to his appearance; his tastes were never to change.

On February 4 he left Philadelphia with other members of the commission and rode north to the little town of Easton, Pennsylvania, on the Delaware River. Representatives of the Seneca, Mohawk, and Iroquois were gathering in Easton, and were joined by chiefs of the Algonkian and several other northern tribes. The question, which was not resolved, was whether the Indians were willing to join forces with the rebellious colonies or would cast their lot with England. The meetings, which opened on February 8, were held in the new German Reformed Church, built the previous year, and the routines were established on the first day. According to Paine's later accounts, everyone helped himself to a glass of rum and, while the liquor was being consumed, a local musician played hymns on the church organ. No participant was allowed a second glass until the day's business was concluded, but thereafter everyone drank what he pleased. A brief reference in a letter Paine wrote to Franklin indicates that he made here his first acquaintance with the raw rum commonly served in America, which was far different from the more refined liquor sent to England. He thoroughly enjoyed drinking, but appears not to have allowed it to interfere with business.

This was the first time that Paine had met any Indians, and he was fascinated by them. He went to great lengths to know and understand them. He became friendly with the chief of 'one of the northern tribes', who spoke a little English, and attempted to learn the language of the Iroquois, which most of the natives spoke. He made sufficient progress so that, by the time the talks ended in mid-March, he could understand without an interpreter much that the Indians said.

At best, the accomplishments of the conference were questionable. A treaty was signed, with each side promising to respect the borders of the other's territory, but, like a score of other agreements concluded during the American Revolution, it was broken with impunity by both sides. Paine wrote the report that was submitted to the Philadelphia Council and the Continental Congress.

After his return to Philadelphia he continued to work on his *Crisis* pamphlets. But the £300 he had received would not pay his expenses forever. His friends were determined to find him suitable employment, other than military service, that would aid the war effort. On April 17 the Continental Congress transformed its ineptly named Committee of Secret Correspondence into the Committee of Foreign Affairs. This group was dominated by Samuel Adams and Richard Henry Lee, and, when they submitted a bill to hire Paine as the new committee's salaried secretary, the measure was passed unanimously by the Congress.

No appointment better illustrates the lack of experienced talent in the United States. Paine's selection was considered wise because less than two and a half years earlier he had been a 'foreigner'. Now he was expected to deal with France, Spain, Prussia, the Netherlands, imperial Russia, and other countries, but he could speak no language other than English. If he had paid even fleeting visits to any of these lands, it had been as an ordinary seaman. He could scarcely qualify as a British political expert, his only experience having been the part-time lobbying he had done on behalf of the excisemen. Nevertheless, he performed his duties brilliantly.

Immediately before taking the position on the staff of the Congress, Paine wrote his *Crisis III* pamphlet, which he dated April 19, 1777. In it he tackled an issue of such delicacy that every other American writer had avoided it.

Ironically, the man who had been reared as a Quaker and who still believed in many of the precepts he had been taught as a boy became engaged in a confrontation with the Society of Friends. The Quakers were the wealthiest, most respectable religious group in Philadelphia, and regardless of their sympathies with the cause of American Independence, an overwhelming majority of them were opposed on religious grounds to the struggle to obtain it. Paine could not share their view that physical combat should be avoided at all costs, and he attacked the Quaker ideology by paraphrasing sayings common to the Quakers themselves. Members of the Pennsylvania Society of Friends were traitors, he said, harshly accusing them of being secret Tories who labored in private to secure a British victory. He proposed that all Quakers be required to take an oath of allegiance to the new United States, an oath, he pointed out, that other Americans would take voluntarily. In June of that same year, Pennsylvania required all males of eighteen years and over to take an oath of allegiance to the state.

The validity of the issue raised by Paine is questionable. Although it might be argued that the new pamphlet may have raised the patriotic blood pressure of most Americans somewhat, Paine did not succeed in persuading any Quakers in either Pennsylvania or Rhode Island, where most were living, to join either the Continental Army or the militia. The only notable result was a further deterioration in the relations between the Quakers and other residents of those states, many of whom were already alienated by a philosophy that they failed to understand.

Consequently the influence of *Crisis III* must be regarded as divisive and harmful to the American cause.

Paine's charges against Quakers were as unfair as they were vicious. No more than a very few members of the Society of Friends harbored Loyalist sympathies, and even these few engaged in no overt anti-American activities. The vast majority were patriots who supported the American cause financially and politically, although they did not take part in the fighting. Many became Paine's enemies, and it was they who first called him an agnostic, insisting that he was an active anti-christ. At that time, however, no one else raised a similar charge against him, and the claim was not taken seriously.

In April or May of 1777, Paine found a new place to live, and soon afterward his life became more complicated. He took a suite consisting of a bedroom and a study in a pleasant, shingled house on Walnut Street in Philadelphia. The house was the property of Mrs Martha Daley, a widow with three young children, who rented the quarters out because she needed the revenue. She was in her early thirties, blonde and vivacious, a literate woman who had been a subscriber to the *Pennsylvania Magazine* and was an admirer of Paine's pamphlets. Whether he had been celibate since coming to America or had frequented the Market Street brothels from time to time, he had been starved of feminine warmth and companionship. His good fortune brought him into the home of a discerning, attractive young woman who believed that he was one of the most important American leaders. He ate most of his meals with the family, guided Mrs Daley's reading, and, almost inevitably, drifted into an affair with her.

The depth of their relationship is unknown, Paine's letters to Mrs Daley having been subsequently lost or destroyed. However, a number of contemporaries who enjoyed occasional evenings in the Daley parlor and saw them together assumed that they would be married. That, at least, is what Richard Henry Lee said in a letter to his brother, Arthur, and Thomas Jefferson made a similar comment in a letter to Franklin. John Adams, who did not particularly care for Paine, considering his manner too didactic, wondered in a letter to his wife written a number of years later why Paine and Mrs. Daley had not married. Adams's tone indicated that, had Paine been a gentleman, he would have salvaged the lady's reputation by offering her his name.

The reasons for the failure of Paine and Martha Daley to marry

are obvious to anyone who knows Paine's background; it may
be that his colleagues and friends were unfamiliar with his past.
He and Elizabeth Paine were formally separated but not divorced.
The Church of England maintained strict standards on the question, and, even if Elizabeth had applied for a divorce, her request
would have been rejected.

Whether Mrs Daley was aware that her lover already had a wife
is unknown. Be that as it may, the affair lasted until 1781, at
which time Paine left the Daley house for good. In the following
year Martha Daley married a retired lieutenant colonel of the
Continental Line, and she and her children moved with him to a
farm in western Pennsylvania.

During the years she and Paine were together they were
separated only once – during the period of the British occupation
of Philadelphia, when he was forced to flee from the city. Except
for that momentary interruption, he knew normal living of a kind
that had been denied to him since his brief first marriage. He felt
a contentment that had been lacking; his appearance was neater
and he gained weight. The presence of the Daley children may
have spoiled his pleasure somewhat; Paine never enjoyed a
rapport with youngsters and on occasion wrote that he felt
uncomfortable in their presence. In the main, however, he was
happy, and he found the energy to work more vigorously than
ever.

Paine's duties as secretary of the Committee of Foreign Affairs
corresponded, roughly, to those of a foreign minister; it would be
no exaggeration to say that he served as the first U.S. secretary of
state. Representatives of the Continental Congress, called agents,
were sent to the major neutral islands in the West Indies, and
Paine corresponded regularly with them, supplying them with
information, receiving their reports, and directing their activities.
He also coordinated the work of the various missions in Europe,
but he did not make policy, that function being performed only
by the members of the committee. All major questions were
referred to the entire Congress for a vote.

When Philadelphia fell to the British on September 27, 1777,
Paine accompanied members of the Congress to York, Pennsylvania, the temporary capital, and, after Sir Henry Clinton
was forced to evacuate America's largest city the following June
18 after overextending his supply lines from New York, Paine
was one of the first to return.

During that period, when American fortunes were at their lowest ebb, Paine also performed a difficult and delicate feat for the Pennsylvania Assembly, which paid him for his services. The state legislature heard very little about the activities and plans of General Washington, who was spending the winter with his battered forces at Valley Forge. In order to correct that situation Paine went to Valley Forge, visited the commander in chief, and established a new method of passing along intelligence to the assembly.

Writing his *Crisis* pamphlets in addition to his other activities, Paine was always busy and had little time to himself. He had no hobbies and appeared happy to be spending all of his energies in the fight for American independence. He was a prodigious correspondent, taking it upon himself to write long, informative letters to members of the Committee of Foreign Affairs when they were absent from the capital on personal or official business. Less than two weeks after Lieutenant General John Burgoyne surrendered his entire army to the Americans at Saratoga, New York, thus opening the way to the granting of French aid to the United States, Paine wrote a letter to Richard Henry Lee in Virginia. In his communication, dated October 30, 1777, he described the disposition of the British troops who had become captives and he exhaustively explored legal, diplomatic, and political alternatives. Typically, the letter was more than seven thousand words long.

At the end of October, 1777, he allowed himself the brief luxury of trying to fulfill his yearning for military glory. General Greene had beeng iven command of the American defenses on the Delaware River, and Paine, accompanying Colonel Christopher Greene to the general's headquarters, went out onto the river in an open boat. While inspecting enemy positions on the far side of the river, they were subjected to heavy bombardment. The British gunnery was inaccurate, however, and the two occupants of the boat returned to their camp unscathed.

During Washington's long, terrible winter at Valley Forge, Paine wrote *Crisis V*, one of the most significant and influential of his pamphlets. Most Americans had not yet recognized the importance of the victory achieved by Generals Horatio Gates and Benedict Arnold at Saratoga. All they knew was that Washington and the remnants of his army were spending the winter at Valley Forge, a 'natural fortress' in the Pennsylvania hills, and that the British had occupied Philadelphia. Not until the following spring, when a hardened, disciplined American corps of Continentals would emerge from Valley Forge, would the true meaning of that winter's suffering become clear.

Many Americans became discouraged, and there was talk everywhere of making peace with the British on almost any terms. Even a great many members of the Continental Congress lost hope and went off to their homes to await the end of the war.

Thomas Paine, in *Crisis V*, gave them some encouragement. First, writing in lucid language that any reader could understand, even one who had no knowledge of military principles, he explained that the total defeat of a major British army had been 'an achievement unparalleled in the brief history of American arms'. Not only would it improve the morale of every American fighting man, he maintained, but it would achieve concrete results as well. France had been fence-sitting, waiting to see how the Americans fared on their own before committing herself to giving aid. With an assurance based on his own correspondence with the American commissioners in Paris, Paine wrote that France was certain to provide men, money, ships, munitions – all that the Americans needed from a strong ally to ensure eventual victory over Britain.

Turning to another, far more delicate subject, Paine wrote bluntly of a plan to replace Washington as leader of the American troops. Some members of the Continental Congress had become disillusioned with General Washington and had been hoping to name General Gates commander in chief. Gates, a former British Army officer, had been flattered by the proposal and had maintained a correspondence with his backers. Washington, acting with a typical lack of selfishness, had sent some of his best troops to reinforce Gates, among them the brigade of sharpshooters commanded by Daniel Morgan of Virginia. Paine emphasized the role Washington had played in the Saratoga victory and declared that Gates was aware of it and was grateful to his superior. In addition, Paine pointed out, the victory at Saratoga was but one phase of Washington's long-range plan. The time would soon come when the growing strength of the main army at Valley Forge would compel the British to evacuate Philadelphia and return to their garrison in New York. This prophecy came true, of course, in June of 1778. *Crisis V* was significant not only because it helped to raise the spirits of bewildered civilians but also because it drove the final nails into the coffin of the so-called 'Gates conspiracy'. Neither Horatio Gates nor any of his supporters in Congress could hope to win him the top military post in the country in the face of Paine's clear exposition.

The service Paine performed on Washington's behalf was more remarkable than appears on the surface. The truth of the matter was that Thomas Paine and George Washington did not enjoy close personal relations. The Virginia planter was an aristocrat, and the former corset-maker from Thetford, who had known only dire poverty for almost four decades, was habitually uncomfortable in the presence of any members of the general's class. Washington, for his part, regarded the slovenly Paine as too ungentlemanly and, above all, too forthright in his views. But Paine had the good sense to recognize Washington's importance to the American cause. Like so many others, he marveled at the commander in chief's level-headed patience, his refusal to become discouraged in the face of overwhelming odds. Only Washington could achieve ultimate victory; under Gates or someone like him the cause of American liberty would be lost. Aware of this, Paine did all he could – which was a great deal – to bolster Washington's position. It is not surprising to note that, although Paine and the general continued to feel professional respect for each other, their relationship never ripened into friendship.

Paine wrote *Crisis V* in virtual isolation at the home of a crony, William Henry, Jr, in the sleepy little town of Lancaster, Pennsylvania, which makes his ability to foretell the future all the more surprising. Not even the members of the Foreign Affairs Committee shared his certainty that France would come to America's assistance. Most military men, including a number of American general officers, had failed to grasp the intricacies of Washington's long-range strategic planning. But the one-time craftsman from rural England, a man with no training in military affairs or international relations, had understood the whole situation.

It was impossible to quarrel with his advice. Americans, he said, should leave petty wrangling to the enemy. 'We never had so small an army to fight against,' he wrote, 'nor so fair an opportunity of final success as *now*.' He also pointed out that France would not act out of altruism. She would enter the war, as might Spain, for sound reasons of her own. Great Britain had been weakened by her three-year struggle to conquer her rebellious colonies, so the French and the Spaniards had an opportunity such as they had not had in many years to trounce her in a major war.

No sooner was *Crisis V* completed than Paine turned to the preparation of *Crisis VI*. He also was concerning himself with many matters that were outside his official range of interests. One of these was the plague of counterfeiting that continued to harm the American economy. The situation was complicated because not only was the Continental Congress printing its own money, but each of the thirteen states had its own currency, too. And when, for example, a Connecticut counterfeiter was captured in Pennsylvania, he was released without trial because Pennsylvania did not want to go to the trouble of sending him to prison and caring for him there.

Paine realized that American finances would become even more of a shambles unless strong, positive steps were taken. In April, 1778, he was upset when some counterfeiters of Continental dollars appeared to be on the verge of release from a Lancaster jail because the Pennsylvania authorities cared only about their own money. Writing a long letter to Henry Laurens of South Carolina, who had succeeded John Hancock as president of the Continental Congress, Paine offered a series of specific proposals that would end the chaotic situation. The core of the problem, Paine wrote, was the lack of authority vested in the Continental Congress. Here he identified precisely the greatest single weakness of the system of government established under the Articles of Confederation, which were in force in 1778 – a weakness that would persist until the adoption in 1789 of the new constitution, which would establish a strong federal government. Arguing that the counterfeiting of money in any state hurt all thirteen of the states and 'placed the entire continent in danger', Paine urged that the Congress obtain from the states the right to prosecute all counterfeiters, regardless of whether they printed and passed state money or Continental money. Paine closed on an angry note, declaring that forgery was a 'sin against all men alike'. But, at that time, several prominent American forgers had taken refuge in British-occupied Philadelphia. The Congress, he suggested, should demand that Sir William Howe turn these men over to American authorities for punishment without delay. If Howe refused, he would become a personal accessory to their crimes, and 'the apprehension of Personal Consequences may have some effect on his conduct.' Paine could not be accused of lacking either imagination or ingenuity.

Paine was three writers in one: He was a news reporter who depicted events with crisp accuracy, never wasting a word; he was a 'color' writer who described scenes with the sensitivity of a novelist and the delicacy of a poet, and, above all, he was the military and political analyst who did not hesitate, even when writing to the man he admired more than all others, to interpret the significance of what had happened and to predict the future in the light of what had transpired.

Although Paine did not regard himself as a military expert, he did not hesitate to express his opinions on that subject or on any other. He had become a member of the inner circle of the American leadership, and his relations with the rest of the new Establishment were informal. Most men were reluctant to offer advice directly to the austere Washington, but Paine dared to speak out when others were silent. A letter he wrote to Washington late in the spring of 1778 is reproduced here in its entirety:

York Town, June 5, 1778.–
Sir,–

As a general opinion prevails that the Enemy will quit Philadelphia, I take the Liberty of transmitting you my reasons why it is probable they will not. In your difficult and distinguished Situation every hint may be useful.

I put the immediate cause of their evacuation to be a Declaration of War in Europe made by them or against them: in which case, their Army would be wanted for other Service, and likewise because their present situation would be too unsafe, being subject to be blocked up by France and attacked by you and her jointly.

Britain will avoid a War with France if she can; which according to my arrangement of Politics she may easily do – She must see the necessity of acknowledging, some time or other, the Independance of America; if she is wise enough to make that acknowledgement *now*, she of consequence admits the Right of France to the quiet enjoyment of her Treaty, and therefore no War can take place upon the Ground of having concluded a Treaty with revolted British Subjects.

This being admitted, their apprehension of being doubly attacked, or of being wanted elsewhere, cease being of consequence; and they will then endeavor to hold all they can, that they may have something to restore, in lieu of something else which they will demand; as I know of no Instance where conquered Plans were surrendered up prior to, but only in consequence of a Treaty of Peace.

You will observe, Sir. that my reasoning is founded on the

70

supposition of their being reasonable Beings, which if they are not, then they are not within the compass of my System.

I am, Sir, with every wish for your happiness, Your Affectionate and humble Obt. [obedient] Servant,

THOS. PAINE.

His Excellency, Genl. Washington, Valley Forge.

Regardless of whether Paine's reasoning was sound or specious, it remains remarkable that he could address himself to such matters with complete self-confidence. Only four years earlier he had been a total failure in life, a minor tax collector who had been dismissed from his post, a craftsman who had made ladies' undergarments in return for starvation wages. Now that he had been given the opportunity to live and work on a far higher plane, he had responded to the challenge and was meeting every test. In the light of his further development, it must be said that he was a genius who had required the chance to demonstrate his extraordinary talents.

7

A Feud with Silas Deane

Thomas Paine, like most followers of what had become his true vocation, was a compulsive writer. By 1778 he was the most widely read author in the United States, each of his pamphlets selling at least a quarter of a million copies. Thousands of additional copies mysteriously found their way across the Atlantic and were smuggled into Great Britain, where he had an enthusiastic Whig readership. But Paine was not satisfied with his efforts; still regarding himself as something of a disciple of Oliver Goldsmith's, he turned back to poetry.

Vast numbers of Americans knew he was the writer who signed his pamphlets 'Common Sense', but he was sensitive about his poems. Demonstrating a shyness that was lacking in the presentation of his prose works, he published his poetry anonymously. The most famous of his poems, one that achieved a wide circulation, was written in 1778 and was called 'The American Patriot's Prayer'. In spite of its popularity Paine refused to admit he had written it, and not until a quarter of a century had passed was he willing to let the truth be known. According to Moncure Daniel Conway, the most perceptive of Paine's nineteenth-century biographers, this brief work expressed the author's personal creed with more success than any of his other writings.

> Parent of all, omnipotent
>   In Heaven, and earth below,
> Through all creation's bounds unspent,
>   Whose streams of goodness flow.
>
> Teach me to know from whence I rose,
>   And unto what designed;
> No private aims let me propose,
>   Since link'd with human kind.
>
> But chief to hear my country's voice,
>   May all my thoughts incline;
> 'Tis reason's law, 'tis virtue's choice,
>   'Tis nature's call and thine.
>
> Me from fair freedom's sacred cause
>   Let nothing e'er divide;
> Grandeur, nor gold, nor vain applause,
>   Nor friendship false misguide.
>
> Let me not faction's partial hate
>   Pursue to this Land's woe;
> Nor grasp the thunder of the state
>   To wound a private foe.
>
> If, for the right to wish the wrong
>   My country shall combine,
> Single to serve th' erroneous throng,
>   Spight of themselves, be mine.

The personal sacrifices Paine had already made amply demonstrated that he practiced what he preached. He could have been wealthy by 1778, but he had no funds other than the small salary paid to him by the Continental Congress. In his correspondence he swore he was willing to give all he possessed for the sake of liberty, and he continued to contribute all he made from his pamphlets to the cause of independence.

As a result of one of the more complicated political struggles that took place within the American camp during the Revolution, Paine was required to demonstrate that he meant every word of his pledge. His genius was remarkable, but tact was never one of his assets, and his lack of it created a controversy that had dire consequences for him. The case hinged on the oath of office that Paine had written for himself, which he had prepared in such a manner that it would give him sufficient opportunity to pursue his career as an author in almost any manner he saw fit. According to the archives of the Continental Congress, it was required of one who held his post 'that the said secretary, previous to his entering on his office, take an oath, to be administered by the president, well and faithfully to execute the trust reposed in him, according to his best skill and judgment; and to disclose no matter, the knowledge of which shall be acquired in consequence of his office, that he shall be directed to keep secret.' In all fairness to Paine, he did not violate his oath, not having been told to remain silent on the issue that caused the uproar. He had every right, technically speaking, to say whatever he pleased on the matter. His error was one of judgment: He said too much, too forcibly, and in the process he offended many members of the Congress, who were afraid that the basic integrity and reputation of that body were at stake. Paine miscalculated, and, although he was always eager to do battle for what he believed to be right, he was surprised, in this instance, to discover that he was merely tilting at windmills. He was engaged in a combat that he could not win.

The idea of France supplying aid to the American colonists who were fighting for their independence actually was initiated in France rather than in the United States. The first spark was provided by Pierre de Beaumarchais, one of the leading French playwrights of the eighteenth century, who had considerable influence at court because he had acted for over a decade as a secret agent for the French Crown – or so the Paris press of the period claimed. Long an admirer of America, he was the first to propose in May, 1775, that such aid be sent, and both King Louis XVI and his foreign minister, the comte de Vergennes, were receptive to the idea. France wanted to avoid another war with Great Britain at that time, so a scheme was conceived whereby government funds would be channeled to the United States through Beaumarchais on a supposedly private basis. On June 10, 1776, an initial payment of 1 million livres (the French unit of currency then in use) was made to Beaumarchais, but it was not enough to send to the Americans, and he waited until he accumulated more. (The Frenchman ultimately gave substantial sums for the American cause out of his own pocket, too, thanks to his growing enthusiasm for their enterprise.) The first payment from the French treasury to Beaumarchais was made one month before the arrival in Paris of Silas Deane, a native of Groton, Connecticut, who had served as a delegate to the Continental Congress from 1774 to 1776 and who had been sent as a member of the commission to obtain assistance from France. The second of the commissioners to arrive was Benjamin Franklin, who left Philadelphia in December of 1776; the third, Arthur Lee, did not reach France until late in 1777.

Many aspects of the case are still unsolved two centuries later, but it appears that Deane's worst error was that of claiming credit for the gift of the 1 million livres that had already passed into the hands of Beaumarchais by the time of the American's arrival in France. On the other hand, Deane may have been completely innocent; down to the present day his apologists have claimed, first, that he was deceived by Beaumarchais, who supposedly did not want to share the glory of his diplomatic mission with anyone else and, second, that Deane did not know that the initial payment to the supposedly private company had already been made. In any event, Deane was given the money soon after his arrival, and he forwarded it to Philadelphia. This sum was a tiny fraction of what the Americans actually needed, and a formal treaty was arranged by the American commissioners after the victory at Saratoga convinced Louis XVI and his government that the United States would win the war. Large-scale aid began to flow in the early spring of 1778, and included tens of millions of livres in cash.

Deane's personal situation was complicated by the renewal of an old friendship in Paris with Edward Bancroft, a seemingly harmless physician who was actually a British spy. Whether Deane knew his real identity, and accepted bribes from him, or was ignorant of Bancroft's mission, as he claimed until the end of his days, has never been determined.

Beaumarchais sent a representative named de Francy to America in the spring of 1778, to demand repayment of his 1 million livres and other expenses. The name of Silas Deane figured prominently in the accounts that Beaumarchais sent to the Continental Congress, and Deane was called home to give a full explanation of what had been happening in Paris. Deane returned home in July of 1778 and immediately appeared before the Congress, which met as a committee of the whole to question him. He may not have been guilty of wrong-doing, but his defense was so badly prepared that he was under grave suspicion from the outset of the investigation. He could not remember many of the details of his various transactions with the French. This was natural enough because he had been in almost daily contact with either Beaumarchais or the foreign ministry, but his lapses annoyed members of the Congress. Even more important, he had left in Paris virtually all of the documents pertaining to his mission, and he could produce nothing in writing to substantiate his claims. Worst of all, he had borrowed fairly large sums of money from Beaumarchais for personal expenses and had lived far more lavishly in Paris than had either Franklin or Lee.

The United States was not yet strong enough to tolerate a public scandal, so Deane was interrogated in closed session by the Congress on August 9, 1778. The hearing proved inconclusive, so a second secret meeting was held on August 21. Deane requested a third session, but by this time the Congress had heard enough, and he was refused. The members of the Congress were reluctant to charge Deane with embezzlement and other crimes when the charges already made against him could not be proved. On the other hand, he had not been cleared either; so the Congress temporized, hoping that new evidence of some sort would be forthcoming in due time.

Deane was anxious to have his good name restored, of course, and late in the year he lost patience. The people of the United States learned of his case for the first time from an open letter that he wrote, an 'Appeal to the Free and Virtuous Citizens of America', published in the press on December 5. No member of the Continental Congress replied, but the secretary of the Committee of Foreign Affairs, who believed without reservation that Deane was guilty of all charges against him, was so indignant he could not keep silent. On December 15 a letter over Paine's signature was published in the *Pennsylvania Packet*. Of greater significance than the piece itself was a letter of explanation, dated that same day, which Paine sent to Henry Laurens, president of the Congress:

In this morning's paper is a piece addressed to Mr Deane, in which your name is mentioned. My intention in relating the circumstances with wch. it is connected is to prevent the Enemy drawing any unjust conclusions from an accidental division in the House on matters no ways political. You will please to observe that I have been exceedingly careful to preserve the honor of Congress in the minds of the people who have been so exceedingly fretted by Mr Deane's address – and this will appear the more necessary when I inform you that a proposal has been made for calling a Town Meeting to demand 'justice' for Mr Deane. I have been applied to smoothly and roughly not to publish this piece. Mr Deane has likewise been with the printer.

Henry Laurens believed, as Paine did, that Deane might be guilty of malfeasance and that, in any case, he had no right to claim credit for the French treaty. But Laurens, as it happened, had just resigned as president of the Congress. His place had been taken by John Jay of New York (who would become chief justice of the United States after the adoption of the Constitution in 1789). Jay, as it also happened, was one of Silas Deane's strongest supporters in the Congress.

Jay had a right to be annoyed with Paine, who had conferred with no one before taking it upon himself to issue a public reply to Deane. Jay and the other members of the Deane faction let their displeasure be known, but the matter would have been forgotten had Paine considered his duty done. Incapable of keeping silent, however, he felt that Deane should be exposed no matter what the cost.

In another letter to the *Pennsylvania Packet*, published on January 2, 1779, Paine wrote:

> If Mr Deane or any other gentleman will procure an order from Congress to inspect an account in my office, or any of Mr Deane's friends in Congress will take the trouble of coming themselves, I will give him or them my attendance, and shew them in handwriting which Mr Deane is well acquainted with, that the supplies he so pompously plumes himself upon were promised and engaged, and that as a present, before he ever arrived in France; and the part that fell to Mr Deane was only to see it done, and how he has performed that service the public are acquainted with.

Paine was treading on delicate ground. No official, American or French, had publicly admitted that any help had come to the rebellious colonies before the signing of the treaty in the spring of 1778. France was still trying to avoid an open break with Great Britain, and such an admission might goad Lord North's ministry into a declaration of war against the French.

All still might have been well had Paine let the Silas Deane affair rest. There were no repercussions, even though he had been indiscreet. But he was determined to make certain he won his case. Basically a propagandist, he had learned to hammer at a theme until victory was ensured. So, on January 5, 1779, he wrote yet another public letter, and this time he went too far when he said, 'Those who are now her [America's] allies, prefaced that alliance by an early and generous friendship; yet that we might not attribute too much to human or auxiliary aid, so unfortunate were these supplies that only one ship out of three arrived; the *Mercury* and *Seine* fell into the hands of the enemy.' This was too much. Although everyone in the American and French governments – and, presumably, the British Government as well – was familiar with the facts, no one had admitted them in public. Was Paine trying to goad France and Britain into formal declarations of war against each other? It would not have been beyond him, to be sure, but neither then nor at any later time did he confirm this possibility.

The French minister to the United States, Conrad Gérard, was compelled to issue a formal protest. The Continental Congress, to soothe him and his government, unanimously voted a resolution that lied blandly, stating that the King of France 'did not preface his alliance with any supplies whatever sent to America'.

One question remained: What should be done about the civil servant who had blundered? It was obvious that some punishment had to be meted out to Paine in order to satisfy France. But there were documents in his office to prove the veracity of every word he had written, and, if he should be pushed too far he might reveal his sources. On the other hand, Jay and his fellow members of the pro-Deane faction saw an opportunity to be rid of a man who in their opinion had flouted the dignity of the Congress. Paine did not help his own cause. On January 5 he wrote a letter to the members of the Congress within an hour after the French minister had presented his protest. He began in humility, but he was so annoyed that he could not resist becoming sarcastic, and, after pointing out that he had served them faithfully, he said that his only mistake, perhaps, had been that of selling himself too cheaply. He received only $70 per month, and he reminded them that such a salary barely paid his expenses. On January 6 Paine was summoned to a closed session of the Congress. President Jay asked him whether he had written the various public letters about Deane, and Paine replied, 'Yes, sir.' Those were the only words he was allowed to speak before the president ordered him to withdraw.

Paine angrily wrote yet another letter of protest to the Congress, saying he found the atmosphere unfavorable and demanding a fair hearing if any disciplinary action against him was contemplated. 'I cannot in duty to my character as a freeman submit to be censured unheard,' he declared. Samual Adams and other friends informed Paine privately that he would not be called to another hearing. Whether he would have been dismissed from his office on the ground that he had broken his oath by revealing state secrets is difficult to establish. The pro-Deane faction lacked the votes to exonerate their friend, and it is doubtful they could have mustered the votes to discharge Paine.

Thomas Paine could not bear the slowness of the official deliberations. On January 7, 1779, he sent the Congress a formal letter of resignation, in which he explained the motives for his conduct in the Deane affair:

My wish and my intentions in my late publications were to preserve the Public from error and imposition, to support as far as laid in my power the just authority of the Representatives of the People, and to cordiallize and cement the Union that has so happily taken place between this country and France.

I have betrayed no Trust because I have constantly employed that Trust to the public good. I have revealed no secrets because I have told nothing that was, or I conceive ought to be a secret. I have convicted Mr Deane of error, and in so doing I hope I have done my duty.

It is to the interest of the Alliance that the People should know that before America had any agent in Europe the public-spirited gentlemen in that quarter of the world were her warm friends. And I hope this Honorable House will receive it from me as a farther testimony of my affection to that Alliance, and of my attention to the duty of my office, that I mention that the duplicates of the Dispatches of Oct. 6 & 7, 1777, from the Commissioners, the originals of which are in the Enemy's possession, seem to require on that account a reconsideration.

His Excellency, the Minister of France, is well acquainted with the liberality of my sentiments, and I have had the pleasure of receiving repeated testimonies of his esteem for me. I am concerned that he should in any instance misconceive me. I beg likewise to have it understood that my appeal to this Honorable House yesterday for a hearing was as a *matter of Right* in the character of a freeman, which Right I ought to yield up to no Power whatsoever. I return my utmost thanks to the Honorable Members of this House who endeavored to support me in that Right, so sacred to themselves and to their constituents; and I have the pleasure of saying and reflecting that as I came into office an honest man, I go out of it with the same character.

Paine had written a lucid, convincing letter, and he naïvely assumed that when it was made public the American people would clamor for his reinstatement. What he failed to take into account was that the president of the Congress had no intention of making the contents of the communication public. It was John Jay's opinion that more than enough had already been said. The ruffled feelings of the French minister had by that time been smoothed, and no further action could be taken in the Silas Deane affair because the members of the Congress were so badly split on the subject. A revelation of the Thomas Paine case would only create additional dissension while the nation was still struggling to achieve unity.

A wildly indignant Paine reacted as might be expected when he discovered that the Congress intended neither to reply to his letter nor to publish it. Within a week he conceived the idea of publishing it himself, and only the intervention of Samuel Adams, Richard Henry Lee, and other friends prevented him from carrying out his plan and making an unpleasant situation even worse. Lee, who was in such poor health that he would soon be obliged to resign his seat in the Congress, was afraid that Paine would engage in some impulsive act, and he wrote to Thomas Jefferson, asking him to calm the outraged propagandist. Jefferson wrote to Paine immediately, emphasizing that a prolongation of the controversy in public would in no way advance the cause of freedom in America. Paine was calmed, at least to an extent, and agreed not to publish his letter. But this did not prevent him from badgering the Congress, and he sent the honorable members four more letters, each running to several thousand words, between January and March, 1779. There was no reply, which infuriated him, and on April 23 he sent the Congress a final letter, saying:

On inquiring yesterday of Mr Thompson, your Secretary, I find that no answer is given to any of my letters. I am unable to account for the seeming inattention of Congress in collecting information at this particular time, from whatever quarter it may come; and this wonder is the more increased when I recollect that a private offer was made to me, about three months ago, amounting in money to £700 a year; yet however polite the proposal might be, however friendly it might be designed, I thought it my duty to decline it; as it was accompanied with a condition which I conceived had a tendency to prevent the information I have since given, and shall yet give to the Country on public affairs.

I have repeatedly wrote to Congress respecting Mr Deane's dark incendiary conduct, and offered every information in my power. The opportunities I have had of knowing the state of foreign affairs is greater than that of many gentlemen of this House, and I want no other knowledge to declare that I look on Mr Deane to be, what Mr Carmichael calls him, a rascal.

The offer of an annual salary of £700 was not a figment of Paine's imagination. This sum, which would have provided him with the largest income he had ever received, had been made to him on behalf of the French Government by Minister Gérard, who had asked him to become a propagandist for France in America. One of the diplomat's motives, of course, had been that of rendering it virtually impossible for Paine to embarrass Louis XVI and his government by making further revelation of pre-treaty French aid to America. That, however, was not his only reason. Knowing that Paine was a genuine friend of France, he assumed, mistakenly, that he also approved of the monarchy. If the minister had read the *Crisis* pamphlets published up until that time he would have been aware that Paine's contempt for monarchy was boundless.

At Gérard's request Paine paid a visit to the French legation in Philadelphia a scant two days after resigning his position with the Congress. Paine was flattered by the offer but wanted to know more about it, and two more meetings were held within the next week. He finally rejected the offer, however; as he told Congress, he believed his integrity was at stake. Thereafter, in his many letters to the press, he ignored the delicate subject of French aid, but Gérard kept a close watch on everything he wrote; the minister's reports to Paris indicated his fear that the matter might be reopened at any time.

Paine was furious at the members of the Continental Congress; he sincerely believed that they were betraying the ideals for which the War of Independence was being fought. This conviction led him to express in print a number of opinions that, although they had no effect on his popularity in his own time, have caused his reputation to suffer somewhat in the eyes of posterity. The most foolish of his ideas appeared in a letter he wrote to the *Pennsylvania Gazette* on May 29, 1779, when he was still seething with anger. He was the only honest man who had ever been employed by the government of the United States, he declared indignantly, and he requested that the people of the country demand his appointment to a new post, that of 'Censor-General'. Once in office, he said, it would be his solemn duty to 'reform and purify' the Continental Congress.

Did Paine seriously contemplate his appointment to such a post? That is difficult to believe. He had spent five years in the New World, he was thoroughly familiar with the emerging American system of democratic government, and it is unlikely in the extreme that he believed any man would be given such powers. His suggestion must be viewed in the light of his primary occupation as a propagandist, in which he had achieved a popularity greater than that of any other writer in the New World.

It seems probable that the very concept of a censor-general whose duty it would be to purify the Congress was intended as a form of propagandistic ridicule. One of the great weaknesses of the Continental Congress was its lack of public support. The United States was just beginning its existence as a nation; men were loyal, first and foremost, to the individual states in which they lived. The central government was granted only those powers that the jealous states believed they could not handle separately. Furthermore, most of the men of national standing and reputation who had been members of the First and Second Continental Congresses in the early days of the Revolution no longer sat in the Congressional chamber. Jefferson, John Adams, and Richard Henry Lee had departed; and Samuel Adams would soon be gone. Benjamin Franklin was in France, John Hancock had returned to Massachusetts, and George Washington had resigned his seat in 1775 when he had taken command of the forces in the field. Most of the present members were nonentities, second-rate politicians who had replaced the group that later became known as the Founding Fathers of the Republic.

Paine's readers enjoyed his attacks on the unpopular Congress. Every time a letter from him on the subject appeared in the *Pennsylvania Gazette*, the newspaper's circulation increased sharply. What good he accomplished is another matter. He was venting his spleen on what his contemporaries called a 'dead Indian', and he was not achieving that unity of will directed toward the winning of the war that was his paramount consideration in the *Crisis* pamphlets.

It is wrong, however, to accuse Paine of allowing his vanity to get the better of him, or to insist that he was striking back after being reprimanded for his indiscretion. The greatest single weakness in the emerging American system of government could be found in the Continental Congress. Paine was aware of that, and, although neither he nor most other thinking men had as yet conceived of a solution to the problem, he felt it his duty to call the attention of the public to the situation as it existed.

He believed in telling the truth, even at the expense of tact, and he was no less devoted to the cause of independence because of the humiliation he had suffered.

8

Semiprivate Citizen

It is difficult to know whether Thomas Paine's resignation of his public office was prompted by principle, pique, or a combination of motives. In any case he was unemployed, he had saved no money, and his financial situation was precarious. The Revolution's leading propagandist could not be allowed to starve; so friends came to his aid. Although he had had no training as an attorney and had not expressed any interest in entering that profession, they found him a position as clerk in the Philadelphia law office of Owen Biddle. He was paid $80 per month, slightly more than he had received from the Continental Congress.

It is unlikely that Paine did much work as a law clerk or that any such labor was expected of him. He continued to write his *Crisis* pamphlets and stubbornly and somewhat quixotically insisted that all of the profits from their sale be given to the cause of American independence. By the summer of 1779 it was becoming obvious that the United States would win the war and that, although the fighting continued, Great Britain was beginning to lose interest in the struggle. Paine could have used the royalties himself because he was desperately poor, but he felt that to do so would be to subvert the purpose of his pamphlets.

While casting about for other sources of income, he was free to devote more of his thoughts to America's future. He wrote a series of letters to the press, most of them concerned with the terms the United States should demand in the peace treaty that would eventually be signed with Great Britain.

He had been outraged by a letter that had appeared in the *Pennsylvania Gazette* on June 23, 1779, urging that the United States not request fishing rights in the Grand Banks region off the coast of Newfoundland. The author of the letter had argued that Britain would stand firm in a refusal to grant such rights, France would be in no position to insist that the American claim be honored, and the United States herself lacked the naval strength to enforce such a treaty obligation. Paine wrote three long letters in reply and demonstrated that, no matter how inept he might be in the handling of his own financial affairs, he had a firm grasp of the principles governing national economic needs. Independence, he said, was more than a political entity, more than a state of mind: It also included a nation's economic freedom, and no country could survive unless it had the right to pursue prosperity. 'There are but two natural sources of wealth,' he declared, 'the Earth and the Ocean, and to lose the right to either is, in our situation, to put up the other for sale.' The United States needed the Grand Banks rights, he said, as a source of employment, as a means of 'producing national supply and commerce', and to provide a 'nursery for seamen'. When Britain wanted peace, he felt certain, she would not balk at granting America the right to use the fishing grounds, and 'to leave the fisheries wholly out, on any pretence whatever, is to sow the seeds of another war'.

Paine proved less realistic in thinking of his own future. In a long letter to Henry Laurens, written on September 14, 1779, he admitted that he was 'curiously circumstanced' and that his financial situation was truly precarious. 'I have . . . lived so very sparingly,' he wrote, 'that unless I alter my way of life it will alter me.' During the coming winter he hoped to collect all of his written works, 'from *Common Sense* to the fisheries,' and publish them in two volumes. He felt certain that the subscription would be large, but he would have difficulty obtaining paper for the enterprise. He had written to Arthur Lee in Paris, hoping that his friend could obtain the paper he needed from the French Government. He also wanted to write a 'history of the Revolution' and to support himself by obtaining subscriptions in advance. This study had been in his mind for a long time; he had first mentioned it in a letter to Franklin two years earlier. It would reveal 'the secrets of the other side', including the complicated politics of Britain in the years leading to the outbreak of the war. He wanted to publish it in three volumes 'and to make an abridgment afterwards in an easy agreeable language for a school book'.

Britain had cornered the bulk of Europe's paper supplies, and Paine told Laurens he was afraid that sufficient quantities might not be available for his project in France, even if Lee found the government sympathetic. The possibility of additional obstacles to his projects made Paine uneasy, and he confided to Laurens that, if driven to extremes, he would borrow money from various friends so that he could live while his projects were in preparation.

On September 28 he began an intensive hunt for other sources of income, and in a pathetic letter to the Executive Council of Pennsylvania he reminded the state's leaders not only of his great needs but of his many services as well. He had been promised payment for what he had done, but as yet he had received no compensation. The members of the council, including Joseph Reed, the president, were well aware of all that Paine had done for the cause of freedom. Their treasury was empty, however, which embarrassed them, but Reed conceived the idea of creating for Paine a position on the council. Some of his colleagues wanted to make certain that the French legation would not be offended; so a letter of inquiry was sent to Minister Gérard. Gérard waited until October 11 before sending an equivocal reply that neither approved nor disapproved the idea.

Meanwhile Paine, who knew nothing of the efforts on his behalf, became so impatient that he wrote a second long letter to the council and, unable to curb his irritation, proved to be his own worst enemy. Complaining that he had received no reply to his initial letter, he wrote, 'It is to me a matter of great concern to find in the government of this State, that which appears to be a disposition in them to neglect their friends and to throw discouragements in the way of genius and Letters.' Telling the

Council about his own writing plans and his fear that it might take Arthur Lee some time to obtain paper for him in France, he requested a loan of £1,500 'for which I will give bond payable within a year'. If this unusual request could not be met, he demanded immediate payment for services rendered. His tone and wording were certain to arouse the antagonism of the council.

Joseph Reed, himself something of an eccentric, faced a dilemma. He had to appease his colleagues but at the same time felt it necessary to take a long view of the situation. He was well acquainted with Paine and liked him, although they had never been close friends, and sincerely wanted to do something for a man who badly needed money. He also realized that Paine enjoyed enormous national and local popularity and that Pennsylvania could not afford to treat him in a niggardly fashion. No reply to Paine's letter was sent, but Reed found a way out of his dilemma. On November 2, 1779, Thomas Paine was elected clerk of the Pennsylvania Assembly; the legislature passed a bill that same day granting its new clerk a salary of $210 per month, the largest sum that Paine had been paid since his arrival in America. A committee headed by Reed called on the clerk-elect that evening, and Paine happily accepted the offer. His immediate crisis was ended.

He went to work with a vengeance and spent that same night writing a bill, introduced in the assembly the following day, that abolished the institution of slavery in Pennsylvania. It was passed and became law on March 1, 1780. The preamble of the act shows Paine at his best:

When we contemplate our abhorrence of that condition, to which the arms and tyranny of Great Britain were exerted to reduce us, when we look back on the variety of dangers to which we have been exposed, and how miraculously our wants in many instances have been supplied, and our deliverance wrought, when even hope and human fortitude have become unequal to the conflict, we are unavoidably led to a serious and grateful sense of the manifold blessings, which we have undeservedly received from the hand of that Being, from whom every good and perfect gift cometh. Impressed with these ideas, we conceive that it is our duty, and we rejoice that it is in our power, to extend a portion of that freedom to others, which hath been extended to us, and release us from that state of thraldom, to which we ourselves were tyrannically doomed, and from which we have now every prospect of being delivered. It is not for us to enquire why, in the creation of mankind, the inhabitants of the several parts of the earth were distinguished by a difference in feature or complexion. It is sufficient to know that all are the work of the Almighty Hand. We find in the distribution of the human species, that the most fertile as well as the most barren parts of the earth are inhabited by men of complexions different from ours, and from each other; from whence we may reasonably as well as religiously infer, that He, who placed them in their various situations, hath extended equally his care and protection to all, and that it becometh not us to counteract his mercies. We esteem it a particular blessing granted to us, that we are enabled this day to add one more step to universal civilization, by removing, as much as possible, the sorrows of those who have lived in undeserved bondage, and from which, by the assumed authority of the Kings of Great Britain, no effectual, legal relief could be obtained. Weaned, by a long course of experience, from those narrow prejudices and partialities we had imbibed, we find our hearts enlarged with kindness and benevolence towards men of all conditions and nations; and we conceive ourselves at this particular period particularly called upon by the blessings which we have received, to manifest the sincerity of our profession, and to give a substantial proof of our gratitude.

And whereas the condition of those persons, who have heretofore been denominated Negro and Mulatto slaves, has been attended with circumstances, which not only deprived them of the common blessings that they were by nature entitled to, but has cast them into the deepest afflictions, by an unnatural separation and sale of husband and wife from each other and from their children, an injury, the greatness of which can only be conceived by supposing that we were in the same unhappy case. In justice, therefore, to persons so unhappily circumstanced, and who, having no prospect before them whereon they may rest their sorrows and their hopes, have no reasonable inducement to render their service to society, which they otherwise might, and also in grateful commemoration of our own happy deliverance from that state of unconditional submission to which we were doomed by the tyranny of Britain.

Inspired anew because he no longer had to worry about money for his living expenses, Paine threw himself into his work with fresh vigor. By his own account he wrote more, principally on his *Crisis* pamphlets, than ever before. Then, unexpectedly, the United States faced a new test. Continental paper money had become almost worthless. Soldiers deserted and returned to their homes because they had not been paid. Farmers refused to furnish the army with supplies unless they received hard cash in return. The British added to the confusion by printing leaflets urging the American Army to absent itself from the ranks and visit bountiful

New York, where pleasures of every kind awaited the weary. Even General Washington lost some of his perennial optimism. Writing to Joseph Reed from his headquarters at Morristown, near Philadelphia, he said, 'Every idea you can form of our distress will fall short of the reality. There is such a combination of circumstances to exhaust the patience of the soldiery that it begins at length to be worn out, and we see in every line of the army the most serious features of mutiny and sedition.' He expounded on the theme at length and for the first time in years was in despair.

It was the duty of Thomas Paine to read that letter to the members of the assembly, and when he was done there was a deep silence. Then a legislator arose and said in a bleak voice, 'We may as well give up first as last.' Paine asked for the right to say a brief word. His voice was high and thin, his delivery was halting, and by no stretch of the imagination could he be called an accomplished speaker. What he had to say, however, required little oratorical skill. He proposed that a cash subscription be raised for the relief of the army and, having just received his own salary, recklessly offered a contribution of $500. A patriot, he believed, should do more than pay lip service to a cause in a time of true crisis. Within a short time the handsome sum of £300,000 had been raised, and a new bank was established to handle the funds and make disbursements to the army. Additional money continued to pour in throughout the year, and in December, 1780, the bank was incorporated under the terms of legislation passed by the Continental Congress.

Paine published two more *Crisis* pamphlets in 1780, both of them filled with cheerful optimism, even though the British had just occupied Charleston and it seemed that the war might drag on indefinitely. In private, however, he was far more cautious. In a personal letter to Reed, he wrote on June 4 that the exhaustion of credit was at the root of the present problem, and he suggested a variety of ways to raise cash, even proposing that the money be taken by force from those who could pay it, if they refused to give voluntarily. A rich man, he declared, apparently quoting King James I, 'makes a bonny traitor'.

Paine's popularity was probably not in any way lessened by the Silas Deane case or his own resignation from the congressional staff. By heading the subscription for General Washington, he actually had raised himself to a heroic stature. This, together with the *Crisis* pamphlets he published in March and June, 1780, had made him one of America's foremost citizens.

The University of the State of Pennsylvania, as Philadelphia's local institution of higher learning was then called, took cognizance of his stature by conferring on him the degree of master of arts in a ceremony held on Independence Day. Six candidates for divinity degrees and one doctor of medicine were also given diplomas. The fact that Paine had never attended any university and had never been awarded a bachelor's degree bothered none of the participants. Representatives of all of the major religious denominations in Philadelphia were present, as was a delegation of state officials headed by Joseph Reed. It was customary for the recipients of honorary degrees to make brief addresses, but Paine's shyness overcame him at the critical moment, and he merely said that he was writing a new pamphlet, *Crisis Extraordinary*, which would speak on his behalf. Such enthusiastic applause greeted his few words that he became confused and covered his reddened face with his hands as he sat down.

Paine now took complete charge of publishing his pamphlets himself. It was no wonder that inflation, exacerbated by the worthlessness of Continental money, was very much on his mind. In order to keep up with skyrocketing prices, the Pennsylvania Assembly increased his salary to $1,000 per month, but the real value of his wages was actually shrinking. On one occasion in 1780 he paid $300 for a pair of socks, and he wrote that a loaf of bread cost $10. So it is not surprising to find that he had to pay the outrageous sum of $360 for the printing of 120 copies of his new pamphlet, arranging with the printer to print more as soon as cash became available from sales. *Common Sense*, by way of comparison, had cost five cents per copy.

The new pamphlet dealt exclusively with the financial situation. Paine took his title from a letter written by General Washington in which the commander in chief had said, 'This crisis, in every sense, is extraordinary.' Showing impressive understanding of finance and economics, Paine first proved that the war, which was being waged simultaneously by the Continental Congress and the separate governments of the thirteen states, was costing £2 million per year. The population of the country was approximately 3 million people; so the annual cost per person was thirteen shillings and fourpence. Even so, Paine said, Americans were better off than the average Englishman, who paid a tax of £2 per year. When the war ended and the cost of its expenses no longer had to be borne, Americans would pay only five shillings per year to sustain their various governments, and, if the central government were strengthened, with the state governments reducing their responsibilities, the costs would drop still more. Paine appears to have been one of the first to lobby for the establishment of what became, almost a decade later, the new federal system of government.

It was obvious, he wrote in *Crisis Extraordinary*, that taxes had to be raised in order to meet the continuing costs of the war. His specific ideas on the subject were sensible and far ahead of his time: Taxes should be levied on 'landed property' and private dwellings; imports should be taxed; and a heavy tax should be laid on prize goods captured at sea. He also believed that all liquors should be taxed, and he observed, 'It would be an addition to the pleasure of society to know that, when the health of the army goes round, a few drops from every glass become theirs.' *Crisis Extraordinary* enjoyed great popularity with the masses, who were virtually disenfranchised, but gentlemen of substance found Paine's ideas of taxation too radical for their tastes and pocketbooks. They were not pleased by the clamor for property taxes and taxes on liquor and imports that arose in every state.

Paine's duties on behalf of the Pennsylvania Assembly were light, particularly as the legislature met for only three or four months during the year. All the same, his literary output in 1780 was prodigious. Late in December he published yet another pamphlet, which he called *Public Good*, and which was devoted to another difficult problem facing the new nation, that of land development and the related conflicting claims of various states. Under its original charter Virginia laid claim to all territory extending westward as far as the Pacific Ocean. Connecticut and New York, among other states, had similar though slightly less ambitious claims. In *Public Good* Paine concentrated on the Virginia claim and called it invalid. Although several others had had the same idea at about the same time, his thesis was original and was considered wildly radical. The government of the United States, Paine declared, had sovereignty over all American territory that lay beyond the actual boundaries of the thirteen states at the time of the outbreak of the Revolution. The British Crown had claimed such lands as its own, and the United States was the legal, logical, and proper successor to that claim. Paine substantiated his position by citing many precedents, historical and legal, and his pamphlet was used in the courts, after the formation of the federal government in 1789, to obtain possession of vast tracts of land from the states. Above all, Paine declared, the land belonged to the people; the policy of making cheap land available to all who wanted it would enable the new nation to expand and become strong. He proved an accurate prophet; it was precisely this policy that the government was to follow for more than a century and a half.

Public Good, however, did not increase its author's popularity in Virginia in 1781. Patrick Henry and a number of other prominent Virginians had sponsored a movement to offer Paine a cash 'memorial' in return for his services to the United States. But the new pamphlet so infuriated them that the bill authorizing this fund became 'lost' in the files of the House of Burgesses and never reached the floor of the legislature. North Carolina and Georgia, which also had extensive claims to western lands, likewise took umbrage at Paine's arguments. Although Paine's popularity diminished somewhat in the South, ordinary citizens continued to buy his works as rapidly as the published editions appeared. What is more, as the eventual establishment of the separate states of Kentucky, Tennessee, and West Virginia proved, they agreed with him. All of these states occupied territory originally claimed by Virginia, North Carolina, and Georgia.

By 1781, when Paine was living alone again, he discovered he was no longer satisfied to eke out his existence in a tiny room, much less eat his meals in waterfront taverns that catered to sailors. He had become accustomed to spacious dwellings, and he rented a suite for himself in an old house off Walnut Street. His quarters consisted of a parlor, study, and bedroom, and he could entertain there in a relatively decent style because the place could hold as many as a dozen guests without being crowded. He still ate sparingly and remained painfully thin, but he had developed a taste for good food and fine wines. He always drank wine with his meals now and was not averse to a glass of liquer-rum, a dry, white product that was the best of all rums made either in the West Indies or the United States.

The correspondence of his friends is filled with references to his hospitality, and a number of letter-writers mention the quantity and variety of liquors he served them when they dropped in for an evening of conversation in his suite. As nearly as can be gathered, however, alcohol had not yet become a problem for Paine. He was drinking somewhat more heavily now that he could afford the luxury, but there is no mention anywhere of his being unable to control himself. If he drank himself into a state of intoxication, he did it only in private, and his friends were none the wiser. It seems likely that his problem drinking did not begin until a much later date.

Clothes still meant nothing to him. At a time when other men were wearing velvet coats of various colors, silk breeches, and satin vests, he continued to dress in suits of unadorned black broadcloth. Someone, probably a woman, whose identity has been lost to posterity, made him a gift of a black silk waistcoat, and he wore it for many weeks, until it became threadbare. He wore black shirts without silver or pewter buckles, and there were few ruffles on his shirts or stocks. Perhaps he was influenced more than he realized by his Quaker upbringing. Occasionally he was troubled by rheumatism in his left hip; so he began to use a walking stick. Being an incurable romantic, he carried a sword cane, a walking stick from which a sword could be drawn. Because he was an exceptionally amiable man who never sought personal danger when it could be avoided and who rarely allowed himself to become embroiled in social arguments, he never used the sword, at least according to record.

Having tasted semiconnubial bliss, Paine was reluctant to resume a celibate existence, and he appears to have had a succession of 'housekeepers' who lived with him after he had moved into his new quarters. Various friends wrote about visiting Paine and 'his new housekeeper', or 'another housekeeper, the last having found him too dyspeptic'. But no names were ever mentioned.

If Paine ever wrote letters to the various women with whom he lived, they have never been discovered, and he did not talk to any of his friends about his romances, or, if he did, they shared his silence.

Apparently no woman had meant much to him since the death of his first wife, and many more years passed before he became involved in the most important romantic relationship of his life. There had been a time when he had been willing and able to live without women, just as in the past he had been satisfied with bread and cheese, a cramped room, and soiled linen. By 1781, however, at the age of forty-four, he had become a distinguished man. He had been living in America for seven years and was acclaimed everywhere as one of the new nation's leading citizens. He had dined in the mansions of wealthy families, beautiful ladies had flirted with him, and he had developed an appreciation for the finer things in life.

By the standards of others his existence was still spartan, but poverty and abstinence of any kind no longer appealed to him. There had been a time when he had known no luxuries, but those days were over, and now he craved a measure of wealth as well as fame. Although he was only beginning to become aware of it, a new chapter in his life was about to begin.

9

An American in Paris

Lord Cornwallis, the British field commander in America, surrendered his army to General Washington at Yorktown on October 19, 1781, bringing the War of Independence to a successful conclusion for the United States. But it had already been obvious by the latter part of the preceding year that the new nation would win. Most men familiar with the military situation realized it, and no one knew it better than Thomas Paine.

For the first time Paine showed signs of the restlessness that would plague him for the rest of his life. He believed that he had already made his contribution to the cause of American liberty, and he began to think in terms of new challenges. Foremost among them was a project he had long had in mind, the writing of a complete and authoritative history of the American Revolution. In order to accomplish this, he felt, it would be necessary for him to go to France and obtain there the full story of the early aid given by that nation to America. He also wanted to visit

Great Britain but realized that he could not until a formal treaty of peace was signed. For the moment, he would have to rely on his own knowledge of the British situation and on whatever help he could obtain from Franklin and from Arthur Lee.

He had saved a considerable portion of the salary that he had earned as clerk of the Pennsylvania Assembly, and the generosity of his employers made it possible for him to consider going to France in the near future. Thanks to Joseph Reed and other friends, he received an unexpected windfall in the form of £1,700 voted by the assembly for 'extra expenses'. He would live in comfort on that money alone for at least a year and, Arthur Lee having not yet responded to his requests for paper in France, he conceived the idea of buying his own there.

On November 3, 1780, he sent the assembly official notification that he could not serve for another year. Again he was treated with generosity and kindness, the members of the legislature allowing his resignation to be tabled for three months, during which time the state government continued to pay his salary. He intended to devote several months to making intensive preparations for the writing of his book. He also wrote to General Greene, his friend and former commanding officer, about a wild scheme he had in mind: If possible he intended to go 'privately' to England from France and to keep himself 'concealed' there while gathering material for the book. Greene recognized the dangers of the plan and urged Paine not to subject himself to certain arrest and imprisonment by the British, who were sure to regard him as a spy. Paine disagreed, and his romantic fervor got the better of him. He would take an assumed name, he said, and would pretend to be an Englishman who had spent time in America before the outbreak of the war. In that way, he declared, he would be safe.

Before he could put his scheme into operation, however, circumstances forced him to change his plans. The Continental Congress estimated the amount of money needed by the United States to prosecute the war until its end and to establish a secure peace thereafter. Although the estimate was optimistic – slightly lower than Paine's in his *Crisis Extraordinary* – members of the Congress realized that the money could not be raised within the country. There was only one source from which so large a sum could be obtained – the government of France – and it was decided to request from that nation loans of more than one and a quarter million livres (about £1 million) per year until the conclusion of the war.

No delegate to the Continental Congress and no one employed by that body had a pen persuasive enough to write the application for the loan, so Paine was called in and asked to prepare the document for a fee. He, in turn, offered his services and wrote the application free of charge.

Proceeding with great care, the Congress sent one of General Washington's aides, Colonel John Laurens, to explain the current military situation to the French so that they would better understand the reasons for American optimism. Laurens felt himself unequal to the task. The French would ask many questions beyond those concerned with military affairs, and he would be unable to answer them. Someone – it may have been Laurens – suggested that the author of the loan application accompany him. There were few men in the United States who better understood Franco-American relations than Paine, and, moreover, as *Crisis Extraordinary* had so amply demonstrated, he was an expert on American finance. The matter was given additional urgency when members of the French legation staff in Philadelphia indicated that they did not believe their government would grant such a loan.

The Congress met behind closed doors and, with very little opposition, voted to make the offer to Paine. He was delighted to accept. His fare and traveling expenses would be paid, he would be given a salary for the duration of the mission, and he would have ample time to pursue his own interests.

The arrangements were made with unusual dispatch, and on January 31, 1781, Paine and Laurens left Philadelphia for Boston. They sailed a week later on a French merchantman, the *Dauphin*, and took for themselves the best cabin on the brig, as befitted diplomats traveling on an official mission. Since they were the only passengers, they ate all of their meals with the captain and his officers. On several occasions they sighted British warships patrolling the North Atlantic shipping lanes, but the brig ran up the fleur-de-lis banner of Bourbon France and remained unmolested. The uneventful voyage lasted thirty-five days, and the *Dauphin* landed at the little port of L'Orient at the beginning of the second week in March.

Thomas Paine, like countless Americans after him, fell in love with Paris at first sight. The combination of architectural charm and Gallic atmosphere proved irresistible to one who had known only the Anglo-Saxon reserve of England and America, and Paine wrote in ecstasy to Samuel Adams that he had found 'heaven on earth'.

Benjamin Franklin, who had learned only a few days before-hand that his compatriots were arriving, had obtained quarters for them in a house on the Île de la Cité. Less than twenty-four hours after their arrival he took them to the foreign ministry and presented them to the pro-American comte de Vergennes, who, for all practical purposes, determined French foreign policy. International relations were conducted at a stately pace in the eighteenth century, and the eager Laurens almost caused the mission to fail by plunging into the subject of the loan without first observing the necessary amenities. Vergennes was amused by the American's lack of experience and forgave him.

Paine handled himself as though he had been an ambassador all his life, and Franklin paid him the supreme compliment by calling him a 'natural-born diplomat'. He not only ingratiated himself with Vergennes, but was flattered to discover that the foreign minister, who read English fluently, was familiar with his pamphlets and admired them.

Before calling on Louis XVI, who was in residence at Versailles, Paine was taken in hand by Franklin to be made presentable. A tailor was called in, a number of shops were visited, and Paine was transformed into an elegant gentleman. He hated his new clothes, writing to Richard Henry Lee that he felt like a 'lackey' in them, but they helped him to make an exceptionally favorable impression on His Christian Majesty, the King of France. Paine knew only a few words of French and the King's command of English was only a little better, but the two men managed to communicate with only a minimum of assistance from an inter-preter. The monarch honored his guest by seating him on his right at dinner.

That was the beginning of a strange friendship. Thomas Paine, the democrat who despised the institution of monarchy, became the good friend of the bumbling, well-meaning King who would lose his head during the French Revolution because he was the supreme symbol of the absolute tyrant. Paine made many visits to Versailles between mid-March and the end of May, and Louis repeatedly 'loaded him with favors'. Among the gifts were a bolt of gold cloth, a tapestry showing American Indians signing a treaty with settlers, and a gold-headed walking stick, which Paine kept and used for the rest of his life. He took all of this in stride, however; neither the royal reception nor the dazzling splendors of the Versailles palace appeared to make a deep impression on him. He ate sparingly of the rich food, drank only somewhat more copiously of the splendid wines, and never forgot either his identity or the purpose of his mission.

Paine also discovered the fascination of young, attractive French women. Franklin, who was having the time of his own life in Paris, may have introduced him to some of the lovely, available young ladies of the court, but Paine seemed to require no assistance. On a number of occasions he upset the young, ingenuous John Laurens by appearing at their lodgings accompanied by an attractive girl, and the colonel hastily withdrew. According to Laurens's correspondence, what shocked him was the youth of Paine's companions, most of whom were still in their teens. This was a new development, as the women with whom Paine had associated in Philadelphia had been more or less his own age. Now that he was in his mid-forties and visiting a foreign place far from home, however, he may have been trying to recapture his own youth.

One afternoon when Laurens came home, he was dismayed to find the writer with two girls. They may have been daughters of joy, although the colonel doubted it, citing the 'elegance of their dress'. In any event, he hastened to assure his friend that he had no need of the services of either girl. Paine replied that such an idea had not crossed his mind, and added that both girls were 'associated with him'. Laurens fled, and when he returned several hours later he found Paine and the girls were just leaving. All three were in a merry mood, and the innocent colonel wondered how it might be possible for one man and two women to find more or less simultaneous fulfillment.

Paine was becoming more sophisticated, tasting pleasures that previously had been inaccessible, but at no time did he neglect his mission. He inundated the French foreign ministry with memoranda and deluged Vergennes and his assistants with facts, figures, and arguments. From mid-March to mid-May he wrote more than seventy-five thousand words urging the granting of the loan to America. These persuasive documents have never been published; all still repose in the archives of the French foreign ministry. The arguments were elaborations of the themes Paine had sounded in his original application for the loan. The United States was virtually bankrupt, thanks to an unstable currency and runaway inflation. Washington's troops were badly in need of new uniforms, munitions, and supplies, and whole regiments could be expected to desert if the men were not paid in hard currency. Under such circumstances the best the Americans could hope for would be a stalemate, in which case the might of wealthy, solvent Britain would ultimately triumph, and all that France had invested in the American cause to date would be lost. But an appropriate loan granted now and renewed in the years ahead would guarantee a victory for the United States.

Benjamin Franklin augmented Paine's reports, letters, and memoranda with his own verbal powers of persuasion, and in mid-May the French Government granted a loan as generous as anything the Americans hoped to win. The United States would receive without delay two and a half million livres in silver, as well as eleven shiploads of arms, ammunition, medical supplies, and cloth for uniforms and blankets. Paine and Laurens's mission had been completely successful.

Contrary to Paine's original expectations, however, he had not been able to obtain much data in Paris for his history of the American Revolution; he had been too busy. But he consoled himself with the thought that he would put the second part of his scheme into operation and travel incognito into England. Luckily, Franklin was on hand to dissuade him. Anyone else who had tried to talk him out of making the foolhardy journey would have failed, but Franklin, Paine's original mentor, was a man for whom he still had enormous respect. Certainly he had no valid reply to Franklin's strong arguments. Great Britain maintained an active, skilled corps of espionage agents in France. These spies undoubtedly not only knew the loan had been granted, but were keeping Paine under close surveillance, and if he tried to cross the English Channel he would be apprehended the moment he set foot on shore. No matter how well he claimed he knew the Channel coastline, no matter how insistently he declared he was familiar with little-used harbors and inlets because of his past experiences as an exciseman, he was too prominent an advocate of the American cause to escape notice.

Franklin reminded him that he would be punished with more than a prison sentence if he was caught. He was still one of a small group who had been labeled as traitors by Lord North, and the

Tories, who were badly upset because their entire American policy had disintegrated, would have liked nothing better than to hang a man they regarded as one of the prime architects of their humiliation.

Paine was duly dissuaded, and a few days later he received sealed orders from the comte de Vergennes. The French foreign minister had arranged for Paine and Laurens to sail home on a French warship, the flagship of a small but powerful escort for a fleet of merchantmen that would carry the promised silver and supplies across the Atlantic to the waiting Americans. On May 28 Paine and Colonel Laurens reached Brest under escort of a cavalry platoon charged with the responsibility for apprehending all enemy agents who tried to follow the two men.

Brest, the largest seaport on the western coast of France, was one of the largest naval bases and ship-building centers in the world at that time. No unauthorized persons were permitted to visit the city, and the port area was under the guard of marines who had standing orders to shoot anyone they suspected of espionage. Every permanent resident, including shipwrights, longshoremen, tavernkeepers, and even prostitutes, was forced to carry personal papers, and anyone who failed to identify himself to the satisfaction of government inspectors was imprisoned. Only by maintaining these strict precautions could the French prevent Great Britain from learning about sailing schedules and other data that would be of vital interest to the British Navy.

On the afternoon of his arrival in Brest Paine scribbled a brief, affectionate note to Franklin:

> I have just a moment to spare to bid you farewell. We go on board in an hour or two, with a fair wind and everything ready. I understand that you have expressed a desire to withdraw from business, and I beg leave to assure you that every wish of mine, so far as it can be attended with any service, will be employed to make your resignation, should it be accepted, attended with every possible mark of honor which your long services and high character in life justly merit.

The two Americans boarded a 42-gun frigate, the *Resolve* whose captain was acting as commodore of the convoy, and they sailed on the afternoon tide. The quarters assigned to the pair were less spacious than those which they enjoyed on their eastbound crossing, but every effort was made to assure their comfort. They ate their meals in the senior officers' wardroom, they were given the freedom of the ship – a privilege granted few

101

civilians on a man-of-war – and an orderly looked after their personal needs. King Louis had sent Paine a farewell gift of a large box of delicacies; although Paine enjoyed good food, most of these were too rich for his taste, and he gave them to his fellow passengers. To the surprise of Laurens, Paine confessed that he liked the taste of navy hardtack, a water biscuit that had to be dipped in liquid to make it edible. He had acquired a fancy for hardtack in his youth, he said, during his service on a privateer, and he actually preferred it to fresh bread.

The dangers that confronted the convoy were great. In spite of all the precautions taken at Brest, it was almost certain that the British, who kept sloops of war on sentry duty off the port, would learn that the convoy had sailed for the United States. In order to avoid confrontation with a superior force, which would mean almost inevitable defeat, it was necessary for the commodore to sail to the New World by a circuitous route. The French warships were on the alert day and night; no straggling by merchantmen was permitted, and all lights were extinguished after dark. It took nearly three months for a voyage that under less stringent conditions could be made in less than half that time; the convoy did not reach Boston until August 25. Wagon-teams of oxcarts were waiting to carry the silver and supplies to Philadelphia. While Paine and Laurens hurried ahead, bringing the good news to the national capital, two regiments of Massachusetts militia acted as an escort for the precious cargo, which reached General Washington in time for his decisive Yorktown campaign.

The Continental Congress responded with a typical lack of consistency. Laurens was voted an official commendation and was presented with a share of the French silver worth $200. Paine, who had conceived the idea of the loan and was largely responsible for obtaining it, received nothing; the question of thanking him for his efforts was never even put to a vote. According to Robert Morris, the prominent Pennsylvania banker and patriot with whom Paine was on very friendly terms, the Congress's 'reason' for refusing to honor him was that he was not an official employee of either the Congress itself or of the army. In fact, Paine was forced to send three letters to the Congress before he finally received repayment for traveling expenses.

Once again his financial situation was becoming precarious. His little nest egg was dwindling and his publishing projects were at a standstill. He had lacked the opportunity to gather material for his history of the Revolution, and he had apparently failed to obtain paper for the project. Nevertheless, he joined in the celebrations in Philadelphia after Washington won his great victory over Cornwallis at Yorktown. And he thought nostalgically of his recent visit to France, writing to a friend who had just arrived there, 'Make my best wishes to . . . all the good girls at St Germain.'

General Washington came to Philadelphia on November 28, and the Continental Congress gave him a standing ovation when he appeared in person to report. Paine, the nation's leading literary celebrity, was an invited guest at the banquet given that night in Washington's honor, but a letter he wrote privately to the commander in chief on November 30 reveals his bitterness at not being rewarded for his own contributions to the nation's cause. His arrogance may have been exaggerated by the strange combination of circumstances that made him the foremost writer in the United States and at the same time a near-bankrupt.

Second Street, Opposite the Quaker
Meeting House,

Nov. 30, 1781

Sir,–

. . . It is seven years, *this day*, since I arrived in America, and tho' I consider them as the most honorary time of my life, they have nevertheless been the most inconvenient and even distressing. From an anxiety to support, as far as laid in my power, the reputation of the Cause of America, as well as the Cause itself, I declined the customary profits which authors are entitled to, and I have always continued to do so; yet I never thought (if I thought at all on the matter) but that as I dealt generously and honorably by America, she would deal the same by me. But I have experienced the contrary – and it gives me much concern, not only on account of the inconvenience it has occasioned to me, but because it unpleasantly lessens my opinion of the character of a country which once appeared so fair, and it hurts my mind to see her so cold and inattentive to matters which affect her reputation.

Almost every body knows, not only in this country but in Europe, that I have been of service to her, and as far as the interest of the heart could carry a man, I have shared with her in the worst of her fortunes. . . .

Unfortunately for me, I knew the situation of Silas Deane when no other person knew it, and with an honesty for which I ought to have been thanked, endeavored to prevent his fraud taking place. He has himself proved my opinion right, and the warmest of his advocates now very candidly acknowledge their deception.

While it was every body's fate to suffer I cheerfully suffered with them, but tho' the object of the country is now nearly established and her circumstances rising into prosperity, I feel myself left in a very unpleasant situation. Yet I am totally at a loss what to attribute it to; for wherever I go I find respect, and every body I meet treats me with friendship; all join in censuring the neglect and throwing blame on each other, so that their civility disarms me as much as their conduct distresses me. But in this situation I cannot go on, and I have no inclination to differ with the Country or to tell the story of her neglect, it is my design to get to Europe, either to France or Holland. I have literary fame, and I am sure I cannot experience worse fortune than I have here. Besides a person who understood the affairs of America, and was capable and disposed to do her a kindness, might render her considerable service in Europe, where her situation is but imperfectly understood and much misrepresented by the publications which have appeared on that side of the water, and tho' she has not behaved to me with any proportionate return of friendship, my wish for her prosperity is no ways abated, and I shall be very happy to see her character as fair as her cause. . . .

Your obedt. humble servant,
THOMAS PAINE.

His Excellency General Washington.

It is not easy to imagine what Paine believed the United States owed him or how that debt was to be paid. He was irritated by the cavalier attitude the Continental Congress had just displayed toward him, but his ruffled feelings could have been smoothed by a congressional vote of thanks and a gift similar to that which Colonel Laurens had received. What he actually sought, however, was something far more. Having given voluntarily and generously to the cause of American independence, when instead he could have made a tremendous personal profit, he seems to have believed that the United States now owed him a living. In some ways, therefore, he proved himself as naïve as he was sensitive.

Certainly he felt that an author was the sole proprietor of what he wrote; he himself was the first to advocate the establishment of copyright laws in the United States. When one publisher tried to earn a profit of his own on *Common Sense* immediately after the war, adding new material to it and pretending that it had been omitted inadvertently from the original edition, Paine was quick to prosecute him, halt publication by obtaining an injunction against the man, and obtain a small payment in punitive damages.

At the same time, however, he insisted that something should be done by the United States to make his future secure. Until now few men had heeded his requests, but he had been wise when he went to General Washington for help. The commander in chief knew well what Paine's contribution had been, and he was not one to forget the services of a patriot and friend.

10

A Time That Tried One Man's Soul

The winter of 1781–82 was the most trying time that Thomas Paine had endured since he first came to America. His reputation as a writer was secure, and men in high places knew that he had played a major role in obtaining the French loan, but there no longer seemed to be a place for him in the nation's affairs. The war was still being fought, particularly in South Carolina and Georgia, but neither side was initiating any major campaigns, and it was apparent on both sides of the Atlantic that the struggle was drawing to an end. Independence was assured, and Americans were beginning to turn to peacetime pursuits.

Paine, who had no employment and was forced to live on his savings, clung to the belief that America owed him a living. He ignored Benjamin Franklin's suggestion that he establish a new magazine, and he made no attempt to write any new pamphlets or otherwise use his pen to produce income. He seems to have been stricken with a strange lethargy, and the suspicion arises that he could thrive only in a time of crisis and turmoil. He followed this pattern consistently throughout his adult life. He appears to have lost interest in the world around him in times of peace and prosperity. His personality demanded conflict, the existence of foes whom he transformed from state enemies into personal enemies. Perhaps poverty and loneliness in childhood and youth made it impossible for him to enjoy what most men craved. Although he may not have realized it, he needed a world in upset and a personal life hampered by scheming opponents – real or imagined – to achieve a balance.

That winter saw him at his most unattractive. He was petulant, sometimes morose, and he spoke frequently of moving either to France or Holland. But he made no actual plans to move, and, as far as is known, he did not even investigate the possibilities of beginning a new life in Europe. It may be that he was bluffing, making idle threats in the hope that they would be taken seriously.

Fortunately he had friends who had not forgotten his services to America, and chief among them was George Washington. Regardless of his personal opinion of Paine, the general became active on his behalf, suggesting to a number of men in key positions that the country should do something for the propagandist who had wielded such influence. Robert Morris, the brilliant superintendent of finance, who had himself become friendly with Paine, indicated in his diary that on two occasions early in 1782 General Washington urged him to find some way to help the writer. Morris held a number of talks with Paine in January and February. Although there were as yet no vacancies and no new posts had been created, the financier emphasized that the country's need for Paine's services was great. The American people would be required to work together toward common goals if they hoped to create a viable economy. Weaknesses in the developing political system would have to be rectified, and the states would have to establish a common policy on taxation, the settlement of the West, immigration, and a score of other pressing problems. None of these issues could be resolved until someone defined them clearly in print and pointed the way toward possible solutions.

Morris's eloquence succeeded in arousing Paine, who went to work on a new pamphlet which, he wrote, was 'designed to restore the public tranquillity'. He wrote principally on questions of finance and taxation, and he boldly took a stand in favor of

107

strengthening the national government, thereby arousing the opposition of the vocal and powerful advocates of states' rights. The relationship of the separate states to the central government, he argued, was similar to that of the individual to the state in which he lived. In other words, it was the duty of the states to submit to the authority of the national government for the sake of the common good; policies harmful to a minority of states should be adopted if the majority benefited. The national interests were paramount at all times. Nowhere was this more evident than in the unresolved question of the responsibility for settlement of the West. Paine stated unequivocally that all 'vacant land' belonged to the national government, not to the individual states; that the administration of this territory was a prerogative of the national government; and that it alone had the right and duty to establish immigration policies.

While Paine was preparing this controversial document his friends were taking steps to help him. Morris and Robert R. Livingston of New York, a financier and expert on foreign affairs, went to Washington and in mid-February sent a secret letter of recommendation to the Congress:

> The subscribers, taking into consideration the important situation of affairs at the present moment, and the propriety and even necessity of informing the people and rousing them into action; considering also the abilities of Mr Thomas Paine as a writer, and that he has been of considerable utility to the common cause by several of his publications: they are agreed that it will be much for the interest of the United States that Mr Paine be engaged in their service for the purpose above mentioned. They are therefore agreed that Mr Paine be offered a salary of $800 per annum, and that the same be paid to him by the Secretary of Foreign Affairs. The salary to commence from this day, and to be paid by the Secretary of Foreign Affairs out of monies to be allowed by the Superintendent of Finance for secret services. The subscribers being of opinion that a salary publicly and avowedly given for the above purpose would injure the effect of Mr Paine's publications, and subject him to injurious personal reflections.

The proposal was accepted virtually without debate by the Congress, meeting behind closed doors, and the offer was duly made to Paine, who immediately went on the government payroll. He now enjoyed the distinction of being the first full-time secret employee of the United States Government. The arrangement solved his personal financial difficulties, and his enthusiasm was revived.

His *Crisis* pamphlet on taxation, in which his thoughts and those of Robert Morris happened to be similar, was published on March 5, 1782. As expected, officials of the various states protested Paine's ideas vigorously, but his arguments were so clear and forceful that they were instrumental in creating the climate that led, five years later, to the calling of the Constitutional Convention that created the new federal government. In order to understand the significance of this pamphlet it is necessary to examine briefly the American political situation at the end of the Revolution. A truly *national* consciousness was only beginning to emerge, and the individual states were still jealous of their rights. Some of the most prominent of the Patriot leaders during the war years, among them Samuel Adams, Patrick Henry, and John Hancock, were adamant in their insistence that ultimate power be vested in the individual states. Men like Alexander Hamilton and James Madison, who advocated a strong federal government, were just beginning to be heard. Their writings indicate that in 1782 their own ideas on the subject were just being formulated; no leader or group of leaders had as yet appeared to bring about a definitive change in the American Government. Almost without exception the elected state officials and the delegates sent to the Congress were states'-rights men. Paine's pamphlet was one of the first documents to persuade many Americans to start thinking in terms of establishing a more powerful central government at the expense of the states.

Paine immediately went to work on yet another pamphlet. Most people took peace for granted and failed to realize that Great Britain was trying, in secret, to undermine the friendship between the United States and France. Paine believed, as did Morris and Livingston, that the American people would become less complacent when they learned the facts, and the only problem in dealing with the subject was that of approach. When General Washington was visiting Philadelphia in mid-March, Paine invited him to 'spend a part of an evening at my apartments, and eat a few oysters or a crust of bread and cheese', for he wanted to consult with Washington 'on a matter of public business, tho' of a secret nature'. The meeting was held a few nights later, and various long-range strategic and tactical plans were made. The first result was yet another *Crisis* pamphlet, published on May 22, 1782. One brief quotation indicates its essence:

The British parliament suppose they have many friends in America, and that, when all chance of conquest is over, they will be able to draw her from her alliance with France. Now if I have any conception of the human heart, they will fail in this more than in anything that they have yet tried. This part of the business is not a question of policy only, but of honor and honesty.

This document was followed by an open letter to General Sir Guy Carleton, the governor of Canada and British commander in chief for North America. Washington had been trying in vain to persuade the British to give him custody of a redcoat captain who had led a 'band of refugees' from New York into New Jersey and had murdered an American officer. Now, Paine wrote, obviously with Washington's approval, drastic measures would have to be taken. A British officer of the same rank as the murdered American would be selected by lot in a prisoner-of-war camp and executed. The measure, Paine explained calmly, would be harsh and barbaric, but barbarism would be justifiable if the British refused to obey international law. Firm steps were necessary to prevent similar outrages in the future, and it was unfortunate that an innocent man would die, just as it was tragic that an American officer who had offended no one had been killed in cold blood. Whether Washington meant to go through with the plan or was merely bluffing will never be known. Sir Guy took cognizance of Paine's forceful letter, and the murderer, a Captain Lippencott, was duly handed over to the Continental Army for punishment.

In September, 1782, Paine finally published a pamphlet on which he had been working sporadically for almost a year, his critique of the Abbé Raynal's history of the American Revolution. Raynal, a French historian, had published in Paris a fragmentary, inadequate account of the struggle in the New World. It was Paine's original intention to write his own history of the Revolution, a project which never materialized, and his pamphlet is significant principally because it demonstrates his own superior insights as an historian. Most of his interpretations have long been accepted, but in his own day it was far more diffidult to understand the major thrusts of the war and the principles that lay behind the struggle.

Writing in a more florid 'literary' style than had been his custom, Paine went to great lengths to contradict Raynal's assertion that the war was fought over the question of whether 'the mother country had, or had not, a right to lay, directly or indirectly, a slight tax upon the colonies'. The amount of the tax, Paine affirmed, correctly, was irrelevant. The tax on tea was strictly a British experiment to test whether Parliament had the right 'to bind America in all cases whatever'. The Americans denied that right, and recognizing the intent of the tax on tea, rejected it on principle. Paine also dealt severely with Raynal's suggestion that the British commissioners, who came to America in the spring of 1778, would have carried out their mission successfully had not the French formed an alliance with the Americans at that time. This was totally untrue, Paine insisted, saying that the American people had determined to wage war until Britain granted them complete independence. He pointed out that the Continental Congress rejected the proposals of the commissioners eleven days before word was received that Dr Franklin and his associates had signed the treaty with France. He became indignant, too, at Raynal's description of Washington's Christmas attack on Trenton as accidental and lacking military significance. The attack had been deliberate and had achieved its purpose, Paine said, as it not only proved that American fighting men could win, but regenerated flagging American spirits at a time when such a revival was desperately needed.

The pamphlet, written in the form of an open latter to the Abbè, also contained much propaganda. The people of the United States were urged to maintain their ties with France and to establish a close, friendly association with Spain. Britain was advised to conduct her relations with America 'with civility', and to abandon Canada, which constituted a drain on the British taxpayer. The Canadian wilderness was so extensive, he said, that the country would never become heavily populated, no matter how much aid she was given. Consequently, wrote Paine, 'Britain will sustain the expense, and America reap the advantage.'

As soon as the pamphlet was printed, Paine sent General Washington fifty copies for the army's use, and added:

> I fully believe we have seen our worst days over. The spirit of the war, on the part of the enemy, is certainly on the decline full as much as we think. I draw this opinion not only from the present promising appearance of things, and the difficulties we know the British Cabinet is in; but I add to it the peculiar effect which certain periods of time have, more or less, on all men. The British have accustomed them-

selves to think of *seven years* in a manner different to other portions
of time. They acquire this partly by habit, by reason, by religion, and
by superstition. They serve seven years' apprenticeship – they elect
their parliament for seven years – they punish by seven years'
transportation, or the duplicate or triplicate of that term – they let
their leases in the same manner, and they read that Jacob served
seven years for one wife, and after that seven years for another; and
the same term likewise extinguishes all obligations (in certain cases)
of debt, or matrimony: and thus this particular period of time, by a
variety of concurrences, has obtained an influence on their mind.
They have now had seven years of war, and are no farther on the
Continent than when they began. The superstitious and populous
part will therefore conclude that *it is not to be,* and the rational part
of them will think they have tried an unsuccessful and expensive
experiment long enough, and that it is in vain to try it any longer,
and by these two joining in the same eventual opinion the obstinate
part among them will be beaten out, unless consistent with their
former sagacity, they get over the matter at once by passing a new
declaratory Act to bind Time in all cases whatsoever or declare him a
rebel.

General Washington was amused by the observation, which
prompted him to think of the matter in depth. In a reply dated
September 18 Washington wrote:

Your observations on the period of seven years, as it applies itself to
and affects British minds, are ingenious, and I wish it may not fail
of its effects in the present instance. The measures and the policy of
the enemy are at present in great perplexity and embarrassment – but
I have my fears, whether their necessities (which are the only operating motives with them) are yet arrived to that point, which must drive
them unavoidably into what they will esteem disagreeable and dis-
honorable terms of peace, – such, for instance, as an absolute,
unequivocal admission of American Independence, upon the terms
on which she can accept it. For this reason, added to the obstinacy
of the King, and the probable consonant principles of some of the
principal ministers, I have not so full a confidence in the success of
the present negociation for peace as some gentlemen entertain.
Should events prove my jealousies to be ill founded, I shall make
myself happy under the mistake, consoling myself with the idea of
having erred on the safest side, and enjoying with as much satisfaction as any of my countrymen the pleasing issue of our severe
contest.

On October 29, 1782, Paine published another of his *Crisis*
pamphlets. He took as his theme a remark supposedly made in a
speech delivered in July by Lord Shelburne, one of the most

prominent Tory spokesmen, who said, 'The independence of America would be the ruin of England'. The assertion begged for a reply, and Paine took full advantage of his opportunity. 'Was America then the giant of Empire, and England only her dwarf in waiting?' he asked. 'Is the case so strangely altered, that those who once thought we could not live without them are now brought to declare that they cannot exist without us?'

In November, 1782, Paine became involved in a controversy over a proposal by the Continental Congress to levy an import tax. The Dutch Government had promised to grant the United States a substantial loan if she could produce evidence that the interest on it could be raised and paid. Robert Morris proposed that a 5 per cent duty be levied on all imports, and some of the states protested, but all except Rhode Island were hauled into line. The Dutch, however, refused to grant the loan until all thirteen of the states approved the plan to levy the tax. On November 27 Paine wrote a long letter to the *Providence Gazette*, which he signed 'A Friend to Rhode Island and the Union'. The concerned citizens of Rhode Island were so afraid their precious sovereignty might be diluted that his appeal met almost hysterical resistance; abuse, ridicule, and vilification were heaped on him. No outsider, they felt, had the right to interfere in their affairs.

In all, he wrote a series of six letters to the Providence newspaper, and early in 1783 actually traveled there. The Rhode Islanders proved themselves gentlemen. He was greeted cordially, thanks in part to a public letter from Rhode Island's great war hero, General Nathanael Greene, who declared that Paine should be rewarded for his services to the country. In spite of his favorable reception, however, strong efforts were made to prevent the publication of his letters there. These attempts failed, and in the last of his letters Paine made a stirring appeal for a powerful central government: 'What would the sovereignty of any individual state be,' he asked, 'if left to itself to contend with a foreign power? It is on our *united* sovereignty that our greatness and safety, and the security of our foreign commerce rest. This united sovereignty then must be something more than a name, and requires to be as completely organized for the line it is to act in as that of any individual state, and if anything more so, because more depends on it.'

Rhode Island reluctantly accepted the import duty. Robert Morris resigned his own position early in 1783, and in February, after twelve months of employment, Paine was retired, too. Before he left office, however, he wrote a strong memorandum in favor of creating a more viable and powerful national government. Morris gave a private dinner attended by Paine, Livingston, Gouverneur Morris, and other prominent citizens at which the idea was discussed and approved. This session was one of the earliest, if not the first, of the semiformal meetings favoring the establishment of a strong national government that were held prior to the calling of the Constitutional Convention in 1787.

On April 18, 1783, General Washington announced that hostilities between the United States and Britain had come to an end. The next day, the anniversary of the Battle of Lexington, Thomas Paine published the last of his *Crisis* pamphlets, which he called *Thoughts on Peace and the Probable Advantages Thereof*. It was the only one of his pamphlets which he published for personal profit, and it can only be regarded as a conscious valedictory. The need for a central government powerful enough to guard the interests of the entire nation was very much on his mind:

'The times that tried men's souls' are over – and the greatest and completest revolution the world ever knew, gloriously and happily accomplished.

But to pass from the extremes of danger to safety – from the tumult to the tranquillity of peace, though sweet in contemplation, requires a gradual composure of the senses to receive it. . . .

But that which must more forcibly strike a thoughtful, penetrating mind, and which includes and renders easy all inferior concerns, is THE UNION OF THE STATES. On this our great national character depends. It is this which must give us importance abroad and security at home. It is through this only that we are, or can be, nationally known in the world. . . .

The division of the empire into states is for our own convenience, but abroad this distinction ceases. The affairs of each state are local. They can go no further than to itself. And were the whole worth of even the richest of them expended in revenue, it would not be sufficient to support sovereignty against a foreign attack. In short, we have no other national sovereignty than as the United States. . . . Sovereignty must have power to protect all the parts that compose and constitute it: and as *United States* we are equal to the importance of the title, but otherwise we are not. . . .

It is with confederated states as with individuals in society; something must be yielded up to make the whole secure. In this view of things we gain by what we give, and draw an annual interest greater than the capital. – I ever feel myself hurt when I hear the union, that great palladium of our liberty and safety, the least irreverently spoken of. It is the most sacred thing in the constitution of America, and that which every man should be most proud and tender of. Our citizenship in the United States is our national character. Our citizenship in any particular state is only our local distinction. By the latter we are known at home, by the former to the world. Our great title is AMERICANS – our inferior one varies with the place.'

Having come out in favor of the only type of government that, in his opinion, would enable the United States to survive, Paine closed the last of his *Crisis* pamphlets on a rare, personal note:

It was the cause of America that made me an author. The force with which it struck my mind, and the dangerous condition the country appeared to be in, by courting an impossible and an unnatural reconciliation with those who were determined to reduce her, instead of striking out into the only line that could cement and save her, A DECLARATION OF INDEPENDENCE, made it impossible for me, feeling as I did, to be silent; and if, in the course of more than seven years, I have rendered her any service, I have likewise added something to the reputation of literature, by freely and disinterestedly employing it in the great cause of mankind, and showing that there may be genius without prostitution.

Independence always appeared to me practicable and probable, provided the sentiment of the country could be formed and held to the object: and there is no instance in the world, where a people so extended, and wedded to former habits of thinking, and under such a variety of circumstances, were so instantly and effectually pervaded, by a turn in politics, as in the case of independence; and who supported their opinion, undiminished, through such a succession of good and ill fortune, till they crowned it with success.

But as the scenes of war are closed, and every man preparing for home and happier times, I therefore take my leave of the subject. I have most sincerely followed it from beginning to end, and through all its turns and windings: and whatever country I may hereafter be in, I shall always feel an honest pride at the part I have taken and acted, and a gratitude to nature and providence for putting it in my power to be of some use to mankind.

11

High and Low Finance

The sentiments Thomas Paine expressed in the closing lines of his *Crisis* of April 19, 1783 were sincere. The United States had won her independence. He was proud of the part he had played in that struggle, and now he was thinking of moving on and making his home elsewhere. He was devoted to liberty and to democracy as conceived and practiced in America, but he sensed there was no place in a world at peace for a man who needed turmoil in order to spark his best and most convincing writing. In other words, he felt a familiar restlessness and did not quite know where to turn. Unlike the other Founding Fathers, he had known no real roots in America and had established none there. He ragarded Philadelphia as his home, but he still lived in rented rooms, engaged in temporary liaisons with various women, and established no permanent place for himself in society. He was still something of the outsider, the loner.

He made a valiant attempt to settle down quietly. A friend,

Colonel Joseph Kirkbridge, who was like Paine a former Quaker and believed in the principles that Paine espoused, bought himself a small house in Bordentown, New Jersey. Paine soon joined him there and used most of his savings to purchase a tiny cottage that stood on one-fifth of an acre of land. Another friend, a man named Hall who was something of an inventor, moved there, too, and reawakened Paine's interest in developing labor-saving scientific machines, a subject that long had interested him, as he had indicated in the first magazine he had written and edited, the *Pennsylvania Magazine*.

In the meantime, however, he needed cash for living expenses. Robert Morris urged him to send an application to the Congress for money, reminding him that he had never received his full salary of $70 per month while serving as the secretary of the Foreign Affairs Committee and had been paid nothing beyond his traveling expenses for the role he played in obtaining the all-important French loan for the United States. The country was in his debt, Morris said, and he urged Paine to be vigorous in his application. Paine took him at his word and sent the Congress a strongly worded letter.

His claim did not go unsupported. On September 10, 1783, only a few weeks after he moved into his little house, he received from General Washington in Philadelphia a letter which read, in part:

> I have learned . . . that you are at Bordentown. Whether for the sake of retirement or economy, I know not. Be it for either, for both, or whatever it may, if you will come to this place, and partake with me, I shall be exceedingly happy to see you.
>
> Your presence may remind Congress of your past services to this country; and if it is in my power to impress them, command my best services with freedom, as they will be rendered cheerfully by one who entertains a lively sense of importance of your works, and who, with much pleasure, subscribes himself.
>
> Your sincere friend,
> G. WASHINGTON.

Paine immediately wrote the general a long reply. There was a movement in the Congress, he said, to appoint him 'historiographer to the continent', but he had asked that consideration of the appointment be postponed until he could appear before the congressional committee. He welcomed the general's offer of assistance, and once again revealed that he felt hurt by what he regarded as the 'neglect' of the 'collective ostensible body of America'. On November 5 he visited Washington's headquarters in the field, and as it was Guy Fawkes Day, the English holiday commemorating the attempt to blow up the Houses of Parliament, the great soldier and the great propagandist amused themselves by 'setting the river on fire' with a roll of cartridge paper.

In December Paine wrote yet another pamphlet, a very short work in the form of a letter which he called *To the People of America*. In it he again appealed for a powerful national government, insisting that the states 'act in union'. This document was ill-timed. Many of the men currently serving in the Congress were ardent advocates of the rights of the states, and Paine's stand so alarmed them that they decided his application for funds should be rejected. The sentiment against him was so great that Washington was forced to intervene directly on his behalf and threatened to take the matter to the public at large unless the Congress gave Paine what he deserved. Because of the general's action, many of Paine's opponents relented, and congressional approval of financial reward for the writer was assured.

Paine's mind turned to the future. It was safe for him to go to England now that the war was officially ended, and he wanted to visit his aged parents and see a number of friends. Then he would return to America and at long last begin work on his history of the Revolution – a project he planned for the rest of his life but never actually wrote.

Before the Congress could stop wrangling long enough to do something on Paine's behalf, the New York legislature took action, presenting him with a handsome estate in the little town of New Rochelle, a day's ride from New York. It consisted of 277 acres of rich farmland and woods, and a handsome mansion, formerly the property of a Loyalist named Frederick Devoe, who had fled to Halifax. Other lands were eventually added to the gift, and Paine became a major land-owner, the proprietor of ten thousand valuable acres.

He went to New York in June, 1784, and from there to New Rochelle where the entire village turned out to greet him. Paine shook hands with every man, woman, and child in the crowd, and took an active part in the festivities that were held in his honor, ladling out the sugar for the whisky-and-rum toddy being prepared for toasts. He did not remain permanently in New Rochelle, however. The mansion was too large for a man living alone, and his friendships in New Jersey were congenial; so he returned there after spending only a week or two in his magnificent new house.

It is ironic that the advocate of a strong central government realized that the Congress was too feeble to offer him any assistance. Paine wrote to General Washington (enclosing a song for the Order of the Cincinnati, the organization of retired army officers that was just then being established) that he deemed it expedient to request aid from the individual states rather than from the Congress. He said much the same thing in a letter to Thomas Jefferson, and in both communications he indicated that he believed the Pennsylvania legislature would do something for him in the immediate future. Acting without Paine's knowledge Washington wrote to Richard Henry Lee and James Madison, whose followers were in control of the Virginia legislature, and suggested that they too do something concrete for the writer. 'His writings certainly have had a powerful effect on the public mind,' the general said to Madison. 'Ought they not then to meet an adequate return? He is poor! he is chagreened! and almost if not altogether in despair of relief.'

A bill was offered in the House of Burgesses to give Paine possession of lands worth about £4,000, which would pay him £100 annually in rents. Washington exerted pressure by writing a letter in support of the measure to Patrick Henry, the state's most powerful political leader. The bill passed two readings but failed on the third, partly because Richard Henry Lee was ill and could not lend his personal prestige to the measure. Washington was annoyed and did not give up his efforts on Paine's behalf. He used his influence next with the Pennsylvania Assembly where the climate was more favorable, and in December, 1784, the members of the legislature voted Paine a cash gift of £500 in silver, or the equivalent today of about $8,000.

Although Paine was not yet truly wealthy, the action of only two states had at least made him financially independent. He still resented his dismissal by the Continental Congress and made it clear that he wanted no gift from that body, but he insisted on being paid the wages that had been withheld from him. A full review of the matter would have necessitated reconsideration of the unsavory Silas Deane case, which may have been what Paine wanted, as he believed his forced resignation had left a stain on his good name. But the New Englanders in the Congress had no desire to air the Deane case publicly again and therefore side-stepped the issue. Instead a bill bursting with patriotic gratitude was introduced, declaring

> . . . that the early, unsolicited, and continuing labors of Mr Thomas Paine, in explaining and enforcing the principles of the late revolution by ingenious and timely publications upon the nature of liberty, and civil government, have been well received by the citizens of these States, and merit the approbation of Congress; and that in consideration of these services, and the benefits produced thereby, Mr Paine is entitled to a liberal gratification from the United States.

The high-sounding resolution did not please Paine because no specific sum was indicated. But the man who had become the most renowned citizen of Bordentown was enjoying himself thoroughly, perhaps for the first time in his life. He had made many friends in the little community, he went for a daily canter on a horse he had bought, and, according to Conway and other nineteenth-century biographers, he even made it his habit to greet the young ladies of the town with a resounding kiss.

Only two things troubled him. One was the health of his elderly parents, whom he was eager to see again, perhaps feeling guilty because he had neglected them; the other was his compensation for past services to America, which the Congress was loathe to approve.

Members of the special congressional committee that proposed the grant wanted to give Paine the sum of $6,000, but virtually no bill ever went through the economy-minded Congress unaltered. Various friends, among them Richard Henry Lee, Madison, and Livingston, tried without success to halt the congressional action, and at the final vote Paine was awarded only $3,000 in the devalued paper money that was still being printed in large amounts. The disgruntled Paine, accepting the gift because he had no choice, commented that it would barely pay for his round-trip fare to England.

A number of his friends wrote him to express their sympathies, and to let him know that they shared with him the feeling that the Congress had treated him shabbily. The list of names is of interest because it included the men who later became the first four presidents of the United States – Washington, John Adams, Jefferson, and Madison.

Paine refused to allow his defeat, as he regarded it, to hamper his spirits, however. He was solvent, and in the autumn of 1785 he went to New York, where the Congress was now convened. The temporary capital of the United States was enjoying a busy social season, and no man was in greater demand than the nation's leading literary lion. The forty-eight-year-old Paine was a guest at dinners and lunches, assemblies and receptions, and he had the time of his life. His stature as an author gave him the self-confidence that he had always lacked and, less shy now, he was able to expound his views in mixed company. He flirted outrageously with young ladies less than half his age and formed a convivial friendship with one of them – Hannah Nicholson, the daughter of a prominent New York political leader, who became the wife of Albert Gallatin, the future secretary of the treasury.

Benjamin Franklin, who had just returned home from France, sounded a serious note in several letters he wrote to Paine. The nation's affairs were still in a precarious state, he said, and he expressed the wish that some immediate use could be found for the extraordinary talents of his friend, whose services were needed to end the bickering between the states and achieve a spirit like that which had suffused the country during the war.

No offers of a government position were forthcoming, however, and Paine busied himself with an early love – scientific invention. He developed a new bridge, with a single arch and made of cast iron, and in his enthusiasm sought support for it from his prominent friends. For nearly two years he tried to promote his bridge; on various occasions bills authorizing the building of the Paine bridge across one or another major river such as the Hudson or the Delaware almost passed the Congress and the legislatures of New York, Pennsylvania, and New Jersey, but in all instances the vote fell short by a few votes. Paine's work was not in vain, however, as the principles he espoused were incorporated into the bridges built by later inventors.

Perhaps the most curious of the inventions that he worked on late in 1785 was a new type of candle. For many years the French had been making and exporting a smokeless taper, which was unique, much in demand, and exorbitantly expensive. Hoping to take advantage of this profitable market with a candle that would be within the means of most middle-class households, Paine invented a taper that ejected its smoke through a hole in the bottom. His experiments proved successful, and he made a number of the candles and sent a pair to Benjamin Franklin on

December 31, 1785, along with a long letter describing the invention in detail. A few days later he went to Philadelphia and called on Franklin, who expressed his approval of the candle, but the taper was never produced commercially. Others matter intervened to claim Paine's attention.

One was a defense of the Bank of North America, which Paine had helped to found with his gift of $500 initiating the subscription for funds to be passed along to the army in 1780. The bank subsequently had been incorporated, first by the Congress and then by the Pennsylvania legislature, and was very successful. Paper money interests, wanting to get their hands on the large deposits of cash in the bank, initiated a movement to revoke its Pennsylvania and congressional charters. Paine hurried to the bank's defense, and between December 22, 1785, and February 26, 1786, he wrote a new pamphlet, which was published on February 28. Called *Dissertations on Government, the Affairs of the Bank, and Paper Money*, it strongly defended the bank. It was immediately successful and was credited by Robert Morris with saving the bank. More philosophical than he had been in the past, Paine stated a number of basic principles:

- 'Sovereignty, when applied to a people, does not mean the arbitrariness it signifies in a monarchy'
- 'A republic is a sovereignty of justice, in contradistinction to a sovereignty of will'
- 'All laws are acts, but all acts are not laws'
- 'Laws govern the conduct of every individual, and may be altered; acts of agency or negotiation are deeds and contracts'

He went on to say:

The greatness of one party cannot give it a superiority or advantage over the other. The state or its representative, the assembly, has no more power over an act of this kind, after it has passed, than if the state was a private person. It is the glory of a republic to have it so, because it secures the individual from becoming the prey of power, and prevents might from overcoming right. If any difference or dispute arise between the state and the individuals with whom the agreement is made respecting the contract, or the meaning or extent of any of the matters contained in the act, which may affect the property or interest of either, such difference or dispute must be judged and decided upon by the laws of the land, in a court of justice and trial by jury; that is, by the laws of the land already in being at the time such act and contract was made.

This was true justice, Paine declared, and was the true principle of republican government. His concept was incorporated into the Constitution the following year. In 1792 in the case of *Chisholm* vs. *Georgia*, the United States Supreme Court ruled on Georgia's claim of the right to repudiate a contract, and in its decision not only affirmed every principle stated by Paine but also used his actual words.

His influence on the American public was astonishing. Until he wrote his pamphlet it appeared that paper money advocates could revoke the bank's charters, but a drastic shift in public opinion forced them to back off, and the Bank of North America was safe. Paine earned a tidy sum from his royalties but still clung to the idea that he could not accept direct compensation for work he regarded as a public service. He therefore gave his profits to the bank, to be used in the future as a 'fund to protect and defend the institution'. His gesture was quixotic, certainly, as he had far more need for the money than did the Bank of North America, already the most powerful and successful financial enterprise in the United States.

Paine returned to Bordentown in the spring of 1786 and there busied himself making models of his cast-iron bridge. He brought one to Franklin in Philadelphia and won for the project the support of that eminent scientist and statesman. Paine had hoped his first bridge would be built over the Harlem River in New York. When that project failed to elicit the support of the New York legislature he transferred his attentions to the Pennsylvania legislature, but was no more successful there. Engineers and architects said his bridge was sound, but members of the state legislatures were dubious, granting his effectiveness as an author but wondering how a man who put words on paper for a living could possibly design a safe bridge. Paine accepted his defeats cheerfully, believing that in time he would overcome every obstacle. Perhaps, he wrote to several friends, the climate of opinion would improve after he made his frequently delayed trip to England. The wily Franklin suggested that he stop first in France, taking several models of his bridge with him. Americans were impressed by anything French, especially scientific developments, and the legislatures of the various states would clamor for the right to use Paine's design once it had been approved by the leading engineers working in Paris.

Paine accepted the suggestion and made plans to sail early in

May, 1787. This was precisely the time that the delegates to the Constitutional Convention, which was to open on May 25, were beginning to gather in Philadelphia. It is surprising to learn that Paine's name was never mentioned as a possible delegate from any state. At first glance this appears paradoxical, but there were personal and political reasons that made it less than feasible for Paine to become a delegate. At no time had he taken a direct part in politics. He had never allowed himself to become a candidate for office, preferring to do his own work in isolation behind the closed doors of his study. His strength lay in his pen, and he had no wish to exert direct influence by becoming a voting delegate. It must be remembered, too, that he was one of the nation's leading champions of the establishment of a strong national government, and this fact alone would have discouraged his contemporaries from nominating him. It had become increasingly obvious that the Articles of Confederation, which left all real power in the hands of the individual states, were inadequate, and such men as Washington, Madison, and Alexander Hamilton had been agitating on behalf of the formation of a more perfect government. But the states were still arguing over their respective rights, and the Congress, afraid of being disbanded, ignored the proposed convention as long as it could. Then, when it became obvious that there was a groundswell of popular support for the creation of a new constitution, it belatedly sent out notices for the convention to all the state legislatures.

Enthusiasm for the convention was generated in virtually every state. New Hampshire delayed for a time but finally sent its delegates to Philadelphia in June; ultimately only Rhode Island, still going its own way, was not represented. The radicals who had been prominent in the fight for independence, including such men as Samuel Adams, Patrick Henry, and John Hancock, were notably absent. Most of the men elected as delegates were former members of the Continental Congress, and a number had been governors or judges. The rest were moderates – businessmen, well-to-do farmers, and lawyers.

The country was in a strangely apprehensive mood. Every thinking man realized that the union of states under the Articles of Confederation was too weak, too loosely organized, and that a stronger central government had to be established. At the same time, however, the individual states were nervous and fearful, ready to fight for the maintenance of the rights they had enjoyed since 1776. In this atmosphere, therefore, men who advocated extremist positions for either cause were shunned – those who took too insistent a stand in favor of the creation of a more powerful national government as well as the radicals who wanted no diminution of the rights of the individual states.

Because Paine had won universal recognition as a spokesman for those who sought a strong national government, the state legislatures, which elected the delegates in most instances, were not anxious to be represented by someone completely committed to a cause that opposed their own interests.

Curiously Paine seemed to show little interest at this time in the Constitutional Convention and mentioned it only in passing in his correspondence, apparently taking it for granted that the type of government he had long advocated would come into being in the near future. Not until later was his interest aroused. A closer examination of his situation reveals the reasons for his complacency. He had been a member of a select group that called itself the Society of Political Inquiries. Its members, including Franklin, Washington, Robert Morris, and others who favored a strong national government, had been meeting at irregular intervals in Franklin's library. Paine rarely addressed the group, however, preferring to put his thoughts on paper and knowing in any case that his views would be well-represented at the convention. Perhaps, had he realized how difficult the fight for adoption of the new constitution would be in most states, he might have remained in the United States to take an active part in that struggle.

Instead he felt that his work there was finished and late in April, 1787, sailed from New York for France, intending to spend a short time in Paris before going on to England. He planned to spend about a year abroad. Fifteen crowded, dramatic years would pass before he returned to the United States.

12

Bearding the British Lion

Thomas Paine brought with him a thick packet of letters of introduction written by Benjamin Franklin; but when he reached Paris early in the summer of 1787 he discovered that he did not need them. Then as in later times intellectuals were more highly regarded in Europe than in the United States, and Paine, the spokesman of the American Revolution, was given a hero's welcome. France was on the verge of her own revolution, and Paine spent evenings with men of every political persuasion, from Cardinal de Brienne, a member of the Cabinet of Louis XVI, to Georges Jacques Danton, the controversial and complex attorney who became one of the leaders of the French Revolution.

Paine also spent a great deal of time with Thomas Jefferson, the United States minister to France. As a result of Jefferson's influence the Academy of Sciences undertook a study of Paine's bridge, appointing a committee of experts to test his models. Paine felt certain he would win the academy's approval, as he indicated in a brief note to Jefferson written on August 18. At about the same time, he sent a letter to a friend in Philadelphia, George Clymer, saying that the academy's committee had examined all the models and plans for iron bridges in France. 'They unanimously gave the preference to our own,' he declared, 'as being the simplest, strongest and tightest.' The committee reported as Paine had anticipated, and the academy duly voted its approval of his plan; but no state ever appropriated necessary funds, and Paine's bridge was never built.

Before leaving for England Paine held a number of meetings with Cardinal de Brienne and suggested an idea which in that era was regarded as fantastic. He proposed that a 'bridge of friendship' be built across the English Channel, linking Great Britain and France, and he submitted a detailed sketch of his proposed bridge. The bemused cardinal approved of the idea in principle and indicated his opinion in a brief document to that effect, which he signed.

Although Paine was busy in Paris, he found time for activities necessary to his welfare and peace of mind. He made the opportunity to visit the 'girls of St. Germain', usually late at night when he was returning to his lodgings after an evening spent in the company of distinguished gentlemen. The fifty-year-old Paine had developed a distinct preference for young women in their late teens; other women failed to interest him. This was true for his social life as well as his sex life. Now that he enjoyed a moderate financial success, he could make up for the abstinence of earlier years and in association with young women was perhaps living his own youth a second time. The only members of the opposite sex with whom he corresponded after leaving the United States were young girls, to whom he wrote extraordinarily long letters. At no time in his life did he become involved with a mature woman, either romantically or platonically. In this regard it is fair to say that he remained emotionally immature.

He was also secretive in all of his relations with women. He discussed none of his friendships with anyone else, never boasted of his conquests, and went to great lengths to prevent anyone from learning of his affairs with young prostitutes. He was so successful in these efforts that his early biographers believed that he had lost all interest in women after his separation from his wife and that he remained abstinent for the rest of his days. The truth has emerged gradually as his own correspondence and that of friends have come to light.

He also had time to write a new pamphlet, which he called *The Rubicon*. He completed it in Paris in late August and sent it ahead to a printer so the proofs would be ready for his inspection by the time he arrived. On September 3 he crossed the Channel and set foot on English soil for the first time in thirteen years. In spite of his fame – or notoriety – his arrival created no stir and was virtually ignored by all. Hurrying to London, he took lodgings in York Street, Saint James's Square, and then went on to Thetford.

Paine was shocked to find that his father had died the previous year. But his mother was still alive at the age of ninety-one, and he immediately established cordial relations with her, possibly for the first time in his life. Years later family friends revealed a secret that he had never revealed to anyone: From the time he had first gone to America and started earning money, he had sent regular sums to his parents, dispatching the gifts by roundabout means during the war years, when there was no direct contact between the mother country and her former colonies.

During his sojourn in Thetford Paine settled a small income on his mother – the most he could afford – and thereafter she could enjoy a number of luxuries that had always been too expensive for her purse, particularly cakes and other sweets. She had become active in the Society of Friends, and while her son was in Thetford he went with her on a number of occasions to the Quaker meetinghouse. Old Mrs Paine lived until the age of ninety-four, and during the last years of her life she and her son relished the close relationship that, owing to a conflict of personalities, they had not had a half-century earlier. Paine spent the entire autumn of 1787 with his mother; the knowledge that they had made their peace with each other gave him satisfaction until the end of his own days.

His stay in Thetford was one of the most carefree periods he had ever known. He rented a carriage to take his mother and several other elderly ladies on picnics when the weather was sufficiently warm. He went bowling and hiking with boyhood friends and out of deference to his mother's hatred of liquor he avoided the local tavern. Whether Mrs Paine or the author's old friends ever realized that he had become a man of consequence is difficult to determine, as none of them wrote letters. It was probably enough to know that the prodigal son had made good in the world, contrary to early expectations, and had risen to sufficiently high station in life to be regarded as a gentleman.

During his stay at Thetford Paine made some revisions in his new pamphlet, changing its title to *Prospects on the Rubicon; or, an Investigation into the Causes and Consequences of the Politics to be Agitated at the Meeting of Parliament*. It might be noted that another printing of the same work came out in 1793 under yet another title, *Prospects on the War and Paper Currency*. That Paine wrote the work in the first place is surprising. He regarded himself as an American citizen, and the pamphlet concerned itself exclusively with matters of interest to Englishmen. Paine was incapable of keeping silent, however, when he believed an injustice was being done. Although it might be argued that he was aroused because he had spent most of his life as a subject of the Crown, it would perhaps be more accurate to describe him as a citizen of the world. Wherever he saw what he regarded as wrong, he wanted to right it; when he saw principle being abandoned, he called attention to it.

Some people, among them members of the British ruling class, thought of him as a busybody and a nuisance. They believed he had no right to speak out on matters that were none of his business. Paine's troubles with the British, which eventually caused charges of treason and sedition to be brought against him, can be traced to the publication of his *Rubicon* pamphlet. Certainly men of authority, in office and out, were well aware of the role he played in the American Revolution, and some undoubtedly resented him for it. But the war had been lost by Britain and her former colonies were gone; members of the ruling class were willing to allow bygones to be bygones – until Paine so infuriated them that they felt compelled to take action against him, to put him on trial, and to execute him, if necessary, in order to silence him.

The background of the pamphlet may be seen in the efforts of William Pitt the Younger to prepare for a war with Holland. Britain had been spending increasing sums on armaments for that purpose since the end of the American war, and Pitt was planning to ask Parliament for yet another, even larger appropriation. Paine, in the *Rubicon*, argued that Great Britain was courting disaster, that there was little to be gained and much to be lost by such a conflict.

Nowhere is Paine's idealism more evident than in the pages of this work. He urged the government and people of Britain to avoid war with Holland, to cultivate friendly relations with

France, to avoid all alliances which would necessitate giving military aid, and above all to create new liberties at home. This would result in greater wealth for all, he argued, and would more closely unite the people and the Crown. This, he said, was what was happening in France, thus indicating his total ignorance of the developments currently taking place across the Channel.

The *Rubicon* is a somewhat laborious work, and, as Paine had almost no following in Britain it failed to achieve its purpose. But the pamphlet is nevertheless important because it contains a single paragraph that well might be regarded as Thomas Paine's creed:

> When we consider, for the feelings of Nature cannot be dismissed, the calamities of war and the miseries it inflicts upon the human species, the thousands and tens of thousands of every age and sex who are rendered wretched by the event, surely there is something in the heart of man that calls upon him to think! Surely there is some tender chord, tuned by the hand of the Creator, that still struggles to emit in the hearing of the soul a note of sorrowing sympathy. Let it then be heard, and let man learn to feel that *the true greatness of a nation is founded on principles of humanity.* . . . War involves in its progress such a train of unforeseen and unsupposed circumstances, such a combination of foreign matters, that no human wisdom can calculate the end. It has but one thing certain, and that is to increase taxes. . . . I defend the cause of the poor, of the manufacturer, of the trades-man, of the farmer, and of all those on whom the real burthern of taxes fall – but above all, I defend the cause of humanity.

Paine was now fascinated by what little he could find in the London newspapers about the Constitutional Convention in Philadelphia, and bombarded his friends in the United States with letters, in which he asked scores of questions. An undated letter to Thomas Jefferson, probably written early in 1788 from Thetford, may be among the most important declarations Paine ever put on paper.

> After I got home, being alone and wanting amusement, I sat down to explain to myself (for there is such a thing) my ideas of national and civil rights, and the distinction between them. I send them to you to see how nearly we agree.
>
> Suppose twenty persons, strangers to each other, to meet in a country not before inhabited. Each would be a Sovereign in his own natural right. His will would be his law, but his power, in many cases, inadequate to his right; and the consequence would be that each might be exposed, not only to each other, but to the other

nineteen. It would then occur to them that their condition would be much improved, if a way could be devised to exchange that quantity of danger into so much protection; so that each individual should possess the strength of the whole number. As all their rights in the first case are natural rights, and the exercise of those rights supported only by their own natural individual power, they would begin by distinguishing between those rights they could individually exercise, fully and perfectly, and those they could not. Of the first kind are the rights of thinking, speaking, forming and giving opinions, and perhaps are those which can be fully exercised by the individual without the aid of exterior assistance; or, in other words, rights of personal competency. Of the second kind are those of personal protection, of acquiring and possessing property, in the exercise of which the individual natural power is less than the natural right.

Having drawn this line, they agree to retain individually the first class of Rights, or those of personal competency; and to detach from their personal possession the second class, or those of defective power, and to accept in lieu thereof a right to the whole power produced by a condensation of all the parts. These I conceive to be civil rights, or rights of compact, and are distinguishable from natural rights because in the one we act wholly in our own person, in the other we agree not to do so, but act under the guarantee of society.

It therefore follows that the more of imperfect natural rights, or rights of imperfect power we give up, and thus exchange, the more security we possess; . . . the word liberty is often mistakenly put for security. . . . But it does not follow that the more natural rights of *every kind* we assign the more security we possess, because if we resign those of the first class we may suffer much by the exchange; for where the right and power are equal with each other in the individual, naturally, they ought to rest there. . . .

I consider the individual sovereignty of the States retained under the act of confederation to be of the second class of right. It becomes dangerous because it is defective in the power necessary to support it. It answers the pride and purpose of a few men in each State, but the State collectively is injured by it.

No longer under severe financial pressures and with time to think, Paine was rapidly developing into a student of civilization who no longer concerned himself exclusively with immediate issues. His appearance had changed somewhat, too, as a description by Royall Tyler indicates. Tyler, a dramatist, met him in 1788 at his lodgings in London, and apparently Paine had made some slight efforts to improve his dress. He wore a snuff-colored coat, an olive vest of velvet, drab breeches, and coarse stockings. His shoe buckles were plain and about the size of a half-dollar.

Perched on his head was a tattered, bob-tailed wig, which Tyler said made him look like an old soldier who had worn it throughout a long war. He was painfully thin and although tall gave the impression that he was only of medium height. He was 'subject to the extreme of low, and highly exhilarating spirits'. In most company he was reserved, and refused to take part in small talk. But when 'a man of sense and elocution' was present, he 'delighted in advancing the most unaccountable, and often the most whimsical paradoxes; which he defended in his own plausible manner'. When others encouraged him, he would enlarge happily on his theme, but if anyone interrupted with an irrelevant comment – or even if a poker accidentally fell to the floor – Paine retired into silence and would not be drawn out again.

Having a great deal of free time in Thetford, his sojourn there interrupted only by occasional visits to London, Paine turned again to scientific invention. He was undaunted by his failures and continued to turn out ideas at a furious rate. He invented a machine that would plane wood, a new and complicated crane, and a wheel with a double rim; and he attempted to make a completely smokeless candle. He also invented a motor that used gunpowder for fuel and, building a small model, almost terminated his career when the contraption exploded. Fortunately, since his mother was taking a nap at the time, he conducted his experiment outdoors, and thereby saved a wall and the roof of the old Paine homestead, the rest of which was destroyed. Eternally optimistic about matters scientific, he would concede only that his gunpowder mixture had been 'a trifle strong', and he insisted he would try the experiment again. Luckily for posterity and himself, other matters began to occupy his attention.

His bridge was his special joy, and he obtained a patent on it, applying primly to the man he had so long vilified and calling him 'His Most Excellent Majesty King George the Third'. The patent was granted, and when a replacement was built across the Thames after the collapse of the old Blackfriars Bridge, an adaptation of Paine's model was used. The author-inventor was paid the huge sum of £1,500 for his contribution to the new bridge. The money gave him additional financial independence. Although his mother did not want any new clothes, Paine bought her a wardrobe; he also presented her with a horse and carriage and hired a youth in the neighborhood to drive her when she wanted to visit friends.

Meanwhile the *Rubicon* pamphlet, although it failed to influence

British policy, gave the author in intellectual circles a stature independent of the reputation he had acquired in America. He was regarded as a man of standing and substance in London, where his company was eagerly sought in the spring of 1788.

Only one aspect of his life remained secret. London was filled with prostitutes, many of them young, and Paine did not hesitate to avail himself of their services. Apparently he had grown tired of ordinary relations with them and usually took two at a time to his lodgings. Precisely how he cavorted with them was a matter he never discussed.

Certainly his personal situation was difficult. He was still legally married, and, divorce being out of the question under the restrictions of the Church of England, he could not even contemplate marrying again. Therefore, not wanting to become dishonorably involved with someone when he could offer no permanent relationship, he avoided single ladies of breeding and family. Apparently it did not cross his mind to see his wife again or to write to her. He had developed his habits in America and France, and in England they remained true to form. He was gallant to the wives of his friends, he avoided widows and other eligible ladies, and he satisfied his own needs with street-walkers. His sexual appetite grew steadily – and would continue to grow – but he did not permit this aspect of his life to interfere with his other activities.

The Messrs. Walker, a firm of bridge builders, set up a workshop in the little town of Rotherham, Yorkshire, and there Paine labored intermittently on his designs for the new Blackfriars Bridge and for several other projects that were presented to him. Sometimes he remained in Yorkshire for several weeks at a time before going to London again. For the time being his financial problems were at an end, and before long he became the good friend of some of the most prominent and powerful men in Great Britain.

In fact, Paine became as much the American social lion in England as Benjamin Franklin had been in Paris. He spent a week late in 1788 at the country house of Edmund Burke and often dined with Charles James Fox, the peripatetic former Cabinet minister whose friendship for America had never wavered. He visited the ancestral home of the Duke of Portland and frequently was invited to Wentworth House, the home of the enormously wealthy Whig leader Lord Fitzwilliam. Sir Joseph

Banks, the physicist, dined with him and discussed scientific matters with him; Lord Lansdowne and Sir George Staunton, prominent government officials, consulted him on public affairs. He also played an active, prominent part in the life of the small but influential American colony in London. Benjamin West, the distinguished painter, became his friend, as did West's student and colleague, John Trumbull. He dined with them frequently and out of modesty resisted their repeated requests to paint his portrait.

Paine's personality and approach to others remained unchanged. He never put on airs; he was still candid, sometimes brutally honest. Having been on terms of close friendship with the leading Americans of his day, he dealt with great lords and cabinet members in England on the same open basis. And he treated the workmen in his engineering shop as equals, an attitude that was startling in class-conscious England. Above all, Paine regarded himself as an American temporarily living in Britain, never a prodigal Englishman who had come home. He thought of himself as an unofficial representative of the United States, and he went to great efforts to explain American democracy and the American system of government to Britons in high places. They in turn invariably regarded him as an American, despite the fact that he had been born in England and had spent most of the first four decades of his life there.

In spite of an active career and social life, however, Paine was lonely. It may be that he thought of marrying again, as he hired an attorney in London to study his separation agreement with his wife. The lawyer advised him that he was in fact divorced, but the issue was clouded, and Paine preferred not to take a risk that could prove mortifying. He revealed his feelings in a long, frank letter he wrote to the youngest of the Nicholson daughters, Kitty, whom he had known in New York and at her school in Bordentown. She had just been married, and on January 6, 1789, he sent her his congratulations, and then spoke freely of his own situation:

> Though I appear a sort of wanderer, the married state has not a sincerer friend than I am. It is the harbour of human life, and is, with respect to the things of this world, what the next world is to this. It is home: and that one word conveys more than any other word can express. For a few years we may glide along the tide of youthful single life and be wonderfully delighted; but it is a tide that flows but

134

once, and what is still worse, it ebbs faster than it flows, and leaves many a hapless voyager aground. I am one, you see, that have experienced the fate I am describing. I have lost my tide; it passed by while every thought of my heart was on the wing for the salvation of my dear America, and I have now as contentedly as I can, made myself a little bower of willows on the shore that has the solitary resemblance of a home. Should I always continue the tenant of this home, I hope my female will ever remember that it contains not the churlish enemy of their sex, nor the inaccessible cold hearted mortal, nor the capricious tempered oddity, but one of the best and most affectionate of their friends. . . .

You touch me on a very tender part when you say my friends on your side of the water 'cannot be reconciled to the idea of my resigning my adopted America, even for my native England'. They are right. Though I am in as elegant style of acquaintance here as any American that ever came over, my heart and myself are 3000 miles apart; and I had rather see my horse Button in his stable, or eating the grass of Bordentown or Morrisiana, than see all the pomp and show of Europe.

A thousand years hence (for I must indulge in a few thoughts) perhaps in less, America may be what England now is! The innocence of her character that won the hearts of all nations in her favor may sound like a romance, and her inimitable virtue as if it had never been. The ruins of that liberty which thousands bled for, or suffered to obtain, may just furnish materials for a village tale or extort a sigh from rustic sensibility, while the fashionable of that day, enveloped in dissipation, shall deride the principle and deny the fact.

When we contemplate the fall of Empires and the extinction of nations of the ancient world, we see but little to excite our regret than the mouldering ruins of pompous palaces, magnificent monuments, lofty pyramids, and walls and towers of the most costly workmanship. But when the Empire of America shall fall, the subject for contemplative sorrow will be infinitely greater than crumbling brass or marble can inspire. It will not then be said, here stood a temple of vast antiquity, – here rose a Babel of invisible height, or there a palace of sumptuous extravagance; but here, ah painful thought! the noblest work of human wisdom, the grandest scene of human glory, the fair cause of freedom rose and fell!

Read this and then ask if I forget America.

Obviously Paine was homesick as well as lonely, but it did not make financial sense for him to leave England. Although he was writing almost nothing for publication, as an engineer he was earning a 'tidy fortune', as he called it – far more than he could bring in with his pen in the United States. He was able to save

Rebel!

large sums because he made so few changes in his style of living. He hired a manservant as a bow to convention, and on occasion he took friends to dinner at expensive inns and taverns; but otherwise he spent little.

His work as an engineer, although lucrative, failed to occupy his mind. As his letter to Kitty Nicholson indicates, his thoughts returned constantly to the United States and to the experiment in democracy being conducted there. He did not exaggerate when he called America his first love.

13

The Rights of Man

Not the least of the services Thomas Paine performed for the United States were his unpublicized activities in England. John Adams, the United States minister to Great Britain, returned home soon after Paine's arrival in England, leaving America without formal representation there. The absence of news from London hampered the formation of American foreign policy, and Jefferson, who was coordinating the activities of his nation's diplomats in Europe as well as serving as minister to France, wrote to his good friend Paine, 'I have great confidence in your communications, and since Mr Adams' departure I am in need of authentic information from that country.'

Paine happily volunteered, and served as an informal United States minister, or, in perhaps humbler terms, an accurate listening post. The function he performed was recognized by both the British Government and the opposition. Leading members of both the Whig and Tory parties took pains to keep him informed of views and developments they wanted transmitted across the Atlantic. Paine regarded this work as a labor of love and attended his duties with scrupulous fidelity to fact, even when reporting matters with which he had no sympathy. He made no secret of his activities, but they became known to the general public only after Jefferson's death.

His letters to Jefferson were curious blends of the personal and impersonal; after discussing the patents he was seeking on bridge design and describing his scientific inventions in detail to the friend who shared his interest in such matters, he plunged into long descriptions of the political situation. And he found it impossible to refrain from discussing the essence of democracy with a fellow writer-philosopher who shared so many of his views.

The extensive correspondence of Paine and Jefferson led the early biographers of both men to speculate on the basic contributions that each had made to the concepts of the other. These historians settled nothing because their premise was false. Paine and Jefferson thought remarkably alike on fundamental issues. Both were students of Locke and had shared the same empirical experiences in the founding of a new, democratic nation whose form of government was unique. So their thinking sometimes was identical and sometimes ran parallel. Each bolstered and to an extent refined the views of the other; they did not debate but mutually supported each other.

Both men were pleased by the political developments in France that marked the beginning of the French Revolution – neither was able to envision the vicious bloodbath of the Reign of Terror. Jefferson kept his friend informed of the early developments, and Paine, in his enthusiasm, predicted that a 'crowned republic' would be established in France. Thereafter, he said, the movement would spread to Great Britain, and soon the governments of all Europe would be reorganized on a democratic basis, using the United States as a model.

Jefferson returned to America in September, 1789, and two weeks later Paine arrived in Paris. The moderates and intellectuals who were prominent in the first phase of the French Revolution were familiar with *Common Sense* and the *Crisis* pamphlets, and the author of these works was greeted as a conquering hero.

Paine was warmly welcomed by the marquis de Lafayette, the

idealistic nobleman who had served as a volunteer under General Washington. One night in late October both men were principals in a ceremony that was held in the gardens of the Louvre and witnessed by thousands. Lafayette presented Paine with the key to the Bastille, the ancient prison that had recently been destroyed by mobs as a symbol of autocracy and royal prerogative, and asked him to give it to George Washington, who had taken office as President of the United States the preceding April 30. In a brief acceptance speech which Lafayette translated for the crowd, Paine said, 'the principles of America opened the Bastille'. Paine was soon being hailed as 'the father of democracy'. He protested in vain that he had merely been a spokesman for a movement that had been under way long before he had migrated to the New World. His visit completely eclipsed that of Gouverneur Morris, who had come to France on a financial mission for President Washington. Morris, whose political views were conservative, disapproved of the French Revolution and regarded Paine almost as a poseur, certainly as someone whose talents were being over-rated. Although they had been on friendly terms in Philadelphia, the relationship now cooled and they were never on good terms again.

Paine remained in Paris until mid-March, 1790, when he left for England to see the completion of one of his bridges in York-shire. Before his departure he wrote to friends in the United States telling them that Lafayette was becoming the George Washington of France, that the 'spirit of political reformation' soon would 'sweep over Britain like a tidal wave', and that he himself was becoming desperately homesick for America. When he left he promised Lafayette he would return to carry the Ameri-can flag in the 'great procession' that would take place when France adopted a constitution modeled on that of the United States. He was so convinced these events would take place that after his return to London he wrote to Washington requesting official permission to take part in the celebration.

In May, 1790, Paine vanished from London for several weeks. To explain his disappearance a strange story was circulated that lasted until the middle of the nineteenth century. It was alleged that he returned secretly to France and conspired there with some of the elements who were causing the Revolution to take a more radical turn. Nothing could have been further from the truth: Old Mrs Paine had fallen ill, and her son hurried to her bedside, remaining there until she died at the end of May. He returned to London in June and wore a mourning band on his arm for the next six months.

An exhibition featuring Paine's bridge, a span of 110 feet, opened in London in June, sponsored by the inventor and an American merchant, Peter Whiteside, who was living in London. The public was charged one shilling per person to view the structure, and Paine estimated that he would be making a profit by August. But Whiteside got into financial difficulties in July, and Paine and several other friends helped him to avoid bankruptcy. The gesture cost Paine more than £600 and seemed to ruin his enthusiasm for engineering, at least for the moment.

The exhibition continued to draw visitors, and by October Paine was in the clear; but he had lost interest in the venture and went off to France for a few weeks. He returned early in November, 1790, imbued with a new fervor. The United States was prospering under a democratic form of government and France was following her example; now it was the turn of Great Britain. What she was unwilling to do for herself, Thomas Paine would do for her. At no time in his life was his revolutionary, restless spirit in his crusade on behalf of democracy more evident than at this moment. He was the true missionary, and he sincerely believed the time had come for Great Britain to be saved.

He was inspired to take action at this time by Edmund Burke's *Reflexions on the Revolution in France*, published on November 1. Paine who landed at Dover the following day, immediately obtained a copy of the pamphlet; twenty-four hours later he had taken quiet quarters at the Angel Inn, Islington, and there began to compose his reply.

Until now, Paine had admired Burke more than any other living Englishman. It had been Burke who had offered constant support for the Americans and their ideals through the darkest days of their revolution; who had called the Crown 'almost dead and rotton'; who had cried out that the ancient rights of free Englishmen were being subverted and nullified. Burke had become the symbol of British Liberalism to Paine, and in the past two years they had become friends. But Paine had misjudged Burke, failing to recognize the solidly conservative core of his friend's ideas. In the *Reflexions* Burke had attacked the very principles of the French Revolution, calling them anarchistic and declaring that they would destroy French civilization. Paine therefore regarded him as a traitor to a sacred cause; the initial purpose of his reply was to challenge Burke's theses. The pamphlet over which he labored soon turned into something far more, however, than a rebuttal. Even more than *Common Sense*, this document must be regarded as his masterpiece. He called it *The Rights of Man* and dedicated it to George Washington.

The people of a nation, Paine said in his new essay, have the right to choose any form of government they wish. If they want a democracy, they are entitled to it; if they prefer a hereditary monarchy, an oligarchy, an autocracy – whatever – it is their prerogative to live under that form of government. But a real constitution must be 'of the people and for the people and by the people', a phrase that, slightly altered, would later be heard in Lincoln's Gettysburg Address. People make a constitution for themselves, and have no right to bind those as yet unborn to it. All men are born equal; and every child, said Paine, derives his existence from God. 'The world is as new to him as it was to the first man who existed, and this natural right to it is of the same kind.'

The natural rights of man are inviolable: This is the rock on which Paine founds his thesis. Man's civil rights grow out of his natural rights. To secure his natural rights man deposits some of them, such as the right to judge in his own cause, in 'the common stock of society'. There are two types of government, Paine said – those which grow out of this social compact and those which do not. Some governments are founded on superstition, others on power. Still others are founded on the common interests of society and the common rights of man, regardless of whether these be 'priestcraft', conquest, or reason. A national constitution is the act of the people that is antecedent to government; therefore a government cannot determine or alter the law that it *temporarily* represents. Pitt's bill to reform Parliament, for example, is ludicrous because it involves the absurdity of trusting an admittedly corrupt body to reform itself. In other words, the judges would sit on their own case. 'The right of reform is in the nation in its original character,' Paine declared, 'and the constitutional method would be by a general convention elected for the purpose.' The organization of the aggregate of rights which individuals concede to society for the purpose of making all rights secure is what creates a republic. Insofar as those rights are surrendered to such extraneous authority as priestcraft, hereditary power, or conquest, despotism is created.

Having stated his principles, Paine presented the history of the French Revolution to date, relying in part on his own observations and, for the rest, on what he had been told by Lafayette, Danton, and others. Until this time few outrages had been committed by the mobs. Burke made the most of these incidents in his *Reflexions*, but Paine took the opposite approach and played them down. The French nation could no more be blamed for these excesses than the entire English nation could be blamed for the London riots of 1780, in which the poor had rebelled against high prices. And in any event, he emphasized, mobs are the inevitable consequence of misgovernment:

> It is by distortedly exalting some men, that others are distortedly debased. A vast mass of mankind are degradedly thrown into the background of the human picture, to bring forward, with greater glare, the puppet show of state and aristocracy. In the commencement of a revolution, those men are rather followers of the camp than of the standard of liberty, and have yet to be instructed how to use it.

It was Paine's intention to publish Part One of *The Rights of Man* in time for the opening of Parliament in February, but the printer to whom he gave the work, a man named Johnson, became frightened because so many of the sentiments expressed by the author appeared to be clearly seditious. Johnson gave up the enterprise after printing only a handful of copies. A more daring printer, J. S. Jordan, whose shop was at 166 Fleet Street, agreed to take the work, and Paine added a preface to it tracing the background of Burke's work and his own. He left the publication in the hands of progressive-minded friends – the philosopher William Godwin and the playwright Thomas Holcroft – and prior to the publication of Part One of *The Rights of Man* on March 13, 1791, he left for France.

Godwin, the husband of feminist Mary Wollstonecraft and the future father-in-law of Percy Bysshe Shelley, was responsible for the story that no reputable bookseller in England would admit that he kept a single copy of Paine's pamphlet in his shop but on demand, however, would produce one from beneath the counter. The first printing of 10,000 copies sold out overnight, and thereafter Jordan kept his presses running twenty-four hours each day in an attempt to meet the demand. Within the next year many hundreds of thousands of copies were sold in Great Britain and the United States, and still more, in a translated edition, in France. No accurate records were kept, but it has been estimated that at least 2 million copies of the work were sold in the three countries. A single copy cost three shillings, and had Paine kept the money for himself he would have become a wealthy man. Following the course he had set with his pamphlets in America, however, he refused to accept pay for what he regarded as the necessity to tell the truth, and he insisted that the proceeds be paid to a little-known organization called the Society for Constitutional Information, which acquired vast sums as a result of his generosity.

The principles elucidated by Paine have been so completely accepted by the Western world that today nothing he said in *The Rights of Man* appears unusual or shocking. But the pamphlet created a sensation in the tradition-bound monarchy in which it was first published. Great Britain was split by the publication of the work. A great many people wondered if Paine was slightly mad. Certainly his attack on cherished institutions caused him to be regarded as a wild radical, and even Whigs who could find no fault with many of his arguments were shocked and dismayed by his assault on the monarchy. The Society for Constitutional Information, however, which had branches in Scotland and Ireland, immediately adopted the work as its Bible. Great ferment was caused in Dublin, where copies disappeared as rapidly as they were produced, and the Whigs of that city appointed a committee to insure that the pamphlet was widely disseminated.

The first American edition was published in the summer of 1791 and was openly hailed by Jefferson and Madison. The American conservatives, however, reacted to it as did the Tories in England, and for the first time the great propagandist of the American Revolution failed to win the almost unanimous support of the American people. Vice-President John Adams heartily disapproved of the work. President Washington remained aloof and expressed no opinion of the pamphlet. But since it was dedicated to the President and publicly praised by Secretary of State Jefferson, many people thought it bore the official approval of the administration.

The greater the controversy raged, the more tranquil Paine became. A stream of letters from friends in England and the United States kept him abreast of developments. He was content; he rented a small flat for himself on the Île Saint-Louis and settled down to watch what he felt certain would be the peaceful, bloodless development of the French Revolution. He was delighted when Lafayette was appointed commander in chief of the National Guard. To Paine's way of thinking France was following in America's footsteps, his own influence was increasing in Great Britain, and soon democracy would be universal. One sentence that had appeared in the original Johnson edition of *The Rights of Man* had been eliminated from Jordan's edition but reappeared in the United States because the printer there made his copy from Johnson's edition: 'Every thing in the English government appears to me the reverse of what it ought to be, and of what it is said to be.' Members of the British legation staff in the United States saw the sentence, of course, and duly reported it to an outraged government in London.

In his spare time Paine was making notes for Part Two of *The Rights of Man*, an incendiary work that would include a call for revolution in Great Britain. But he spent most of his time in Paris meeting various leaders of the French Revolution. It was during this period that he became friendly with the middle-class, impeccably dressed Maximilien de Robespierre, who became the dictator of France during the Reign of Terror, 1793–94. Paine was charmed by his new friend and heartily approved of the sentiments he expressed in his speeches. Robespierre hailed universal suffrage and freedom of religion, attacked the abuses of royal and ministerial power, and demanded the abolition of slavery throughout the world. He also publicly endorsed *The Rights of Man*.

In June Paine witnessed the true beginning of the downfall of the monarchy. King Louis XVI, Queen Marie Antoinette, and other members of the royal family became fearful for their safety and attempted to escape in disguise. They were recognized, returned to Paris, and imprisoned, and public sentiment began to turn against Lafayette, who was suspected of having deliberately allowed the King to depart.

The people of Paris were in an increasingly ugly mood. On the day Louis was returned to the city Paine went into the streets, where huge crowds were milling about, and suddenly the mob turned on him. He was manhandled and might have suffered a severe beating if a man who spoke English had not intervened. Paine, it seemed, was not wearing a red, white, and blue cockade in his hat; so the crowd assumed that the absence of the tricolor emblem, which was a symbol of those who wanted to abolish the monarchy and establish a republic, meant that he was a nobleman.

Paine, conscious of the irony of the situation, apologized for the oversight and after promising to wear the tricolor in the future returned to his apartment.

By July he was in London again and wrote a long letter to President Washington. He was proud of the success of the first portion of *The Rights of Man* and was now hard at work on the second, more important part. 'As I have got the ear of the country,' he wrote, 'I shall go on, and at least shew them, what is a novelty here, that there can be a person beyond the reach of corruption.' After presenting Lafayette's regards, he indicated a sufficient understanding of affairs in France to say that a new crisis was building to a climax there, and that what was at stake was whether the government should be 'monarchical and hereditary or wholly representative'. As to his own activities, he wrote with great candor:

> After the establishment of the American Revolution, it did not appear to me that any object could arise great enough to engage me a second time. I began to feel myself happy in being quiet; but I now experience that principle is not confined to time or place, and that the ardour of '76 is capable of renewing itself. I have another work on hand which I intend shall be my last, for I long much to return to America. It is not natural that fame should wish for a rival, but the case is otherwise with me, for I do most sincerely wish there was some person in this country that could usefully and successfully attract the public attention, and leave me with a satisfied mind to the enjoyment of quiet life: but it is painful to see abuses and errors and sit down a senseless spectator. Of this your own mind will interpret mine.

President Washington's reply was cordial, although he made no mention of the dedication of *The Rights of Man*. Unlike the author he did not believe the American Revolution could be exported, or that the form of government now established in the United States could be effectively transplanted to the eastern shores of the Atlantic. In a letter dated May 6, 1792, he wrote:

> To my friends, and those who know my occupations, I am sure no apology is necessary for keeping their letters so much longer unanswered, than my inclination would lead me to do. I shall therefore offer no excuse for not having sooner acknowledged the receipt of your letter of the 21st of June (July). My thanks, however, for the token of your remembrance, in the fifty copies of *The Rights of Man*, are offered with no less cordiality than they would have been had I answered your letter in the first moment of receiving it.
> The duties of my office, which at all times, especially during the

session of Congress, require an unremitting attention, naturally become more pressing towards the close of it; and as that body have resolved to rise tomorrow, and as I am determined, in case they should, to set out for Mt. Vernon on the next day, you will readily conclude that the present is a busy moment with me; and to that I am persuaded your goodness will impute my not entering into the several points touched upon in your letter. Let it suffice, therefore, at this time, to say, that I rejoice in the information of your personal prosperity, and, as no one can feel a greater interest in the happiness of mankind than I do, that is the first wish of my heart, that the enlightened policy of the present age may diffuse to all men those blessings, to which they are entitled, and lay the foundation of happiness for future generations.

Paine's enthusiasm caused him to write a 'Republican Manifesto' for France, a document of about 1,000 words in which he urged the establishment there of his favorite form of government, at the same time suggesting the abdication of Louis XVI and requesting the people of France to permit the King to go peacefully into exile without harm to his person. The manifesto was translated and published, and thousands of copies were distributed in Paris by members of a small group called the Republican Society. Within a few months, under the leadership of such men as Nicolas de Bonneville and Achille Du Châtelet that organization became one of the most important and powerful in France. Although the manifesto was unsigned, leaders of the various political movements in France knew that Paine was its author, and his renown increased accordingly.

Paine's primary interest lay in extending the principles of the American Revolution to Great Britain, but he could not refrain from speaking his mind on French affairs as well. In 1791 he wrote a letter to the Parisian newspaper of the moderates, the *Moniteur*, attacking the concept of monarchy. Regarded with note by horrified members of the British legation, the letter was forwarded to His Majesty's government in London. It read:

I am not the personal enemy of Kings. Quite the contrary. No man wishes more heartily than myself to see them all in the happy and honorable state of private individuals; but I am the avowed, open, and intrepid enemy of what is called monarchy; and I am such by principles which nothing can either alter or corrupt – by my attachment to humanity; by the anxiety which I feel within myself for the dignity and honor of the human race; by the disgust which I experience when I observe men directed by children and governed by

146

brutes; by the horror which all the evils which monarchy has spread over the earth excite within my breast; and by those sentiments which make me shudder at the calamities, the exactions, the wars, and the massacres with which monarchy has crushed mankind: in short, it is against all the hell of monarchy that I have declared war.

No doubt Paine had intended the letter for France. At the time of the letter's publication in July, however, he had already returned to London, a situation which resulted in unfortunate consequences. The Crown and the Cabinet were indifferent to the opinions expressed by Paine when he was separated from them by the Atlantic, but the painfully candid expression of a creed that attacked the institution of monarchy, written by a man who was making his home and earning his living in London, could not be ignored. Complicating Paine's situation further was the question of his citizenship. He regarded himself as an American, as did other citizens of the United States, but it did not necessarily follow that the Crown so regarded him. He had been born in England, and after living in America for a relatively short time he was residing in England again. The question of what constituted British or American citizenship had not been settled by the Treaty of 1783; indeed, it remained an unresolved issue until the War of 1812. Paine was therefore treading on dangerous ground, and his friends tried to warn him that he was placing himself in grave personal jeopardy. If he chose to engage in polemical discussions in print with the Abbé Sieyès, the philosopher of the increasingly powerful Jacobins in France, that was his prerogative. But he was courting almost certain arrest and prosecution on serious charges in Britain if he persisted in attacking all monarchies rather than the French monarchy alone.

Paine may have been a trifle mad, as even some of the people closest to him suspected; but he was no fool, and he had no desire to be forced into posing either as a hero or as a martyr. By the very nature of his personality, however, he could not allow himself to surrender his right to speak his mind honestly in the face of threats. He considered his integrity at stake, and he was determined to speak his thoughts to the world. Etienne Dumont, one of the leaders of the French Revolution, who traveled with Paine to London in July, 1791, said the author was convinced 'the world would still be benefitted if all books in the world other than *The Rights of Man* were burned'. He had, Dumont said, a 'sublime faith' in the 'sacred nature of his testimonies' against the institution of monarchy, and the Frenchman was unable to decide whether Paine's supreme confidence in the words he put on paper were due to humility or vanity.

Paine was scheduled to attend the celebration in Piccadilly of the second anniversary of Bastille Day, but the authorities were taking the dimmest of all possible views of the demonstration. Because it seemed likely that riots might break out, he wisely stayed at home. A meeting was to be held in a tavern called the Crown and Anchor, at which the presence of Paine and others had been advertised in advance. The proprietor, not wanting glass broken and furniture smashed, was persuaded to close his doors thus effectively canceling the meeting. The propagandist in Paine could not resist exploiting this situation. Declaring that Englishmen had been denied the right of freedom of assemblage, he wrote an inflammatory statement of about 2,000 words which he called 'An Address and Declaration of the Friends of Universal Peace and Liberty'. It was adopted at a meeting held by a group of radicals on August 20 at the Thatched House Tavern in London.

Paine was intentionally goading the King, Parliament, and all who believed in the British system of government; he made it very plain to all who would listen to him that he was trying to foment a revolution in Britain like those undertaken in America and France. 'Wilful misrepresentations are industriously spread by partizans of arbitrary power,' he wrote in the 'Address', so he deemed it important to 'declare to the world our principles and the motives of our conduct'. He rejoiced over the French Revolution, which meant 'much to us as Englishmen'. Here, apparently, he allowed his fervor to conquer his judgment; he was saying in effect that he was an Englishman! If that were the case, then he could not claim the protection of the United States or take refuge as an American citizen. He went on to rejoice in the freedom of 25 million Frenchmen and 'in the prospect which such a magnificent example opens to the world'. He congratulated the people of France for 'having laid the axe to the roots of tyranny, and for erecting government on the sacred hereditary rights of man'. He knew of no human authority superior to that of a whole nation and claimed the right of every nation to act as France had done. Then, making his own situation even more precarious, he added, 'As Englishmen we also rejoice, because we are immediately interested in the French Revolution'.

It should be noted that he was not a very accurate observer of the passing scene. As yet he seemed unaware of the anarchistic elements of the French Revolution, of the growing undertones of mob violence and mob rule, or of the increasing tendency toward autocracy in that upheaval. Allowing for the differences in the temperaments of the people of the two nations, he regarded the American and French Revolutions as more or less identical and believed they sprang from virtually identical causes. Being stubborn, he clung to those beliefs.

He continued his attack on Britain by listing what he regarded as the grievances of the British people: The government was the most expensive in the world – taxes were oppressive, the national debt was heavy, and millions were poverty-stricken; the 'moral obligation' of providing for the aged, for infants, and for the poor was not being met; the government was on friendly terms with 'the most despotic and arbitrary powers in the world', among them Prussia, Turkey, and the German principalities; the government was crippled by intrigue and corruption; and the nation still struggled under the burden of an outmoded feudal system.

Unlike his direct attack on monarchy in his letter to the *Moniteur*, his recent address made no mention of the Crown. Either he was showing at least the vestiges of caution, or perhaps, as some nineteenth-century students of his life claimed, he believed the British monarchy to be unrelated to the actual government of and by the people. His polemic was so extreme, however, that men of all classes were alarmed. Certainly Paine was not then the only one in Britain who supported the French Revolution; but his writing made him conspicuous beyond all others, and he was credited – or blamed – for what several newspapers called 'the importation of a plague'. He seemed to seek – indeed, to demand – recognition as a radical.

In his private life Paine seemed blissfully unaware of the turmoil that he was provoking. He made his home now with an old friend from Lewes, Thomas Rickman, a bookseller, who lived quietly with his wife and children in a comfortable flat above his shop. According to Rickman, Paine spent most of his time writing, engaging in correspondence, and visiting with various friends, a number of whom were authors, artists, or philosophers. He occasionally stopped at a coffeehouse for an hour or two, generally took a nap after dinner, and sometimes in the evenings played chess or dominoes, but never cards. He enjoyed music, particu-

larly singing, and regularly walked to the homes of friends so he
would not become too sedentary. In short, he had settled into the
tranquil life of a middle-aged gentleman of some means. Nothing
in his conduct indicated that in the opinion of the government he
was the most dangerous, radical firebrand in all of Britain. At
this very time, the autumn of 1791, he was in fact writing and
polishing the incendiary Part Two of *The Rights of Man*.

Others, including his friends, recognized the part he was
playing and the place he was achieving in British society, as is
evidenced by a poem, 'Paine's Welcome to Great Britain',
written by an anonymous bard:

> He comes – the great Reformer comes!
> Cease, cease your trumpets, cease, cease your drums!
> Those warlike sounds offend the ear,
> Peace and Friendship now appear:
> Welcome, welcome, welcome, welcome,
> Welcome, thou Reformer, here!
>
> Prepare, prepare, your songs prepare,
> Freedom cheers the brow of care;
> The joyful tidings spread around,
> Monarchs tremble at the sound!
> Freedom, freedom, freedom, freedom, –
> Rights of Man, and Paine resound!

These less-than-immortal words inspired the muse that had
lain dormant within Paine, and at a dinner in his honor tendered
him that same autumn by such friends as the painter George
Romney and the iconoclastic author Mary Wollstonecraft, he
responded with a poetic effort of his own, a new set of lyrics set
to the tune of 'Rule Britannia':

> Hail, Great Republic of the world,
> The rising empire of the West,
> Where famed Columbus, with a mighty mind inspired,
> Gave tortured Europe scenes of rest.
> Be thou forever, forever great and free,
> The Land of Love and Liberty.
>
> Beneath thy spreading mantling vine,
> Beside thy flowery groves and springs,
> And on thy loft, thy lofty mountains' brow,
> May all thy sons and fair ones sing.

The Rights of Man

From thee may rudest nations learn
To prize the cause thy sons began;
From thee may future, may future tyrants know
That sacred are the Rights of Man.

From thee may hated discord fly,
With all her dark, her gloomy train;
And o'er thy fertile, thy fertile wide domain
May everlasting friendship reign.

Of thee may lisping infancy
The pleasing wondrous story tell,
And patriot sages in venerable mood
Instruct the world to govern well.

Ye guardian angels watch around,
From harm protect the new-born State;
And all ye friendly, ye friendly nations join,
And thus salute the Child of Fate.
Be thou forever, forever great and free,
The Land of Love and Liberty!

The effort was creditable, although not destined to be printed in anthologies of the great poetry of the period. As usual, to be sure, Paine was guilty of an indiscretion: There were a great many in Britain, certainly a majority of the ruling classes, who still smarted when they thought of the loss of the North American colonies. And words in praise of America set to the tune of a patriotic British song was no balm to their wounds.

Before the evening ended, however, Paine recited another poem, this one calculated to outrage every Briton who loved his country and was loyal to the Crown. The new words, written to the tune of the national anthem, 'God Save the King', verged on sedition:

God save the Rights of Man!
Give him a heart to scan
Blessings so dear;
Let them be spread around,
Wherever man is found,
And with the welcome sound
Ravish his ear!

The startled press reported the affair in such circumlocuitous language that no reader could make sense of it, and not one newspaper reprinted Paine's scandalous lyrics. But there was far worse to come in the immediate future.

14

The Lion's Roar

Part Two of *The Rights of Man* was a call to arms to the people of Great Britain, urging them to engage in a revolution, abolish the monarchy, and establish a republic. It created an unprecedented sensation not only in Britain but in the United States and France as well. Even in its own time this work was recognized as being more influential than *Common Sense* and has since become the cornerstone of Thomas Paine's fame.

It was published in London in February, 1792, and was dedicated to the marquis de Lafayette. The public response was immediate, and the pamphlet sold at a rate far greater than that of Part One; approximately 1.5 million copies were sold during the author's lifetime.

The blatant call for the abolition of the monarchy and the establishment of a British republic first terrified, then outraged the ruling classes in Britain. Unofficial attempts had been made by representatives of Prime Minister Pitt, who had heard rumors of the impending work, to bribe the printer so he would not publish it. These efforts failed, and so more forceful tactics were adopted.

Men were hired by the government at five shillings each to demonstrate against Paine. Huge crowds roamed through the streets of London, chanting slogans against him, and one night in late February he was burned in effigy in four different parts of the city. A spurious biography of Paine was written by one 'Francis Oldys, A.M., of the University of Pennsylvania', and hurriedly printed. This slanderous work, which presented Paine as a perverted, rather moronic antichrist, contained little that was true. Paine's friends discovered that the author was actually a minor government official named George Chalmers, who received the handsome sum of £700 from the Pitt administration for his efforts.

None of these activities hampered the sale of Part Two of *The Rights of Man*, and Pitt realized that the challenge to the Crown – to the authority of the government – could not be ignored. First, a royal proclamation was issued against seditious works of literature; this decree temporarily halted the sale of the pamphlet. Then, Paine was indicted for sedition; the government planned to put him on trial and, if possible, execute him.

What did Part Two of *The Rights of Man* contain that so provoked the official wrath of Great Britain against the fifty-five-year-old author? The pamphlet, over a hundred pages long, was by far the longest work Paine had yet written.* Its philosophy, summarized as follows, reflects Paine's strong belief in representative democracy as the best form of government for all nations: Government is the organization of the aggregate of those natural rights which individuals are not competent to secure as individuals, and which they therefore surrender to the control of society in exchange for the protection of all human rights. Republican government is that whose object is the welfare of the whole nation. Monarchy is government, more or less arbitrary and often capricious, in which the interests of an individual, the monarch, are paramount to those of the people. Aristocracy is government, in part arbitrary and sometimes capricious, in which the interests of one privileged class are paramount to those of the people as a whole. Democracy is self-government of the whole people, governing themselves directly and without secondary

* See Appendix, pages 319–325, for excerpts.

means. Representative government is that in which the people of a whole nation voluntarily surrender control of the apparatus of government to officials whom they elect for the purpose, and who are responsible to the people because they are elected for limited periods of time. The rights of man, according to Paine's definition, means that all people are entitled to such representation.

Pure democracy, Paine said, is effectively operative in simple and primitive societies, but degenerates into chaos when attempted in heavily populated, advanced countries. Monarchy, which as an institution was an outgrowth of this confusion, itself degenerates into incapacity when extended to a complex society whose interests require 'an assemblage of practical knowledges which no one individual can possess'. The aristocratic form, or oligarchy, has vices and defects virtually identical to those of the monarchy, except that more men of ability will appear; their number depends on the size and extent of the aristocracy.

The representative republic, he declared, is the only form of government suited to a modern nation, the only form that can be effective. 'Representation,' he said resoundingly, 'is the true delegated monarchy of a nation.' The representative is not a mere delegate who carries out the instructions of those who elect him; 'the representatives of a people are clothed with their sovereignty'. In other words, sovereignty has been transferred to them by their constituencies, and they do not merely follow the directives and accept the opinions of their constituents.

These abstract concepts, which Paine discussed at great length in their historical and philosophical perspectives, would not have offended anyone had he confined himself to that level of study. But the 'philosopher of the English Revolution', as he liked to think of himself, was no theoretician merely defining political systems. He was still the propagandist of the American Revolution and regarded himself as a spokesman for the French Revolution. He wanted to sway men's minds in favor of the cause in which he believed and, above all, to impel men to take direct action immediately on behalf of that cause. That was the purpose of his argument, the essence of his inspiration – the very reason he had written *The Rights of Man*.

Prime Minister Pitt was keeping a close watch on Paine's publication schedule; Part Two of *The Rights of Man* was put on sale on February 16, 1792, and only forty-eight hours later the so-called biography of Paine by 'Oldys' made its appearance.

Paine, who had become aware of the author's real identity, was irritated by this scurrilous work but made no attempt to expose the man, perhaps because too many other matters of greater consequence were occupying his full attention. The Oldys-Chalmers effort had no effect on the sale of Paine's pamphlet, but it may have harmed his personal reputation. Chalmers's story that Paine was physically abusive to his wife persisted through the nineteenth century and into the present century; even Theodore Roosevelt, among others, believed it.

Soon after the publication of the pamphlet Paine went off to Bromley, Kent, and on May 14 learned that the government had issued a summons to Jordan, the printer. He hurried back to London, intending to supply the funds for Jordan's defense. But he found that the printer had deserted him completely: Jordan had agreed to plead guilty and had already surrendered his correspondence with the author, in return for which the government rendered a verdict 'to the author's prejudice'. Jordan was thus relieved of any possible guilt, which was satisfactory to Paine; but complications quickly followed.

On the morning of May 21 a royal proclamation against seditious writings was issued, and less than three hours later a summons was left at Paine's lodgings in London ordering him to appear before the Court of King's Bench on June 8. Ignoring the advice of friends who urged him to say nothing and to leave the country as quickly as he could, Paine wrote a long, defiant letter to the attorney general. Concentrating his fiery sarcasm on the summons to Jordan, the author made it clear that he alone was responsible for *The Rights of Man* and that he stood by every word he had written.

Among the writers and philosophers who influenced Paine, most were contemplative rather than active. Although Paine considered himself a fireside thinker, he not only demanded that others man the barricades without hesitation, but was willing to do so himself, as he had proved when he had joined the Pennsylvania militia in the early days of the American Revolution. Paine's friends couldn't help wondering whether he was trying to become a martyr. The official charges against him called him 'a wicked, malicious, seditious, and ill-disposed person'. He was 'disaffected', his writings were 'scandalous', and he was trying to destroy the Crown, the Constitution, Parliament, and the entire British system of government.

Paine blithely sent an official notice to the court that he was not guilty. He looked forward to a trial, confident not only that he would be cleared, but that the publicity would help the sale of *The Rights of Man*. His friends were unable to persuade him to leave, and on June 8 he appeared in court. To his disappointment the trial was postponed until December, the prosecutor having asked for additional time to prepare his case. The author had to accept the delay, and to make certain that men in high places understood what was at stake he sent copies of *The Rights of Man* to every member of Parliament, the Cabinet, and the subcabinet.

In spite of the royal proclamation against sedition the pamphlet was sold openly, and approximately a quarter of a million copies were purchased by the end of the year. Meanwhile, Pitt launched his well-orchestrated campaign to discredit the author. Paine's works were burned in a score of towns, and he was hanged in effigy in London, Canterbury, Worcester, and elsewhere. His friends printed copies of his portrait painted by Romney, and government agents tried to destroy them wherever they appeared, which was a hopeless task.

It should be noted, however, that Paine's accounts of the official opposition to *The Rights of Man* were exaggerated, and that his concept of reality was at variance with the facts. The Pitt administration could have seized and confiscated all copies of the pamphlet but instead allowed it to circulate freely. Paine himself could have been arrested and sent to prison, but he remained – at least for the moment – a free man. Only when the government feared he was leaving the country did it finally try to take decisive action against him.

The rapidly deteriorating situation across the English Channel made Britons who believed in the *status quo* increasingly apprehensive. Paine's predictions about France were coming true; mobs were rioting, pitched battles with troops loyal to Louis XVI were becoming increasingly frequent, and the Royal Swiss Guard in Marseilles killed at least a score of people in a bloody fight there. Had Paine remained silent it is possible that Great Britain would not have connected him with events in France, but he made his involvement there quite conspicuous by his frequent public pronouncements and newspaper interviews. Always his theme was the same: 'The mob is what the cruelty of governments has made it.'

On August 26, 1792, the Legislative Assembly granted French

citizenship to Paine, one of a dozen foreigners so honored including Washington, Madison, and Alexander Hamilton. On September 25 the departments of Pas-de-Calais, Oise, and Puy-de-Dôme each elected Paine as its representative to the National Convention, and in all three the vote was apparently unanimous.

By the early part of September affairs in England were moving toward a climax. Paine was spending most of his evenings making enthusiastic, inflammatory speeches to potential recruits for a new society that had been formed, the Friends of Liberty. He was either trying to force the government's hand, or acting naïvely. In any case neither the Prime Minister nor the attorney general could or would permit him such a free hand.

The French were worried about him, and on the day after Paine's election to the National Convention, one of Calais's leading legislators, Achille Audibert, came to London to extend to him personally an invitation to come to France. Uncertain of how Paine would react to the proposal, Audibert first conferred with several of the author's friends. On their advice he based his plea on France's need for Paine's services, rather than urging him to flee for his life. He suggested to Paine that he would be serving the cause he cherished if he left immediately for Paris.

The same argument was used by Thomas Pinckney, the United States minister to Great Britain, who was aware of Paine's great vulnerability to prosecution as an Englishman. He knew that the government felt it had to obtain a conviction at all costs, and indicated in his reports to the State Department his belief that Paine would be imprisoned for life, at the very least, and that he well might be hanged. Pinckney, too, suggested that he go to France without delay.

That night at a meeting of the Friends of Liberty, Paine made another provocative speech, urging the abolition of the monarchy and the establishment of a republic in the British Isles. The government was trying to silence him, he declared, but no threat would force him to remain quiet.

William Blake, who was no more worldly than Paine but had a more realistic approach to practical matters, encountered his fellow author the following day in a coffeehouse that both men frequented. Whether Blake had learned something specific or acted on instinct is not known, but, according to one of his biographers, Alexander Gilchrest, he 'laid his hand on the orator's shoulder, saying, "You must not go home, or you are a dead man." '

Paine gathered that he was in earnest and heeded the advice. Buying a few toilet articles, a spare shirt, some underclothes, and a small case in which to carry these belongings, he caught the afternoon stage to Dover. Bailiffs appeared that very afternoon at Rickman's house, armed with a warrant authorizing them to arrest and imprison Paine without bail.

Early the following morning Paine presented himself at the Dover customs house and went through the formalities required of departing travelers. He showed identification papers, and his small suitcase was opened for inspection. A few moments later he boarded the first sloop making the Channel crossing. By noon, when customs house officials received a court order directing them to apprehend one Thomas Paine if he tried to leave the country, the newly elected member of the National Convention was well on his way to France.

15

On the Rise

In retrospect the French Revolution appears to have been the inevitable outgrowth of the shortsighted policies of the house of Bourbon. The rich had become wealthier, the poor were on the verge of starvation, the government was as corrupt as it was inefficient, religion had become a mockery, and justice for the common man was a thing of the past.

Under the wise, forceful rule of Henry IV – known to his compatriots as Henry the Great – France at the beginning of the seventeenth century became the wealthiest and most powerful nation on the Continent. He ended her religious civil wars and encouraged agricultural production and the establishment of such industries as tapestry making, silk manufacturing, and wine making. He founded a modern army and navy, encouraged French exploration and colonization in North America, and was responsible for a vast increase in trade with other countries.

Subsequently two chief ministers, cardinals Richelieu and

Mazarin, followed the guidelines established by Henry, and the nation became even stronger and wealthier. During the reign of Henry's grandson, Louis XIV, called the 'Sun King'. France achieved greater international power and influence than ever before. But Louis sowed the seeds of future discontent and destruction, waging expensive wars, revoking his grandfather's Edict of Nantes (which guaranteed Protestants religious tolerance), and emasculating the nobility by concentrating powers in the Crown.

These trends became more pronounced during the reign of his great-grandson, Louis XV, and on the eve of the Revolution, under Louis XVI, life had become unbearable for most Frenchmen. Louis XVI was a lethargic king, and his government was corrupt and inefficient. The burden of taxation on the middle class was too great to be tolerated, and the urban working man and the peasant were mired in poverty from which they could not escape. The idle nobles were draining off the profits earned by a wealthy nation while making no contribution in return, and the Church was arrogant and unresponsive to the urgent needs of the people.

Under the circumstances, even initiating reforms overnight could not have prevented the outbreak of the Revolution in 1789. Inexperienced representatives of the people assumed power, 'abolishing' the nobility and making Louis XVI a prisoner. They confiscated the property of the Church, prohibited religious worship, and established a republic. But the Anglo-Saxon tradition that guaranteed the liberties of the individual was sadly lacking, and justice was at best theoretical, with uncounted thousands suffering from abuses that had never been tolerated in the United States and had been unknown for centuries in Great Britain. The 'liberty, equality and fraternity' that the French Revolution promised in 1789 were illusions, unattainable goals. And into the maelstrom came Thomas Paine, the most idealistic exponent of the principles of human liberty and dignity.

Paine was accompanied on his flight from England by his fellow deputy to the National Convention, Audibert, and although the details of their journey are hazy, they appear to have left the Dover stage at its first stop after leaving London. They traveled by a roundabout route through Rochester, Sandwich, and Deal (and, ironically, halting briefly only a few miles from the home of Paine's wife) before proceeding finally to Dover.

The stories told about Paine's near-arrest by customs officials are legion; all are romantic and probably inaccurate. It is unlikely that he was saved from arrest because of a letter from President Washington which he carried in his pocket. Paine himself made this claim in a letter to a friend in London, but it may be that he exaggerated his tale so that it could be used effectively as propaganda. The details of his arrival in Calais, however, have been authenticated. A regiment of troops was lined up at the dock in Paine's honor when the packet cast anchor, and a band played republican airs, according to a report in the *Moniteur*. He was presented with a red, white, and blue cockade, and an attractive young lady placed it in his hat. Speeches were made by the senior military officer and other dignitaries, and Paine rode through the streets in an open carriage while his fellow citizens of France lined the streets and cheered him. At the Hôtel de Ville he was given an official welcome by the mayor and several aldermen, all of whom also made speeches.

That night Paine was led in a torchlight procession to a meeting of the Constitutional Society of Calais. The crowd was too large to squeeze into the hall intended for the purpose so the gathering moved to the cathedral, where Paine's election to the National Convention was confirmed and more speeches made. The new deputy neither understood nor spoke French, although he had visited the country previously when negotiating for the loan to America. But he smiled steadily, and when asked to reply he held aloft a recently translated copy of Part Two of *The Rights of Man*. Later that evening he sat in a box of honor at a theatrical performance.

The British by pursuing Paine and trying to apprehend him had inadvertently made him a bigger hero to the French than he otherwise would have been. Thanks to this 'persecution by royalists' he was now a national figure in France, and was treated accordingly. On September 28 he left for Paris, having been elected the chairman of Calais's five-man deputation to the National Convention.

On his arrival in Paris Paine took up lodgings overlooking the Tuileries gardens in White's Hotel, a hostelry frequented by Americans and, to a lesser extent, Englishmen. Plunging into his new work with a fervor that was in no way diminished by his lack of familiarity with the French language, he presented his credentials to the Convention, and took his seat for the deliberations being held in the Tuileries. For the first time in his life he was an active legislator, a participant in the republican form of government that he advocated.

It was a time of great change and excitement. On September 21 the French monarchy had been abolished, and on Paine's first day as a deputy a motion to remove from office all administrators and judges was being pushed through the Convention before the mobs could take matters into their own hands. Paine, speaking through a fellow member who interpreted for him, suggested that acting with such haste would still leave many secret royalists in the positions which they now occupied. A thorough investigation should be made, he declared, and reforms carried out completely. He was supported by Danton, the foremost leader of the moderates in the Convention, and the question of the eligibility of candidates for public office was tabled subject to further review.

On October 11 a special committee was named to prepare a new constitution for France, with the Abbé Sieyès as chairman and Paine as vice-chairman. The new citizen of France, acknowledged as 'the most formidable of all experts on constitutions', would have been made chairman had he not been handicapped by his inability to speak French. But he was able to make his views known through at least four and possibly six members of the committee who knew English.

On October 25 the first article written by Paine specifically for a French readership appeared in a Paris newspaper, *Le Patriote Français*. It was translated by the paper's editor, Jacques Pierre Brissot, a fellow deputy, who – like so many of Paine's associates at this time – was executed two years later. The article contined no new ideas, but it is noteworthy for Paine's style and for his statement, 'A talented king is worse than a fool'. Conscious of the fact that he was writing for Frenchmen, he adopted a stylistic approach similar to that with which Parisians were familiar and which scarcely resembled his usual writing:

> We are astonished at reading that the Egyptians set upon the throne a stone, which they called king. Well! such a monarch was less absurd and less mischievous than those before whom nations prostrate themselves. At least he deceived no one. None supposed that he possessed qualities or a character. They did not call him Father of his People; and yet it would have been scarcely more ridiculous than to give such a title to a blockhead whom the right of succession crowns at eighteen. A dumb idol is better than one animated.

On the surface Paine here appears to be joining in the popular sport of attacking the imprisoned Louis XVI, but his real purpose was more devious than that. The radicals were demanding that the King's head be severed from his body by the guillotine, the ingenious instrument of execution used in the French Revolution. Paine, like other moderates, was intent upon saving the life of the harmless monarch and sending him safely into exile. This could best be accomplished, the American reasoned, by convincing the people that Louis was an eccentric near-imbecile, and that, as a consequence, his life wasn't worth the risk of Europe's monarchies declaring war on France. True to his humanitarian principles, Paine was firmly opposed to bloodshed.

In his personal life Paine was already established at the center of an adoring cult. Never in America, not even when he had been the literary lion of New York, had he known such consistent admiration. In London he had enjoyed the company of his intellectual equals. But in Paris he became the magnet for young Americans and Englishmen who had been drawn to France because they had idealized the Revolution, and they saw in Paine the personification of all they believed and held dear. Many of these young men lived at White's Hotel. The most prominent of them was Lord Edward Fitzgerald, who wrote to his mother, 'I cannot express how kind he is to me; there is a simplicity of manner, a goodness of heart, and a strength of mind in him, that I never knew a man before possess'. Others felt as Lord Edward did, and soon Paine was surrounded by a worshipful coterie that gave him little peace. They joined him at breakfast, dinner, and supper, whether at the hotel or a public restaurant. They asked him questions and respectfully took notes when he replied. They escorted him to the Tuileries for sessions of the Convention. They waited for him and marched back to White's with him when the sessions were over.

Paine suffered discomfort when his English and American admirers surrounded him, but he accepted their friendship with good humor. One reason, as he wrote to a friend in London, was because they shared his taste in food. He found most French dishes too rich for his 'palate, spleen, and liver' and preferred to eat the simple meals to which he was accustomed.

In other areas, too, he maintained his old habits. His mode of dress still resembled that of a somber scarecrow, and the new suits made for him in Paris resembled those he had left behind in

London. His sex life followed its usual pattern, but was more active. His American and English friends conveniently turned a deaf ear when Paine, after spending several hours at the home of one or another colleague, returned to White's late at night with two very young strumpets, one on each arm. His young friends, being eighteenth-century gentlemen, regarded his sexual eccentricities as strictly his own business and carefully refrained in their correspondence from mentioning the subject except to their intimates. The young commentators were impressed by Paine's prowess, and occasionally there was a tinge of envy in these references.

Sieyès appears to have been somewhat jealous of Paine's stature, and the two men never became close. Brissot, Danton, Condorcet, and Barère, however, all of whom spoke fluent English, became the American's good friends. Paine tried to become conversant in French but was never completely successful, and even after living in France for several years he never gained a mastery of the tongue.

From the time of his arrival in France Paine became one of the leaders of the informal campaign to save the life of the King. He always took care to speak of him as Louis Capet, however, as did all members of the Revolution, and he made every effort to temper the ire of his less charitable colleagues. On October 27 he represented the delegation from Calais in offering the Convention his congratulations on the abolition of the monarchy, and even in this communication he took advantage of the chance to plead for humanitarian clemency:

Citizen President:– In the name of the Deputies of the department of Pas de Calais, I have the honor of presenting to the Convention the felicitations of the General Council of the Commune of Calais on the abolition of royalty.

Amid the joy inspired by this event, one can not forbear some pain at the folly of our ancestors, who have placed us under the necessity of treating seriously the abolition of a phantom.

Paine and his colleagues on the committee to draw up a constitution for France went to work with a vengeance, hoping to complete the task in a few months. The author found hotel living too distracting, so he moved to a small but comfortable flat at 7, passage des Petits Pères, a narrow, winding mews adjacent to a chapel of the Capucines. A fellow citizen consented to prepare his meals and take care of the apartment, and Paine settled into domesticity.

But his work on the constitution was constantly being interrupted by his concern for the fate of Louis XVI. Public demands for the execution of the deposed monarch were becoming increasingly strident, and Paine spent several hours each day arguing with other members of the Convention about Louis's ultimate fate.

The French armies were victorious throughout the Continent in the war waged by the Convention against a coalition of European monarchies, and it seemed probable that, if the life of the King were spared, the other European powers would no longer interfere and would allow France to proceed in peace with her political experiment, or so Paine and others believed. The radicals were reckless, however: By mid-November it appeared inevitable that Louis would lose his life.

'Revolutions are not made of rose water,' Danton said, but Paine was so horrified by the unanimous vote of the Convention in finding the King guilty that he felt compelled to do something dramatic. On the night of November 20 he wrote a long address to the Convention, and it was translated and read the following day. By standing alone as the King's champion Paine was placing his own life in jeopardy. Once again this stubborn, idealistic man was motivated by principle; he would not condone what he regarded as a murder that would betray the ideals of the French Revolution.

Paine agreed that Louis XVI should be tried on a charge of treason, on which grounds the Convention planned to execute him. But he insisted that justice, not vengeance, should be the motivating force impelling the people of the Republic of France to conduct such a trial. If innocent, Louis should be allowed to prove it; if guilty, he should either be punished or pardoned. Louis as an individual, Paine stressed, was beneath the dignity of the nation's consideration. The French monarch was accused of having participated in a conspiracy of Europe's 'crowned brigands'. A trial would be valuable because it would reveal, not just to the people of France but to all the people of Europe, that their monarchs were secretly working against the best interests of their subjects. The trial should be held *only* because it would be in the interests of all European people:

> If, seeing in Louis XVI only a weak and narrow-minded man, badly reared, as all like him, subject, it is said, to intemperance, imprudently re-established by the Constituent Assembly on a throne for which he was unfit, – if we hereafter show him some compassion,

165

this compassion should be the effect of national magnanimity, and not a result of the burlesque notion of pretended inviolability.

The distinguished nineteenth-century French author-statesman Louis Blanc was well aware of what Paine tried to accomplish. 'He had learned in England,' Blanc wrote, 'that killing a monarch does not kill monarchs.' Experience had taught Paine to be clever, and he did not base his plea for clemency on the argument that the King stood above the law and therefore could not be tried. Let him be tried, by all means, Paine cried, and then show him mercy. Pardon him, then set him free and send him into exile; or, if you insist, confine him to a castle in a rural retreat and hold him hostage for the good conduct of other monarchs. But don't cut off his head!

The Convention listened to the reading of Paine's words in stony silence; not one deputy applauded, not one even glanced in the direction of the author. He could not help but realize that his campaign was failing, but he was determined to persist. It was beyond his grasp that, although he might instinctively understand the Anglo-Saxons, he could fail to comprehend the volatile nature of the French people or the undercurrent of violence that was forcing their revolution into bloodier channels.

That he knew England and her people is confirmed by the way in which he overcame certain difficulties involving publication there of Part Two of *The Rights of Man*. Friends wrote him from London to inform him that the demand for copies of the pamphlet were unfulfilled, in part because of the royal proclamation against sedition, in part because Jordan was unable to print enough copies of the pamphlet. Chester, Leicester, Sheffield, and other towns were clamoring for the work, but no copies were available. Paine responded by granting to any publisher in Great Britain the right to publish *The Rights of Man* provided the work was offered to the public at a low cost. A score of printers leaped at the opportunity to capitalize on the author's willingness to waive his royalty rights, and by the end of 1792 more than half a million copies of new editions of both Part One and Part Two were in print.

Adding fresh fuel to the flames, Paine spent the early part of November, 1792, writing yet another pamphlet. He called it *Address to the Addressers*, but it soon became known in Great Britain as Part Three of *The Rights of Man*. In this short, pungent work Paine hurled a defiant challenge at the authorities who were trying to suppress his writings:

> It is a dangerous attempt in any government to say to a Nation, *'Thou shalt not read.'*
>
> Thought, by some means or other, is got abroad in the world, and cannot be restrained, though reading may.
>
> Whatever the rights of the people are, they have a right to them, and none have a right either to withhold or to grant them.
>
> The project of hereditary Governors and Legislatures was a treasonable usurpation over the rights of posterity.
>
> Put a country right, and it will soon put government right.
>
> When the rich plunder the poor of his rights, it becomes an example to the poor to plunder the rich of his property.
>
> Who are those that are frightened at reform? Are the public afraid their taxes should be lessened too much? Are they afraid that sinecure places and pensions should be abolished too fast? Are the poor afraid that their condition should be rendered too comfortable?
>
> If to expose the fraud and imposition of monarchy, and every species of hereditary government – to lessen the oppression of taxes – to propose plans for the education of helpless infancy, and the comfortable support of the aged and distressed – to endeavor to conciliate nations with each other – to extirpate the horrid practice of war – to promote universal peace, civilization, and commerce – and to break the chains of political superstition, and raise degraded man to his proper rank – if these things be libellous, let me live the life of a Libeller, and let the name of Libeller be engraven on my tomb.

The British and American editions sold out promptly, and a translation of the pamphlet achieved enormous popularity in France. Paine consented to accept royalties from the French edition in order to pay his living expenses because he had refused to accept a salary as a deputy to the Convention. The people of Britain were delighted at the spectacle of the middle-aged David baiting the national Goliath. At least a dozen printers brought out the work, and approximately a quarter of a million copies were sold during the first week of its publication.

The 'Oldys' biography had been discredited, and all that the British Government could do to thwart Paine – short of bringing legal action against the various printers, which would have fanned the controversy still more – was to have him appear to be repudiated by the people. So government hirelings staged new spectacles, burning Paine's works in a score of cities and hanging him in effigy. The author, living far from friends who might have reassured him, was upset by the government's campaign and for a time failed to recognize these actions as the highest compliment Prime Minister Pitt could have paid him. Morris, the American minister, dined with him on December 19, 1792, and noted in his *Diary* that Paine 'looks a little down at the news from England'.

The campaign was thorough, and by mid-December Paine had been hanged in effigy 'in every town of more than three thousand persons in the British Isles'. On December 18, 1792, in Guildhall, London, the reasons for the high-pressure campaign became evident: A special jury convened to try Thomas Paine, in absentia, on a charge of high treason.

A battery of distinguished attorneys had volunteered to represent the defendant, but Paine himself was so certain of being found guilty that on November 11 he had already written a letter of protest to the attorney-general. His friends made the letter public on the day the trial began. Concerned only with the propaganda value of what he was writing, Paine was indifferent to the effect his communication would have on the court:

> My necessary absence from your country affords the opportunity of knowing whether the prosecution was intended against Thomas Paine, or against the Rights of the People of England to investigate systems and principles of government; for as I can not now be the object of prosecution, the going on with the prosecution will show that something else was the object, and that something else can be no other than the People of England. . . .
>
> But I have other reasons than those I have mentioned for writing this letter; and however you chuse to interpret them they proceed from a good heart. The time, Sir, is becoming too serious to play with court prosecutions, and sport with national rights. The terrible examples that have taken place here upon men who, less than a year ago, thought themselves as secure as any prosecuting Judge, Jury or Attorney-General can now do in England, ought to have some weight with men in your situation.
>
> That the Government of England is as great, if not the greatest perfection of fraud and corruption that ever took place since governments began, is what you cannot be a stranger to; unless the constant habit of seeing has blinded your sense. But though you may not chuse to see it, the people are seeing it very fast, and the progress is beyond what you may chuse to believe. Is it possible that you or I can believe, or that reason can make any other man believe, that the capacity of such a man as Mr Guelph, or any of his profligate sons, is necessary to the government of a nation? I speak to you as one man ought to speak to another; and I know also that I speak what other

people are beginning to think. That you cannot obtain a verdict (and if you do it will signify nothing) without packing a jury, and we both know that such tricks are practised, is what I have very good reason to believe. . . .

Do not then, Sir, be the instrument of drawing away twelve men into a situation that may be injurious to them afterwards. I do not speak this from policy, but from benevolence; but if you chuse to go on with the process, I make it my request that you read this letter in Court, after which the Judge and Jury may do what they please. As I do not consider myself the object of the prosecution, neither can I be affected by the issue one way or the other, I shall, though a foreigner in your country, subscribe as much money as any other man towards supporting the right of the nation against the prosecution; and it is for this purpose only that I shall do it.

Nothing Paine could have written could have been better calculated to antagonize a judge and horrify a jury. The 'Mr Guelph' of whom he spoke so slightingly was King George III, and 'his profligate sons' were the Prince Regent (later to become George IV) and his younger brothers. Not only did the intemperate author call the jury corrupt, but he threatened the members with unspecified retaliation, presumably at the hands of an outraged public. A great many intelligent people had sympathized with Paine before the trial began, believing he was the object of persecution because he had dared to suggest that the British government was in need of major reforms. But his crude letter lost him large numbers of friends.

It also validated the case for the prosecution, and the attorney-general called Paine's bluff by having the letter read in open court on the day the trial opened. It created a sensation, but not of the sort the author had intended. Even chief counsel for the defense Thomas Erskine, attorney-general to the Prince of Wales, was forced to admit privately that the outcome of the case was a foregone conclusion. Erskine tried in vain to prevent the reading of the letter on the grounds that it was a forgery, but he was overruled.

The defense concentrated on the historical rights of all Englishmen to think and speak and write what they pleased. The judge agreed with most of the sentiments expressed, and so did the prosecutor. But Paine's own words nevertheless condemned him, and the jury, after hearing closing arguments on December 20, retired for a scant half an hour and returned with the unanimous verdict that the defendant was guilty.

Thomas Paine was declared an outlaw and a fugitive from British justice and was forbidden to set foot on British soil again. All Crown officers were ordered to place him under arrest if he defied the injunction, in which event, as one guilty of high treason, he would be conducted to the Tower of London and would be incarcerated there pending the rendering of a final verdict, presumably the sentence of death.

The decision of the court left Paine untouched. He had felt certain he would be found guilty and cared only about the verdict's value as propaganda for the cause he regarded as sacred. He was in fact devoting all of his time and attention in December, 1792, and January, 1793, to another trial, that of King Louis XVI on the same charge of high treason.

It was obvious from the beginning, as it had been in Paine's case, that Louis Capet would be found guilty. Paine was as aware of this as any other member of the Convention, but he refused to agree with Danton, who said that he would try to save the lives of the King and Queen and their children, but that he would vote for their execution in order to save his own neck. Paine insisted that he would vote for acquittal, even if his was the only voice raised in the Convention in defense of Louis and his family.

To stave off the seemingly inevitable outcome of the vote, he tried to make specific plans that would save the King's life. The most ambitious of his ideas was a referendum by the people of France, after the Convention found the King guilty, to determine the punishment that he should receive. Unable to move the members of the Convention, Paine, who had succeeded so notably in influencing public opinion in the United States and Great Britain, was convinced that he could persuade the French people to spare the royal lives. He declared that refuge should be found for them in America, which offered a sanctuary to the persecuted of every land, and he wrote a letter to President Washington suggesting that the United States make a formal offer to France. Morris, the American minister, was far more realistic in his outlook; if Paine's idea were followed and the French people left to decide the deposed monarch's fate, he wrote to the State Department, Louis would be 'massacred'. There were only two choices, he said: The monarch would either die or reign.

By the first days of 1793 Paine had become aware of the mood of the French people, so he abandoned his idea of conducting a national referendum. But he was so disturbed by the thought that he, a civilized humanitarian, could be a member of a body capable of putting Louis to death that he fell prey to wishful thinking: The Convention would in the near future set up a government modeled on that of the United States and fulfill the promise of the rallying cry of the French Revolution – 'liberty, equality and fraternity' – by granting a full pardon to Louis XVI and sending him and his family into exile. He comforted himself with this bit of self-delusion until reality intervened. On January 14 the Convention, from which Paine that day absented himself, unanimously found Louis guilty of high treason. That night Paine wrote a desperate appeal to his fellow deputies, who would determine the deposed monarch's fate the following day:

> Let then those United States be the guard and asylum of Louis Capet. There, in the future, remote from the miseries and crimes of royalty, he may learn, from the constant presence of public prosperity, that the true system of government consists not in monarchs, but in fair, equal, and honorable representation. In recalling this circumstance, and submitting this proposal, I consider myself a citizen of both countries. I submit it as an American who feels a debt of gratitude he owes to every Frenchman. I submit it as a man, who, albeit an adversary of kings, forgets not that they are subject to human frailties. I support my proposal as a citizen of the French Republic, because it appears to me the best and most politic measure than can be adopted. As far as my experience in public life extends, I have ever observed that the great mass of people are always just, both in their intentions and their object; but the true method of obtaining such purposes does not always appear at once. The English nation had groaned under the Stuart despotism. Hence Charles I was executed; but Charles II was restored to all the same powers his father had lost. Forty years later the same family tried to re-establish their oppression; the nation banished the whole race from its territories. The remedy was effectual; the Stuart family sank into obscurity, merged itself in the masses, and is now extinct.

Arguing shrewdly, Paine went on to say that Louis XVI had two younger brothers, both out of France and beyond the reach of French justice, who might naturally desire the King's death. In time, after his execution, one or both of them might become pretenders to the throne of France, and foreign powers – especially foreign kings – might rally to their support. But, he said, as long as the deposed monarch was still alive, there could be no pretenders. He concluded:

171

It has already been proposed to abolish the penalty of death, and it is with infinite satisfaction that I recollect the humane and excellent oration pronounced by Robespierre on the subject, in the constituent Assembly. Monarchical governments have trained the human race to sanguinary punishments, but the people should not follow the examples of their oppressors in such vengeance. As France has been the first of European nations to abolish royalty, let her also be the first to abolish the penalty of death, and to find out a milder and more effectual substitute.

This clever plea, Paine believed, would silence Robespierre and Marat, the two most powerful leaders of the Convention. Paine believed, naïvely, that the aims of all French leaders were similar to his own as those of America's Founding Fathers had been. But the followers of Robespierre and Marat were not hampered by scruples, and their thirst for the blood of Louis Capet intimidated many of the moderates, who might otherwise have voted for clemency. Among them were such men as Sieyès, who had announced that he favored mercy but nevertheless voted for the death penalty.

Paine had written a statement of his position, and a friend translated it for him into French, which he rehearsed prior to the taking of the final vote. When his name was called, he said, 'I vote for the detention of Louis till the end of the war, and after that his perpetual banishment.'

The final vote was close. Almost three hundred deputies voted with Paine, who noted that the majority in favor of the death peanalty won by a scant twenty-five votes. Of these, he declared, a number attached conditions, so that the actual majority was but one vote. His figures, although dramatic, do not match those of Thomas Carlyle, who, in his great history of the French Revolution, wrote that the majority won by 53 votes.

A single question remained: Should the sentence be carried out immediately? Marat, who was afraid Louis might never be executed if there were a delay, pressed for immediate action. This vote was scheduled for January 20, and the advocates of clemency rallied their forces. On the evening of January 18 the *Moniteur* printed Paine's plea for clemency, together with a summary of his own trial in England. That night Paine wrote an address in favor of delay which he was to deliver before the Convention the next day.

The radical Jacobins faced a dilemma. They were afraid that if

172

they threatened Paine with physical violence in an attempt to silence him, as they had threatened a number of French deputies, the candid author would reveal to the public every word of their threats. Moreover, they could not accuse the man who had written *The Rights of Man* of being a secret royalist.

Marat found another way. When Paine's name was called and he made his way to the rostrum to deliver his address, with Brissot standing by to translate it, Marat shouted, 'I submit that Thomas Paine is incompetent to vote on this question! As he is a Quaker, his religious principles are opposed to the death penalty!' The Jacobins cheered, shouted, and paraded in the aisles, many of them shaking their fists and brandishing knives as they filed past the rostrum. Paine stood quietly, his face pale but composed, and waited for order to be restored. Eventually there were demands for the right of free speech; the demonstrators fell silent and Paine was allowed to speak:

> Very sincerely do I regret the Convention's vote for death. I have the advantage of some experience; it is near twenty years that I have been engaged in the cause of liberty, having contributed something to it in the revolution of the United States of America. My language has always been that of liberty *and* humanity, and I know by experience that nothing so exalts a nation as the union of these two principles, under all circumstances. I know that the public mind of France, and particularly that of Paris, has been heated and irritated by the dangers to which they have been exposed; but could we carry our thoughts into the future, when the dangers are ended, and the irritations forgotten, what to-day seems an act of justice may then appear an act of vengeance.

> My anxiety for the cause of France has become for the moment concern for her honor. If, on my return to America, I should employ myself on a history of the French Revolution, I had rather record a thousand errors dictated by humanity, than one inspired by a justice too severe. I voted against an appeal to the people, because it appeared to me that the Convention was needlessly wearied on that point; but I so voted in the hope that this Assembly would pronounce against death, and for the same punishment that the nation would have voted, at least in my opinion, that is, for reclusion during the war and banishment thereafter. That is the punishment most efficacious, because it includes the whole family at once, and none other can so operate. I am still against the appeal to the primary assemblies, because there is a better method.

> This Convention has been elected to form a Constitution, which will be submitted to the primary assemblies. After its acceptance a

necessary consequence will be an election, and another Assembly. We cannot suppose that the present Convention will last more than five or six months. The choice of new deputies will express the national opinion on the propriety or impropriety of your sentence, with as much efficacy as if those primary assemblies had been consulted on it. As the duration of our functions here cannot be long, it is a part of our duty to consider the interests of those who shall replace us. If by any act of ours the number of the nation's enemies shall be needlessly increased, and that of its friends diminished, – at a time when the finances may be more strained than to-day – we should not be justifiable for having thus unnecessarily heaped obstacles in the path of our successors. Let us therefore not be precipitate in our decisions.

France has but one ally – the United States of America. That is the only nation that can furnish France with naval provisions, for the kingdoms of northern Europe are, or soon will be, at war with her. It happens, unfortunately, that the person now under discussion is regarded in America as a deliverer of their country. I can assure you that his execution will there spread universal sorrow, and it is in your power not thus to wound the feelings of your ally.

Could I speak the French language I would descend to your bar, and in their name become your petitioner to respite the execution of the sentence on Louis.

The address was a masterpiece, combining humanity, wisdom, reason, and humility, and it presented arguments that were impossible to challenge. Brissot, in reading his translation of the address, used every oratorical trick he knew, and his delivery was far more colorful than Paine's own reading which was flat and monotonous. Deputies looked at each other, murmured, and began to applaud. Only the Jacobins, who were in the minority, remained stonily silent.

Before Paine could return to his seat, Marat raced to the podium, and with the applause making it difficult for anyone else to hear the conversation, appeared to be asking Paine some brief questions in English. Then he raised a hand for quiet, and said, 'I denounce the interpreter. I maintain that he has not expressed the true words of Thomas Paine. The translation is false, wicked, and faithless!'

There was pandemonium as Marat took his seat, and Paine, who had no idea what Marat had said, declared that he had not quite finished his speech.

The indignant Brissot defended himself and added that the

execution of the King might well alienate the friends of France in England, Ireland, and America. Other deputies who understood English jumped to their feet and, one by one, protested that the translation had been accurate. Marat's trick was exposed, but he remained brazen and glared at Paine as the author spoke his final words:

> Your executive committee will nominate a minister to Philadelphia; my sincere wish is that he may announce to America that the National Convention of France, out of pure friendship to America, has consented to respite Louis. That people, your only ally, have asked you by my vote to delay the execution.
>
> Ah, citizens, give not the tyrant of England the triumph of seeing the man perish on the scaffold who helped my dear brothers of America to break his chains!

Again the Convention applauded, and this time many deputies cheered. Marat interrupted a second time. Racing back to the podium, he shouted that Paine had voted against the death sentence because he was a clergyman. Paine, who had not yet resumed his seat, remained calm, and said, 'I voted against it both morally and politically.' Brissot was the first to agree with all that Paine had said, and was followed by others who echoed his sentiments. It is possible, had the final vote been taken that same day, that the death sentence might have been commuted.

Marat had the last word. When the Convention met on January 20, the building was surrounded by a heavily armed mob howling for 'justice'. According to observers, 55 members who saw the menacing crowd as they approached the hall suddenly turned around and went home again. Of the 721 members who answered the clerk's roll call, 361 voted that Louis Capet should die within twenty-four hours. Among those who voted against the execution was Thomas Paine.

Ignoring the jostling crowds he went straight from the Convention to his apartment and, refusing to see anyone, remained there until he received word that the guillotine had severed the head of Louis XVI. Paine was strongly tempted to resign his seat in the Convention, leave France, and return to the United States without delay. Morris noted in his *Diary* that he had never encountered a man 'more filled with disgust and anguish'.

But Paine's French friends persuaded him to stay. The Revolution was as yet unfinished, he was told by such deputies as Brissot, Condorcet, and Sieyès. If he left now, he would be

surrendering to Marat and his bullies, men who had no understanding of true democratic principles and no desire to learn
them. France had erred by killing Louis Capet and undoubtedly
would have to pay a heavy penalty, as Great Britain was sure to
declare war against her. But the new constitution would soon be
completed, a healthy republic would emerge from the bloodshed,
and France would take her place as the bastion of true liberty in
Europe. The author of *The Rights of Man* could not desert her in
her hour of trial.

Paine would make no definite commitment. But a friend had
brought him from London the gold-headed walking stick that
Louis XVI had given him so many years earlier, and although he
had refrained until then from using it, he began to carry it at all
times. For the moment, at least, he would stay.

Great Britain reacted as Paine had expected. The Royal Army
called up its reserves, and the sitting of Parliament was advanced
forty days. Ironically, most of the government's wrath was
reserved for Paine, who was denounced as a barbarian and a cold-
blooded murderer. Brissot, observing the tragicomedy from Paris,
wrote that 'the grievance of the British Cabinet against France is
not that Louis has been executed, but that Thomas Paine wrote
The Rights of Man.' The author's name was raised so often in the
Commons's debates on war and peace that Fox demanded of the
Prime Minister, 'Can you not prosecute Paine without an army?'

To Paine went the dubious credit of being responsible for
Great Britain's declaration of war against France. He had become
the most renowned – or infamous – native-born Englishman of
his era.

16

On the Decline

The unhappiness that Thomas Paine felt over the execution of Louis XVI was genuine, but his lingering grief was perhaps caused more by distress at seeing his principles abandoned than by personal regret, however heartfelt. He grieved because he thought that the death of Louis had complicated and inevitably postponed the achievement of his ultimate goal, a Continent of Europe composed of allied or otherwise interlocking republics. He saw Great Britain going to war against France, the United States turning cool in its friendship with France, and European liberals everywhere losing their enthusiasm for the republican cause. 'Man remains the worst enemy of man,' he said, 'and liberty has suffered a blow from which it will not quickly recover.'

The radical Jacobins failed to appreciate his stand, however, and marked him as an enemy. But the moderate Girondists were still in power, even though they had lost a number of followers, and they remained well-disposed toward the English-born American. In the Convention he was serving on only one committee, which was charged with the responsibility for drawing up a constitution, but early in the summer of 1793 the Girondists gave him a place on another committee as well, the Committee of Surveillance. At that time the guillotine was being used more and more each day, the prisons were being filled with known and suspected enemies of the Revolution, and a mere denunciation by a casual acquaintance was enough to send a man to a cell. The Committee of Surveillance was given the almost impossible task of keeping watch over this loosely organized system and preventing the incarceration of the innocent. Paine made it his task to investigate the cases of foreigners sent to prison, particularly Americans and Englishmen.

The first he helped was an English Tory named Munro, who had been living in Paris for at least a year and whose correspondence with friends in London indicated that he was one of Paine's severest critics. But he was not guilty of espionage and contrary to the vague charges brought against him, had engaged in no acts harmful to the French Revolution. Paine secured his release in September, 1793, when it appeared certain that he would be guillotined, and the grateful Munro became his ardent, lifelong admirer.

Nowhere is Paine's humanitarianism more evident that in the actions he took in the case of a Captain Grimstone, a British artillery officer who had been visiting Paris in the summer of 1793. He and Paine met at a dinner given at the Palais d'Egalité, and Grimstone, a husky young Tory in his twenties, became increasingly hostile to the author. It may be that the young officer drank too much and that liquor made him careless, but whatever the cause, he called Paine a traitor and knocked him down with a blow that left a mark on his face for weeks.

It was against the law to strike a deputy, and Grimstone was arrested, sent to prison, and condemned to death. Paine's indignant friends were willing to see the man executed, but the author refused to go along with them. It was not easy to secure the release of someone who had wounded the person and dignity of a deputy, and Paine had to use all of his powers of persuasion before Barère, who headed the Committee of Public Safety, would sign a release order. When Grimstone got out of prison he discovered that his money and personal belongings had been stolen from his hotel room, and he was penniless. Paine not only obtained a passport for him, but advanced him enough money for his passage back to England.

Paine's generosity was not returned. As soon as Grimstone reached England, he let it be known to all who would listen to him that Paine, the traitor, had been responsible for his imprisonment and had nearly caused him to be sent to the guillotine. He never repaid Paine's loan. But this ingratitude had no effect on Paine, who continued to do his duty as he saw it.

It was a short time later that Paine formed one of the most solid and lasting of his American friendships. Morris was recalled and replaced as United States minister by Captain James Monroe, who became the fifth American President. Whether they had been acquainted in America is not known, but soon after the new minister's arrival, he and Paine discovered that they had much in common. They shared the same ideals and the same passionate love for liberty and democracy; both men were shy and reserved, but they managed to break through the barriers of their inhibitions and to form a warm relationship that would last until the end of Paine's life.

Paine needed Monroe's friendship and sympathy. Many of the author's English friends were being imprisoned in London by Pitt, who was determined to halt sales of *The Rights of Man*, and anyone who had been close to Paine was suspected of treason. A number of booksellers were arrested and imprisoned for dispensing copies of the pamphlet, now officially regarded as a seditious work. Paine's good friend Clio Rickman barely managed to escape to France with his wife and children before he, too, would have been incarcerated.

Few of Paine's enmities were lasting; his humanitarian principles led him to forgive and forget. But he despised the younger Pitt until the English statesman's death.* Late in 1792 and early in 1793 Paine was expending time and energy trying to fight Pitt from a distance, but there was little he could do other than to urge his friends to hold firm. This he did in letter after letter roundly condemning both Pitt and the Crown, but accomplishing little of practical value.

Meanwhile his major efforts were being directed toward the preparation of a constitution for France. Most members of the Constitution Committee were moderates, but it was difficult in the late eighteenth century, just as it was in later times, to per-

* See Appendix, page 325.

suade any two Frenchmen to agree completely on political matters, and discussions often broke down.

Paine and Sieyès sometimes became involved in feuds, usually because they disagreed over the wording of various clauses of the projected constitution, but they settled their differences sufficiently to allow a draft to be completed by January, 1793. Paine regarded this document as unsatisfactory, so he and Condorcet spent the next month revising it.

By February, 1793, the proposed constitution was ready to be submitted to the Convention, but explosive domestic political animosities intervened. The Jacobins, engaged in a deadly struggle for power with the Girondists, regarded the constitution as a document created by the latter for their own benefit, to perpetuate themselves in office. They were determined to prevent its adoption. According to an article in the *Moniteur* of February 15, the Constitution Committee had tried the previous day to submit its document in the form of a report to the Convention, but squabbles between the Jacobins and Girondists prevented this.

The proposed constitution was distributed, however, and each member of the Convention received a copy. It was remarkably similar to the new Constitution of the United States. The Jacobins promptly let loose a barrage of criticism, saying that Paine, as the principal author of the work, had been too American in his outlook and had failed to take French tradition into consideration. This appeal to chauvinism, always effective in the Convention, caused a number of Girondists to waver and join the opposition. On the evening of March 5 a 'council' composed of Convention leaders met in secret, and by the time the session ended the new constitution had been rejected. Thereafter it had no chance of acceptance by the Convention.

Paine and his colleagues on the committee failed to recognize the need for men of power as well as intellectual stature in the group if the constitution they drew up were to find favor with a majority of the delegates. Robespierre was already the single most influential member of the Convention, but in spite of his standing he was not asked to join the committee. Consequently he did not take its deliberations seriously and made no effort to protect it from assault.

The constitution was scheduled to be presented to the Convention on April 15, 1793. By this time Robespierre and Marat had reached the conclusion that they wanted no basic changes in the system of government that had enabled them to become the most powerful men in France. By taking the same stand, they were able therefore to block serious consideration of the constitution. They persuaded the Convention that, prior to a discussion of the main work, they should concentrate their attention on a 'Declaration of Rights', a preamble which Paine had also written. This document of slightly more than a thousand words was submitted to the Convention on April 17, and an endless series of harangues followed, with speaker after speaker demanding petty changes in wording.

From its outset the French Revolution had been strongly anticlerical and antireligious, so Paine and Condorcet had been careful not to mention of God in their constitution. This gave Robespierre an opportunity to delay further, and he cynically said the entire document would have to be rewritten in order to 'include the Supreme Being'. Paine and Condorcet insisted that they had been guided by human reason, which they regarded as sufficient, but the Convention, duly influenced by Robespierre, insisted that references to God be included. Paine said that there was no reason for delay; he could add references to the Deity with a few strokes of the pen. But Robespierre demanded that the entire work be referred back to the committee. This was done, and the preamble was altered to read, 'In the presence and under the auspices of the Supreme Being, the French people declare . . . '.

Aroused, Paine openly challenged Robespierre on the floor of the Convention, something that few of his colleagues would have had the temerity to do. It was his understanding, he said, that the distinguished deputy was an atheist. This was not true, Robespierre replied. Paine asked him to define his concept of God, and after two days of fruitless debate, Robespierre finally said he found the words God and Nature to be identical and interchangeable.

This philosophical-theological dispute having been resolved, a consideration of the constitution was postponed until the middle of June, by which time a variety of charges had been brought against a score of leading Girondists, who were then arrested and, ultimately, executed. Paine, who was beginning to feel that his work had been done in vain and that France would never become the republic he had envisioned, was surprised when Robespierre permitted the new constitution to be freely discussed on June 22 and 23. On June 25 a vote was taken, and the document was adopted by an overwhelming majority. In accordance with the procedure Paine had advocated, it was then referred to the local communes, and they, in turn, ratified the constitution on August 10. Presumably it was now effective, and the Convention should have been dissolved and elections held to establish a new senate and chamber of deputies, which would have become the legislative branch of a new government.

But Robespierre had other ideas, and it soon became plain why he had allowed the constitution to progress this far toward adoption. The nation was at war, he said, and France could not yet afford the luxury of establishing a completely revised form of government. That could not be accomplished until there was an era of universal peace. In the meantime the Convention would continue to sit, and the completion of the Revolution itself would be the country's only immediate goal.

By this time Paine, although still hopeful that a republic on the American model would be established in France, was growing tired of the Revolution. By the summer of 1793 he realized at long last that his efforts were being thwarted at every turn. He should have known it much earlier. In January he and Condorcet had been assigned by the Convention to write an 'Address to the English People' that could be used for propaganda purposes. Both men worked hard on the document, but the Convention delayed whenever the authors wanted to present their draft. They had made two copies of the work, and the original and both copies vanished mysteriously, never again to reappear.

In February Marat openly declared his opposition to Paine, saying the American had supported Louis XVI for secret reasons of his own, and that he should be compelled to resign his seat in the Convention. In March Marat's threats became blunt, and, speaking on the floor of the Convention while glaring at Paine, he said, 'Frenchmen are mad to allow foreigners to live among them. We should cut off their ears, let them bleed for a few days and then cut off their heads.'

In April, 1793, Marat was placed on trial at the instigation of the Girondists, who accused him of fomenting disorders and trying to disrupt the Revolution. His fate was never in doubt, as the Jacobins controlled the Convention. Marat, in an attempt to drag others down with him, tried to denounce Paine, an effort that failed, but which indicated that the American's influence was waning.

Increasingly discouraged, Paine wrote to Thomas Jefferson on April 20:

> We are now in an extraordinary crisis, and it is not altogether without some considerable faults here. . . . There are now so many powers accidentally jumbled together as to render it exceedingly difficult to get them to agree upon any common object.
>
> The first object, that of restoring the old Monarchy, is evidently given up by the proposal to re-establish the late Constitution. . . . To all this is to be added the probable disputes about opportunity, the expense, and the projects of reimbursements. . . .
>
> Had this revolution been conducted consistently with its principles, there was once a good prospect of extending liberty through the greatest part of Europe; but I now relinquish that hope. Should the Enemy by venturing into France put themselves again in a condition of being captured, the hope will revive; but this is a risk that I do not wish to see tried, lest it should fail.
>
> As the prospect of a general freedom is now much shortened, I begin to contemplate returning home. I shall await the event of the proposed Constitution, and then take my final leave of Europe.

A few days later Marat was exonerated. Jockeying with Robespierre for power, he began to take action against the Girondist leaders, and all but the most optimistic were afraid that the moderates – Paine among them – would be imprisoned, tried, and perhaps sentenced to death.

By early May Paine had lost the last of his illusions regarding the French Revolution, and on May 6 he wrote a long letter to Danton, whom he regarded as his friend.

> I am exceedingly disturbed at the distractions, jealousies, discontents and uneasiness that reign among us, and which, if they continue, will bring ruin and disgrace on the Republic. When I left America in the year 1787, it was my intention to return the year following, but the French Revolution, and the prospect it afforded of extending the principles of liberty and fraternity through the greater part of Europe, have induced me to prolong my stay upwards of six years. I now despair of seeing the great object of European liberty accomplished, and my despair arises not from the combined foreign powers, not from the intrigues of aristocracy and priestcraft, but from the tumultuous misconduct with which the internal affairs of the present revolution is conducted.
>
> All that can now be hoped for is limited to France only. . . .
>
> I have no personal interest in any of these matters, nor in any party disputes. *I attend only to general principles.*
>
> As soon as a constitution shall be established, I shall return to

America; and be the future prosperity of France ever so great, I shall enjoy no other part of it than the happiness of knowing it. In the mean time I am distressed to see matters so badly conducted, and so little attention paid to moral principles. It is these things that injure the character of the Revolution and discourage the progress of liberty all over the world.

There ought be some regulation with respect to the spirit of denunciation that now prevails. If every individual is to indulge his private malignancy or his private ambition, to denounce at random and without any kind of proof, all confidence will be undermined and all authority be destroyed. Calumny is a species of treachery that ought to be punished as well as any other kind of treachery.

The letter concluded with a defense of twenty-two Girondist leaders, Brissot among them, who were charged with treason. Paine knew most of them and, he said, there were no better patriots in France. This statement alone could have condemned him as well, in a France where the Terror was daily growing worse and the guillotines were kept busy. In Paris alone there were as many as 400 executions each day.

In a postscript he told Danton that he had also written to Marat that same day, 'but not on the same subject'. Whatever his purpose, he indicated his own desire to return to the United States as soon as the question of the new French constitution was settled. This admission may have saved his life. He is believed to have been included on Marat's original proscribed list, but because of Paine's renown abroad, Marat – who liked being regarded as a civilized man and was extremely sensitive to criticism – hesitated. If Paine were to leave France, the leadership of the French Revolution would be spared the embarrassment caused by a man who constantly preached principles that interfered with their demands for power.

On June 2 the twenty-two Girondists were placed under arrest and imprisoned, after the radicals had incited a large mob to invade the Convention and open its doors to the people. For the moment, Paine and his good friend and literary collaborator, Condorcet, were spared – perhaps because the radicals were not yet ready to attack the 'American hero' or his associates.

On that same day, however, Paine was told by a minor Jacobin functionary that he would be wise to absent himself from the Convention for a time because the atmosphere 'was not convivial to foreigners'. On June 7 Robespierre demanded that the Convention pass a more stringent law governing the conduct of foreigners and permitting their arrest if they transgressed even the most insignificant regulation. As an afterthought, two foreigners residing in France were exempted; both were deputies. One was Thomas Paine; the other was Anacharsis Cloots, a Prussian journalist.

For all practical purposes Paine was isolated, but the worst was yet to come. The moderates were condemned to death, and many of them were executed. Brissot and several others escaped; they were hunted like common criminals, eventually recaptured, and, like the rest, finally executed. Paine was stunned. These murdered men had been his closest friends in France, his intellectual comrades. He had known them intimately, had dined frequently at their homes, and was well-acquainted with their families.

There was no end to the nightmare. On July 13 a young woman from Normandy, Charlotte Corday, by falsely promising to betray some Girondists, gained admission to Marat's home and stabbed him to death in his bath. Four days later she herself was executed, and the Terror began in earnest. Thousands of innocent men and women were sent to the guillotine on trumped-up charges.

Thomas Paine was sickened by the spectacle. The French were making a mockery of the very name of liberty and destroying his hopes for the establishment of a French republic. The ideals and principles to which he had devoted his life for nineteen years and on which his international renown rested were being savagely mocked and subverted. At that juncture he made the biggest mistake of his life. He should have taken passage to America without delay, put his labors on behalf of France behind him, and devoted himself to useful work in the United States. Instead he turned to the brandy bottle and each day drank himself insensible. He used both liquor and sex obsessively to escape: He later told Rickman that 'borne down by private and public affliction, I had been driven to excesses in Paris'. He did not exaggerate. He often invited as many as three young harlots at a time to his apartment and drank himself into a stupor.

It has been said that at this critical time in his life Paine demonstrated his essential weakness of character. Certainly it cannot be argued that he showed strength, but it should be noted on his behalf that he was in a state of shock. Temporarily deprived of his ability to think clearly and reasonably, he was in such despair that he drank to excess. His conduct cannot be condoned, but it demands understanding. Alone in the world at the age of fifty-six, his closest French comrades murdered, he felt lost. All he had striven to achieve had been destroyed. He had refused to recognize the mounting evidence that the Terror was out of control so that he was totally unprepared for the deluge of blood that inundated France.

A number of American and English friends helped to restore him to sanity. The first to act was Joel Barlow, the American writer and businessman who had been one of Paine's disciples in England and again in France, and who had been granted honorary French citizenship in 1792. Accompanied by two of Paine's, British friends, Lord Lauderdale and the author John Moore, Barlow went to the drunken man's apartment, removed him by force, and took him to the Philadelphia Hotel.

There, probably toward the end of July, 1793, while the Terror was raging, Paine's friends stood watch over him until he recovered. A number of others shared their deep concern for the distinguished man who had suffered such a complete emotional collapse, and new arrangements were made for his future. Seven of his American and British friends rented a mansion at 63, faubourg Saint Denis that had once belonged to Mme Pompadour, and before the end of the month they set up house there and moved Paine in with them. All took part in keeping the house clean, but virtually no cooking was done there, and most meals were eaten in restaurants.

Paine, who quickly recovered his equilibrium, described his situation in a letter written to an English friend early in August. The house was 'too remote' from the Convention, he said, but at the same time he admitted that 'it was also remote from the alarms and confusion into which the interior of Paris was often thrown'. In fact, he said, the isolation was so complete that he felt as though he was living in the countryside. In the yard there were fowl, rabbits, and a pair of pigs which the men fed. They also kept a vegetable garden and a small orchard of orange, apricot, and greengage plum trees which, Paine claimed, yielded the best fruit he had ever tasted. His own apartment consisted of three rooms – a sitting room, a bedchamber, and a storeroom in which he kept wood and water. A set of private stairs led from his suite to the garden, and he frequently went below to think in solitude.

He seldom attended the Convention, making occasional, token appearances there for the sake of what he regarded as propriety.

But he took no part in the deliberations of that body 'because I found it impossible to join in their tremendous decrees, and useless and dangerous to oppose them'. He knew that he was already a marked man because he had been more outspoken than any other deputy in defense of Louis XVI; he also realized that even if he put his real thoughts on paper, any fellow deputy who dared to translate them into French would be placing his own life in jeopardy.

For a moment Paine gave up his career as an author. 'No good could be done by writing,' he said, 'and no printer dared to print.' He did no writing, either, for his own edification or amusement, afraid that agents of the Convention might seize his works and interpret them in a manner that would guarantee his arrest, imprisonment, and execution. At no time did Paine forget that as a French citizen he was completely at the mercy of the Jacobins.

Rickman, who often visited Paine at the mansion on the faubourg Saint Denis, wrote at least two long letters describing his old friend's regimen there. Paine usually got up at about seven in the morning, he said, and descended into the garden to pick his breakfast from the fruit trees. He strolled for an hour or two, lost in thought, and the others in the house did not join him unless he hailed them. Later in the morning he played various games with them, usually 'chess, whist, piquet or cribbage', and he was at his light, conversational best, spicing his talk with anecdotes from his past.

The entire party repaired to a restaurant in the neighborhood for dinner, and after their return Paine joined his friends in play 'at marbles, scotch hops, battledores, etc., on the broad and fine gravel walk at the upper end of the garden'. After an hour of mild outdoor exercise he retired to his bedroom, where he was 'up to his knees in letters and papers of various descriptions'. There he remained, alone and unmolested, until it was time to go out for supper. In the evening he sometimes visited the relatives of Brissot or of other French friends who had been guillotined. Otherwise he never went out at night. His conversation, Rickman said, 'was often witty and cheerful, always acute and improving, but never frivolous. Incorrupt, straightforward, and sincere, he pursued his political course in France, as everywhere else, let the government or clamor or faction of the day be what it might, with firmness, with clearness, and without a shadow of turning.'

In mid-evening the landlord, who maintained his own apartment in the mansion, brought them the day's newspapers. Paine went to his suite with a pile of them. From time to time he announced that perusing them helped him to learn the French language; but he usually added that it didn't matter if he failed to understand most of what he read, as the news of the day was, in his opinion, invariably disgusting. He often read until midnight, when his lamp was extinguished.

Why did Paine stay in France during the summer of 1793, when he was not only free to leave at any time, but would have saved the leaders of the Revolution considerable embarrassment had he returned to the United States? He had given up hope for the establishment of a French republic based on truly democratic principles, he knew that liberty had become a misused word there, and he realized that he himself was accomplishing nothing.

It has been said that he clung to the thought that something might be salvaged from the collapse of his dream, that he was incapable of totally abandoning that dream. But nothing in his correspondence with Thomas Jefferson and others suggests this. It is more likely that he was in the process of a long emotional and physical recuperation from the shocks he had suffered. Perhaps he was incapable of thinking and acting decisively; it may have been too much of an effort for him to put France behind him, endure the mockery of his enemies in England, and return to the United States to begin life anew.

For the moment he was content to drift. He accepted each day as it came, contenting himself with simple pleasures, and seemed to give little thought to the future. Barlow has made it clear that Paine knew the time would come when he would return to his life's work, and he sometimes discussed his future plans for writing. The failure of France to live up to his expectations did not mean that the cause of democracy was dead or dying; on the contrary, the success of the American experiment would ultimately inspire Europe anew. Out of the chaos and senseless cruelty of the French Revolution there might emerge a new sense of national dedication to high principles, and this spirit would in turn communicate itself to Great Britain.

So the immediate task was to make certain that the United States did not falter in her resolve. He would go home to carry on the struggle there as soon he felt energetic enough. In another month, perhaps two, he would book passage. The British fleet was blockading French ports again, but that was nothing new, and he was not afraid of the Royal Navy or anyone else. Soon, very soon, he would be ready to leave.

17

A Prison Term

Citizen Barère, the man who proudly claimed responsibility for the Terror as a cathartic agent that would cure France of her ills, was chairman of the all-powerful Committee of Public Safety. On July 27, 1793, only a few days after the murder of Marat, a new member was added to that group, a fact which went virtually unnoticed at the time. Very quickly, however, France would learn that she had a new master – Citizen Robespierre. The announced goals of Robespierre were humanitarian, and for the moment France breathed a trifle more easily. Even the moderates took heart; after all, most of the imprisoned Girondist leaders were still alive, and Robespierre was said to be opposed in principle to the idea of sending Marie Antoinette to the guillotine.

One of Robespierre's first official acts was to enlist the aid of Thomas Paine, the man who understood better than anyone else in France the intricacies of the British governmental system and the moods of the United States. At the request of the new leader

Paine wrote him a series of analytical reports in which he outlined in detail the probable reactions of Britain and America to various political developments in France. In all, these memoranda ran to more than 50 pages, and they demonstrated that Paine would have been a first-rate diplomat had he been given the opportunity. His predictions were shrewd, and he managed to refrain from including his own personal opinions or hopes in the memoranda. But Robespierre did not seem to pay the slightest attention to anything Paine wrote.

Paine also gave the new leader practical advice of all kinds, also ignored, as a brief, undated memorandum, written sometime in the autumn of 1793, illustrates:

> You mentioned to me that saltpetre was becoming scarce. I communicate to you a project of the late Captain Paul Jones, which, if successfully put in practice, will furnish you with that article.
>
> All the English East India ships put into St Helena, off the coast of Africa, on their return from India to England. A great part of their ballast is saltpetre. Captain Jones, who had been at St Helena, says that the place can be very easily taken. His proposal was to send off a small squadron for that purpose, to keep the English flag flying at port. The English vessels will continue coming in as usual. By this means it will be a long time before the Government of England can have any knowledge of what has happened. The success of this depends so much on secrecy that I wish you would translate this yourself, and give it to Barère.

Nothing came of the proposal, but Paine still felt loyal to France, in spite of all that happened. And he continued to write reports and suggestions throughout the autumn and early winter of 1793, although it was becoming obvious to him that his own situation was growing increasingly precarious.

History has never quite decided whether Maximilien de Robespierre was a man of herioc stature who took stern measures to end the chaos that threatened the success of the French Revolution, or whether he was a cruel despot who because of his crimes was sent to the guillotine a scant year after he assumed power. Thomas Paine's nineteenth-century biographers, however, faced no such difficulties of interpretation. To them Robespierre was a madman who persecuted Paine because of personal jealousy. The only evidence that substantiates this theory is a brief word in Robespierre's private *Notebooks*, written early in 1794, after Paine had been arrested and sent to prison: 'Demand that Thomas

Paine be decreed of accusation for the interests of America as much as of France.' Even if it is true that Robespierre conceived a personal hatred of Paine, this cryptic reference does not clarify the situation. The two men actually shared many interests: Both were deists, convinced that God was the Supreme Being and Supreme Intelligence, and they shared many humanitarian goals. They were also men of great integrity, and both were incorruptible.

The mood of France was such in the autumn and early winter of 1793 that almost nothing could have saved Paine from imprisonment. The nation was beleaguered, surrounded by powerful enemies and internally weakened by vicious feuds between factions greedily seeking power. Unwilling and unable to blame themselves for their misfortunes, the people and a majority of their leaders became xenophobic. All foreigners were anathema to them, guards had to be provided for the diplomatic representatives of other nations living in Paris, and private citizens from other lands were in such jeopardy that many of them fled France before they could be arrested.

The chaos that had threatened to engulf France since the beginning of the Revolution now inundated her. Her treasury, once the wealthiest in Europe, was empty. Every other Old World power was either nominally or in fact at war with her; their monarchs were afraid that the Revolution would spread if it remained unchecked. The dissensions were tearing her apart internally, as well. The mob ruled Paris and had to be placated by the men who governed in the name of the people. But the provinces, traditionally more conservative, were reluctant to follow the lead of the capital, and only the presence of troops loyal to the Revolution prevented the outbreak of numerous rebellions. Even the attitudes of these regiments may be questioned, as it has been said that they followed orders from Paris only because of the discipline instilled in French soldiers since the reign of Henry IV at the beginning of the seventeenth century.

People were denounced by relatives, neighbors – anyone bearing a grudge. The machinery of justice had broken down, and investigations of charges were a mockery, as were the so-called trials conducted by Revolutionary tribunals. Men and women were imprisoned on mere pretexts. The life of every prominent citizen was in jeopardy, and the Revolution had become a vicious, aimless monster, a creature ruled by the Terror for terror's own sake.

Paine's brief idyll in the faubourg Saint Denis came to an end. On several occasions, either late at night or early in the morning, squads of soldiers came to the old mansion. Each time Paine thought that they intended to arrest him, but he was mistaken; they had come for one or another of his companions, all of whom had already left the country.

Paine entertained no false illusions about his own situation, and his correspondence in October and November, 1793, indicates that he was aware of being in imminent danger. He was still a deputy, to be sure, and as such he enjoyed immunity from arrest, but this was a mere technicality and could be easily circumvented. When the number of Girondist deputies on the proscribed list had risen from 22 to 29, the Convention had simply expelled them before having them arrested.

The campaign against Paine began in mid-August. Arras, a town in his constituency, sent a formal address to the Convention, saying that its citizens had lost confidence in Paine and that they wanted him discharged. Robespierre, as it happened, was a native of Arras, and there were many – including Paine himself – who wondered if the leader of the Revolution was responsible for the address. Not until much later was it learned that the instigator of the communication was a man named Joseph le Bon, who had been elected as an alternate deputy and could not take his seat in the Convention until Paine vacated it.

On September 10, 1794, after Robespierre had gone to the guillotine, Paine specifically exonerated him in a brief note to James Monroe:

> However discordant the late American Minister, Gouvernoeur Morris, and the late French Committee of Public Safety, were, it suited the purposes of both that I should be continued in arrestation. The former wished to prevent my return to America, that I should not expose his misconduct; and the latter lest I should publish to the world the history of its wickedness. Whilst that Minister and that Committee continued, I had no expectation of liberty. I speak here of the Committee of which Robespierre was a member. My continuing presence here attests that he bore me no such grudge.

In all fairness to Morris, it should be noted that Paine was badly mistaken, and it may be that like many men held in prison he was suffering from the conviction that he was being persecuted. He and Morris had been on increasingly strained terms, partly because of their diverging political philosophies and partly because their personalities clashed. Numerous attempts were made in the years after Paine's imprisonment to prove that Morris had a hand in his arrest, but the evidence is weak. It was also charged that Morris was less diligent than he might have been in making attempts to secure Paine's release. There was nothing the United States minister could have done other than submit a formal protest to the Committee of Public Safety, which he did. The members of that group were united in their hatred of foreigners, and neither cajolery nor threats would have moved them.

In any event, when it gradually dawned on Paine that his days of freedom were numbered, he made no attempt to escape. The fate of Brissot and his other Girondist friends had made him aware that it was useless to run away. He was a prominent figure and was sure to be recognized, particularly because he could speak only a few words of French. Besides, it was beneath his dignity to flee; he stood by every word he had written, and he would neither retract his views nor do anything that would make it appear that he was ashamed of them.

Conscious of his personal freedom as never before and convinced that if arrested, he would be promptly executed, Paine began writing Part One of *The Age of Reason*. As befitted a man who believed he would soon die, this document was the testament of his religious faith. He spent most of his waking hours laboring on it in October and November, and by early December the work was completed.

Paine's greatest fear was that the French authorities would learn of the existence of *The Age of Reason* and would confiscate his manuscript. This dread became so great that he took extraordinary precautions. Telling virtually no one what he was doing, he made three separate copies of his manuscript, giving one to Barlow, one to another American, and the third to an English friend. All three were hoping to leave France in December, and he charged each of them with the responsibility for making certain that his copy reached the United States. Even if only one of the three succeeded, then the pamphlet would still be published.

In spite of his personal difficulties, however, Paine continued to think of the international situation in broad terms. Writing to Jefferson on October 20, he continued to seek an end to the war:

I am every day more convinced and impressed with the propriety of Congress sending Commissioners to Europe to confer with the

Minister of the Jesuitical Powers on the means of terminating the war. . . . I see not how this war is to terminate if some intermediate power does not step forward. There is now no prospect that France can carry revolutions thro' Europe on the one hand, or that the combined powers can conquer France on the other hand. It is a sort of defensive war on both sides. This being the case, how is the war to close? Neither side will ask for peace though each may wish it. I believe that England and Holland are tired of war. Their commerce and manufactures have suffered most exceedingly – and besides this it is to them a war without an object. Russia keeps herself at a distance. I cannot help repeating my wish that Congress would send Commissioners, and I wish also that yourself would venture once more across the ocean as one of them. If the Commissioners rendezvous at Holland they would then know what steps to take. They could call Mr Pinckney to their councils, and it would be of use, on many accounts, that one of them should come over from Holland to France. Perhaps a long truce, were it proposed by the neutral powers, would have all the effects of a peace, without the difficulties of attending the adjustment of all the forms of peace.

Paine's own situation was steadily becoming worse. Two of his English colleagues in the mansion managed to obtain passports one evening early in November, and were so anxious to leave that they departed at four o'clock in the morning, ultimately reaching safety in Switzerland. Two days later a squad of soldiers appeared seeking the pair who had fled. By now Paine was the only lodger left in the house. In December the landlord, a man named Georgeit, was removed by the police, and Paine wrote to a friend in London, 'Ah, France! thou hast ruined the character of a revolution virtuously begun, and destroyed those who produced it.'

Much later Paine wrote to Samuel Adams about those harrowing days, and an excerpt from the letter indicates not only the spirit of the times but Paine's own determination to finish and publish Part One of *The Age of Reason*:

My friends were falling as fast as the guillotine could cut their heads off, and as I expected, every day, the same fate, I resolved to begin my work. I appeared to myself to be on my death bed, for death was on every side of me, and I had no time to lose. This accounts for my writing at the time I did, and so nicely did the time and intention meet, that I had not finished the first part of the work more than six hours before I was arrested and taken to prison. The people of France were running headlong into atheism, and I had the work translated in their own language, to stop them in that career, and fix them to the first article of every man's creed, who has any creed at all – *I believe in God.*

The Convention met on the morning of December 25, 1793; Christmas was no longer officially observed in France since the National Assembly had outlawed the practice of all religion. The session was held in secret, as were so many in a period when new arrests were being ordered daily. One of the more important items on the agenda for that day was the expulsion of Deputy Thomas Paine of the Pas-de-Calais district from the Convention. The official reason cited for this act was that he had 'conspired against the interests of France and America, together with an agent of the British Foreign Office'. No particulars were given, nor could there have been any, the allegation having been invented out of whole cloth.

Paine was relieved of his duties and dismissed from the Convention by the unanimous vote of the deputies; his case was then handed over to the Committee of Public Safety. Justice was being streamlined in the name of 'efficiency', the courts being too busy to handle all the cases of enemies of the state with which they were being inundated. So the committee, still acting in secret, took the parts of both the prosecutor and the judge, and on December 26 Paine, who still knew nothing of what was happening, was tried in absentia. He was found guilty of treason by a unanimous decision and was condemned to death.

On December 27, still working feverishly, Paine completed a revised version of the last portion of Part One of *The Age of Reason*, and had time to make only one copy. Unable to trust more than a few friends still in France with the manuscripts, and not wanting anyone to endanger his own life by carrying them, he mailed them separately to two different addresses in Switzerland. A member of the Convention had apparently warned Paine privately that he would be placed under arrest that same evening. Some have said that it was Robespierre who notified him of the danger he was in, as a gesture of friendship, but this has never been confirmed.

Paine's official address was still the apartment in the passage des Petits Pères, although he had not set foot in the place for at least six months. Apparently, however, he deemed it appropriate that he be taken into custody at his formal residence. That evening he dined, as usual, in a small restaurant near the faubourg

Saint Denis, then returned to his suite there and removed his few belongings. Carrying them with him, he walked across Paris to the passage des Petits Pères, and as the night was very cold he built a substantial fire in the grate. Shortly before midnight he extinguished his candle and waited for the knock on the door. He did not have long to wait. A quarter of an hour later nine representatives of the Committee of General Surety, one corporal, and four privates arrived. Paine was placed under arrest in the name of the Convention, and he submitted with a smile.

The fourteen men could scarcely squeeze into the little apartment, but all busied themselves searching for 'incriminating documents'. Finding nothing, they tore bricks out of the fireplace, ripped open the mattress and even removed several wall boards. At one point Paine, all but forgotten, stood alone outside his front door and presumably could have slipped away. Instead, he waited for the conclusion of the search, which as he knew would reveal nothing.

It was almost dawn when the searchers gave up. Their task was complicated by the fact that Paine could not speak French and they knew no English. After a long consultation they took their prisoner to the Hotel Great Britain in the rue Jacob, and there awakened the manager, who acted as an interpreter. Through this badly frightened man they learned that Paine had just returned to the passage des Petits Pères that night, and that he had been residing for months in the old mansion on the faubourg Saint Denis. This came as no surprise to several of the Committee of General Surety representatives, but they were required to act within the limitations of their instructions, and could not go to the mansion until they had heard from Paine himself that he lived there.

It was by this time seven o'clock in the morning, and everyone was hungry, so the entire group went to a nearby restaurant, and, at the expense of the Revolution, ate a hearty breakfast. No one had a keener appetite than the prisoner, who also consumed a bottle of red wine. Then the party adjourned to the faubourg Saint Denis, and the search for 'documents' was resumed.

Several more employees of the Committee of General Surety joined the group by mid-morning, as did three members of the Committee itself, along with their official interpreter. Various letters and other papers in both French and English were found, but none were in the least 'suspicious'. As the search continued,

Paine was taken in a carriage to the apartment of Joel Barlow, who swore under oath that he had no documents or other papers there belonging to Thomas Paine. His apartment was searched, too, and nothing incriminating was found as he had hidden his copy of the manuscript of *The Age of Reason* elsewhere. Again it was time to eat, so everyone adjourned to another restaurant for dinner, with Barlow also in tow. He, Paine, and the interpreter discussed metaphysical questions throughout the meal, and the members of the committee, for whom the interpreter translated, professed themselves impressed by Paine's erudition.

At four o'clock in the afternoon the group adjourned to the local police station, where they were joined by the searching party from the faubourg Saint Denis. A full report of the day's activities was recorded, and both Paine and Barlow signed the document, as did five of the Frenchmen. The formalities having been completed, Paine embraced Barlow, and then ceremoniously shook hands with the many Frenchmen who had been his companions since midnight. A black carriage drew up outside the door, and 'the enemy of France' was removed to the Luxembourg Prison, a former palace. Paine was received with due ceremony by Citizen Benoit, the warden, who searched him to make sure he carried no weapon other than his dress small-sword, which he was allowed to keep. Benoit personally took him to a large cell with two windows, in which there were no other occupants, a sure sign that the new guest of the Revolution was a personage of standing. Paine, exhausted, dropped to the pallet on the stone floor and slept until the following morning. Thus on December 29, 1793, a month before his fifty-seventh birthday, he became a prisoner. He had every reason to believe that his new existence would be terminated abruptly by the guillotine.

Prison life there was as quaint as it was informal. Inmates were locked in their cells only from midnight until seven o'clock in the morning. Thereafter all doors were opened, and prisoners of both sexes could visit other cells at will or stroll together in the courtyard. Those who could afford the luxury were attended by servants who shared their masters' captivity.

The population of the prison represented a cross-section of France. There were aristocrats and great ladies, clergymen stripped of their clerical robes, middle-class merchants, actresses and others of the demimonde, and even laborers who had been denounced by their comrades. Supposedly only prisoners of standing were incarcerated in the Luxembourg Prison, but all of the city's jails were so full that 'many persons of no consequence' also were housed there. Virtually all had been condemned to death, and the executioners were busy at dawn and again at sunset. Prisoners rarely knew in advance when their turn would come, but the majority bore the strain with amazing courage and good humor. Fornication was a common practice, and while some prisoners played cards or chess, others buried themselves in books or spent their waking hours in prayer.

The affluent prisoners had their meals sent in from the outside, and those who could not were forced to eat the slop served by the state. Ordinarily Paine would have been a member of the latter group, but the deputies did not want to be charged with having mistreated the famous author; so Paine's meals were catered by a restaurant. He could order whatever he wished in the way of food and wine. He never went hungry while in prison and, in fact, gained weight.

He was not lonely, either. Soon after his arrival at the Luxembourg Prison he formed a liaison with Muriel Alette, an actress who had no political leanings but who had been imprisoned because she had been the mistress of a minor member of the nobility, a man already guillotined. She too had been sentenced to death, but she was released without explanation. Perhaps her affair with him, which was no secret, was responsible for her improved situation.

Paine's imprisonment created a furor in the United States, France, and Great Britain. The first to react were seventeen prominent Americans living in Paris, among them Joel Barlow. On January 27 these gentlemen presented an indignant petition to the Convention, and to make certain it received a wide circulation they flooded Paris with copies. In this document they enumerated Paine's many contributions to the cause of liberty, equality, and fraternity, and they offered to stand bond for his good behavior if he were released into their custody.

The deeply embarrassed Convention replied in a letter – also made public – under the signature of its president, Vadier. This communication tried hard, but in vain, to rationalize Paine's arrest. He was a native of England, and 'this is undoubtedly enough to apply to him the measures of security prescribed by the revolutionary laws'. But there were other reasons: 'His genius has not understood that which has regenerated France; he has regarded the system only in accordance with the illusions with which the false friends of our revolution have invested it.' Struggling to justify itself, the Convention admitted that Paine was a republican author and his works were 'justly esteemed'. Unfortunately, he was guilty of errors which could not be reconciled with the principles he had enunciated.

Great Britain was at war with France and her government was opposed to all that Paine represented. But his friends in England busied themselves, and a petition to the Convention on the author's behalf was smuggled out of the country and brought to Paris. It bore more than 300 signatures, many of them distinguished.

The United States sent an official protest, which indicated that the execution of Paine would be regarded as an unfriendly act toward the people of America. This communication was delivered to the Foreign Office by Minister Monroe, who also paid personal visits to the prisoner at least twice a week.

Paine himself was far more concerned about the manuscript of *The Age of Reason*, and soon discovered that luck was in his favor. The sergeant of the guard who was in charge of his cell-block, a man named Brisson, was an ardent admirer of *The Rights of Man*, and regarded the author of that work with an awe that verged on idolatry. Brisson was loyal to the Revolution, but he made it clear to Paine that he would do anything within his power to help such a renowned prisoner.

Paine took him at his word. Joel Barlow had postponed his departure from Paris because of his desire to help Paine and at the author's request brought sections of *The Age of Reason* with him to the prison on his frequent visits. Paine polished the work at his leisure; as he himself commented, he had ample time.

The threat of death persisted, and he knew that his work on behalf of freedom for all mankind would not save him. Far more prominent persons had already been executed by a government that showed no favorites. Marie Antoinette had gone to the guillotine on October 16, 1793, and the surviving Girondist leaders had been killed soon thereafter. Now it seemed that virtually everyone of prominence in France was being put to death. Paine appeared to be reconciled to his fate, and his one concern was the safety of his precious manuscript and the publication of the work.

As the months passed, however, Paine managed to stay alive.

A Prison Term

The sentence of death had been pronounced against him, but his name never appeared on the list of those sent to the guillotine. It has been said that Robespierre, secretly admiring Paine's works and high principles, kept his name off the death list. This may be true, but it should not be forgotten that Robespierre's power was so great in the first months of 1794 that he could have granted Paine a pardon or reprieve, and no one would have been able to protest.

Some of the elite of the Revolution spent time in the Luxembourg Prison with Paine before they themselves went to the guillotine. There was Danton, who said to his American friend, 'That which you did for the happiness and liberty of your country, I tried in vain to do for mine. I have been less fortunate, but not less innocent. They will send me to the scaffold; very well, my friends, I shall go gaily.' Camille Desmoulins, one of the intellectuals of the Revolution, became Paine's close friend before he went to the guillotine, and another intimate was Anacharsis Cloots, the only foreigner other than Paine to sit in the Convention. One of the author's oldest and closest friends in Paris, Hérault de Séchelles, was in the Luxembourg Prison for a time before he went to his death; he had been condemned because he had hidden a lifelong friend from the police.

A number of high-ranking English prisoners were being held in the prison and, regardless of their political beliefs, all of them became Paine's good friends. Ironically, the most distinguished of them was an officer in the British army who had served in the American Revolution, General Charles O'Hara. He had conducted himself with gallantry and at the ceremonies following the Battle of Yorktown had created something of a scandal by offering the sword of Lord Cornwallis to the French commander, Rochambeau, rather than to Washington.

By now O'Hara had reconciled himself to the fact that the former British colonies had formed an independent nation. He was a Tory, and hence should have been Paine's enemy, but politics make very strange bedfellows, and the pair became inseparable. Others were amused when they spent long hours arguing the future of England, with neither altering his stand. O'Hara escaped the guillotine; in fact, when he was released from prison Paine generously gave him £200 in gold coins, enough to take him back to England by way of Switzerland and the German states. O'Hara later repaid the debt, and the two men corresponded for a long time afterwards.

Because of the leniency of the warden and the friendliness of the sergeant of the guard, Paine was able to continue with his writing for some time while in prison. A month after his incarceration he penned the opening lines of his monumental *Age of Reason*, dedicating the work to his fellow citizens of the United States:

> I put the following work under your protection. It contains my opinion upon religion. You will do me the justice to remember, that I have always strenuously supported the right of every man to his own opinion, however different that opinion might be to mine. He who denies to another this right, makes a slave of himself to his present opinion, because he precludes himself the right of changing it.
>
> The most formidable weapon against errors of every kind is reason. I have never used any other, and I trust I never shall.

For many months afterward Paine did not write anything at all. The atmosphere of the prison was not conducive to writing. Each day new victims of the Terror arrived, and each day the guillotine took its toll. Paine's room, which had its own fireplace, was on the ground floor, 'level with the earth in the garden and floored with brick'. When it rained the moisture seeped up through the earth, and the cell was so damp he caught an endless succession of colds. He was required to provide his own firewood and candles, but both commodities became increasingly difficult to obtain in Paris, and he gradually lost his battle to keep out the chill.

He took a fairly large sum of money with him to prison, about £300. To keep this little fortune safe, he found an ingenious hiding place. He removed the lock from his door, hid the money inside the lock slot, and then replaced the lock.

The prison became so crowded that in mid-March Paine was given a cellmate, Denis Jullien, who was French. Some months later, after the fall and execution of Robespierre, Jullien was accused of having been a spy for him, and Paine was asked to testify in the case. The author said that in the two months they spent together he found Jullien to be 'a man of strict honor, probity and humanity'. Both had loathed Robespierre, he declared, for his 'sanguinary malignancy', and because of his 'hypocrisy' in claiming that he believed in God as the Supreme Being and Intelligence. The two prisoners had not spoken their opinions aloud because they had been afraid of being overheard, but had written these views in English and then consigned the paper to the flames in their fireplace.

In May, 1794, Paine prepared a new edition of *The Rights of Man*, his last major work in prison. Writing that it was 'designed for the use and benefit of all mankind', he removed all specific references that had been calculated to appeal strictly to English and French leaders and prepared a totally new preface. Then, in some way never explained, he smuggled the work out of the prison. It was sent to London, and later in the year a printer named Daniel Isaac Eaton brought out the new edition.

Later that spring Paine contracted a severe fever and fell seriously ill. He had to be moved to a larger room in which three Belgian prisoners were being held – Charles Bastini, Michael Rubyns, and Joseph Vanhuele. Paine was unconscious for days, and delirious for several weeks. The Belgians looked after him, and he was treated by two English prisoners, a physician named Graham and a surgeon named Bond, both members of General O'Hara's staff.

Paine's illness lasted about five weeks. When he began to recover he realized that he had been semiconscious for almost the entire period and had no memory of what had occurred. To his horror he discovered that at least 300 of his fellow prisoners had been put to death during that time.

He was bitter about the horrors of the prison, saying: 'That the accused were not guilty of any counter revolutionary conduct is what I also believe; but the case was that they and all the detained saw themselves shut up like sheep in a pen to be sacrificed in their turn, and they daily saw that others of their Camarades had been and every expression of discontent, which the misery of such a situation extorted from them, was converted into conspiration by the Spies of Robespierre, who were distributed in the prisons.'

One of the first things Paine learned when he regained full consciousness was that Robespierre had been executed on July 28, 1794. Eight years later, shortly after Paine's return to the United States, he told the story of his own miraculous salvation. Most of his contemporaries accepted his tale as fact, as well it might have been, since stranger things had happened in France. But modern students are inclined to believe that Paine embellished his version of what had happened with some fictional details:

One hundred and sixty-eight persons were taken out of the Luxembourg in one night, and a hundred and sixty of them guillotined next day, of which I now know I was to have been one; and the manner I escaped that fate is curious, and has all the appearance of accident.

The room in which I was lodged was on the ground floor, and one of a long range of rooms under a gallery, and the door of it opened outward and flat against the wall, so that when it was open the inside of the door appeared outward, and the contrary when it was shut. I had three comrades, fellow prisoners with me, Joseph Vanhuele of Bruges, since president of the municipality of that town, Michael Rubyns, and Charles Bastinit of Louvain.

When persons by scores and hundreds were to be taken out of prison for the guillotine it was always done in the night, and those who performed that office had a private mark or signal, by which they knew what rooms to go to, and what number to take. We, as I have stated, were four, and the door of our room was marked, unobserved by us, with that number in chalk; but it happened, if happened is a proper word, that the mark was put on when the door was open, and flat against the wall, and thereby came on the inside when we shut it at night, and the destroying angel passed us by. A few days after this Robespierre fell.

18

A Question of Release

From the time of his arrest Thomas Paine made strenuous efforts to obtain his release from prison, writing countless letters and appeals on his own behalf. During the first months of his incarceration Gouverneur Morris was still the United States minister to France, and the principal thrust of Paine's effort was directed at him. Morris's failure to obtain his immediate release was a cause of great bitterness, and Paine never forgave him for it, insisting to the end of his days that the American representative deliberately did nothing for him because of personal animosity. This view was subsequently shared by Moncure Conway, Paine's most important nineteenth-century biographer.

The facts do not bear out this contention. It is true that the conservative, elegant Morris disapproved of his former colleague who was fond of rum and brandy, whose dress was slovenly, and who bathed less frequently than many Americans believed necessary for the sake of hygiene. It cannot be denied, either, that

Morris regarded Paine as 'a little mad' and 'full of self-conceit', as his correspondence indicates. The publication of *The Age of Reason* horrified him; he did not read the pamphlet, apparently, but wrote to Jefferson that Paine's new work denied the existence of God. But in spite of his own predilections, the United States minister did his duty. On February 14, 1794, he sent a letter to the French minister of foreign affairs, Chemin Deforgues, saying:

> Thomas Paine has just applied to me to claim him as a Citizen of the United States. These (I believe) are the facts which relate to him. He was born in England. Becoming subsequently a citizen of the United States, he there acquired a great celebrity through his revolutionary writings. In consequence he was adopted as a French citizen, and then elected a Member of the Convention. His conduct since that period is out of my jurisdiction. I am ignorant of the reason for his present detention in the Luxembourg prison, but I beg you, (if there are reasons unknown to me which prevent his liberation) please be so good as to inform me of them, so that I may communicate them to the government of the United States.

Deforgues sent his reply five days later, defending the arrest of Paine on grounds that may have been unusual in his own time, since the entire question of citizenship had not been clarified on an international basis. It should be kept in mind that the United States fought the War of 1812 against Great Britain largely because American merchant seamen were being seized on the high seas and impressed into service in the Royal Navy. Deforgues struck a distinctly twentieth-century note when he said that Paine, by accepting the title of French citizenship and taking a seat in the Convention, 'has submitted himself to the laws of the Republic and has in effect renounced the protection which the law of nations and the treaties concluded with the United States would have been able to assure him'.

Conway saw a conspiracy against Paine in this exchange of correspondence, claiming that Morris was not truly interested in obtaining the release of the author, but merely wanted documentary proof he could submit to the State Department that he had not neglected Paine. He totally ignored a note written in the margin of Morris's letter by a Foreign Office official which said, 'Acknowledge reception and tell him that the minister will take steps.'

Morris sent a copy of Deforgues's letter to Paine, who angrily concluded that the American minister was only going through the motions on his behalf and was not sincerely trying to obtain his release. 'I have made an essay in answer to the Minister's letter,' he wrote on February 24, 1794, 'which I wish you to make ground of a reply to him. They have nothing against me – except that they do not choose I should be in a state of freedom to write my mind freely upon things I have seen. Though you and I are not on terms of the best harmony, I apply to you as the Minister of America, and you may add to that service whatever you think my integrity deserves. At any rate I expect you to make Congress acquainted with my situation, and to send to them copies of the letters that have passed on the subject. A reply to the Minister's letter is absolutely necessary, were it only to continue the reclamation. Otherwise your silence will be a sort of consent to his observation.'

A few days later Paine wrote to Morris again, this time advancing a new argument. He was 'no more French' than George Washington, who had also been granted honorary French citizenship. Gradually his ire against Gouverneur Morris faded somewhat, as he persuaded himself that it would be a simple matter for Washington, his old comrade and friend, to obtain his release. A brief letter from the President of the United States would surely open the gates of the Luxembourg without further delay. This opinion hardened into a conviction during the ten months of Paine's imprisonment, and by the time he was released late in 1794, he had developed an abiding hatred for Washington. Had his contempt remained private, there would have been no repercussions. But Paine was incapable of keeping any of his views to himself, and he caused himself irreparable harm by feuding openly and viciously with the man who was becoming increasingly idolized by most Americans.

Gouverneur Morris had no intention of issuing an appeal to Congress on Paine's behalf. He continued to correspond, as was appropriate, through his usual State Department channels. On January 21 he had written to Secretary Jefferson, 'I incline to think that if he (Paine) is quiet in prison he may have the good luck to be forgotten, whereas, should he be brought into notice, the long suspended axe might fall on him. I believe he thinks that I ought to claim him as an American citizen; but considering his birth, his naturalisation in this country, and the place he filled, I doubt much the right, and I am sure that the claim would be, for the present at least, inexpedient and ineffectual.'

On March 6 Morris wrote a more detailed report to Jefferson which demonstrates that, regardless of his personal dislike for Paine, his analysis of the situation was sound:

Mr Paine wrote me a note desiring I would claim him as an American, which I accordingly did, although contrary to my judgment, for reasons mentioned in my last. The Minister's letter to me of the 1st Ventose, which I enclose a copy, contains the answer to my reclamation. I sent a copy to Mr Paine, who prepared a long answer, and sent it to me by an Englishman, whom I did not know. I told him, as Mr Paine's friend, that my present opinion was similar to that of the Minister, but I might, perhaps, see occasion to change it, and in that case, if Mr Paine wished it, I would go on with the claim, but that it would be well for him to consider the result; that, if the government meant to release him, they had already a sufficient ground; but if not, I could push them to bring on his trial for the crimes imputed to him; seeing that whether he be considered as a Frenchman, or as an American, he must be amenable to the tribunals of France for his conduct while he was a Frenchman, and he may see in the fate of the Brissotins, that to which he is exposed. I have heard no more of the affair since; but it is not impossible that he may force on a decision, which, as far as I can judge, would be fatal to him; for in the best of times he has a larger share of every other sense than common sense, and lately the intemperate use of ardent spirits has, I am told, considerably impaired the small stock he originally possessed.

There may be a small measure of justice in Conway's claim that Morris failed to act vigorously to protect Paine's life and obtain his release from prison. On the other hand, the American minister was using his best judgment in a delicate situation. Certainly his belief that Paine would be executed if called to the attention of the French authorities appears valid. The guillotine was being used indiscriminately, and every day people who had been cast into prison without cause were being sent to their deaths. In Paris thousands were being executed each month; the toll in the provinces, although never accurately enumerated, may have been as high.

Life at the Luxembourg Prison was filled with tension, as no prisoner knew when he might be sent to his death. Paine discussed philosophy with various other unfortunates, but these chats failed to relieve the strain he was feeling, and he turned again to liquor. His favorite alcoholic beverage, rum, was not readily available in France, so he consoled himself with brandy, which many others also drank to numb their fear. The jailers openly sold brandy by the cask or bottle, and Paine's purchases were unstinting. He apparently did not drink himself into a stupor, but his consumption of liquor was steadily heavy up to the time of his illness. When he recovered from his fever he was still too weak to drink cognac, and for a time he led an exemplary existence.

In July, 1794, Robespierre was sent to the guillotine by his colleagues, who were afraid that he was grasping too much power. Paine took this opportunity to make a direct appeal for his own release to the Committee of Public Safety. *The Age of Reason* had just been translated into French by a friend, François Lanthenas, who on August 6 at the author's specific request presented a copy of the pamphlet to Merlin de Thionville, chairman of the committee. Attached was a brief appeal written by Paine under Lanthénas's signature requesting the committee to reconsider the grounds on which the author had been imprisoned. On the same day Paine wrote a letter under his own name to the committee and sent a copy to the Convention at large. The letter never reached the floor of the Convention, but remained bottled up in the Committee of Public Safety. Conway has written that the members were sensitive to the fact they they had sent Robespierre to the guillotine on dubious grounds and did not want to call attention to their own 'crimes' by releasing a man who was Robespierre's self-proclaimed foe. This, however, stretches the truth and overemphasizes Paine's importance. The real facts speak for themselves: Every member of the Committee of Public Safety was fighting for his own security, and no one had the time to waste on a foreign gadfly who even if released from prison was in no position to help anyone else. So Paine's appeal was placed in a file and was immediately forgotten. At no time during the remainder of his imprisonment or, for that matter, after his release, did he receive a reply.

Meanwhile, on August 2, a new United States minister arrived in Paris to replace Gouverneur Morris. James Monroe, a tall, backwoods Virginia lawyer who had served as a captain in the Continental Line during the American Revolution, had impressive connections at home: He was highly regarded by Washington and was a protégé of Jefferson and a close friend of Madison. Even then, farseeing friends predicted that he might become President at some future time.

On August 28 the New American minister presented his

credentials to the Convention, and was granted the honor of hearing a number of speeches lauding France's noble ally. The event was duly reported in the press, and as copies of newspapers circulated freely in the Luxembourg Prison, Paine soon learned of America's latest representative in Paris. He immediately sat down and wrote Monroe a note asking for help.

Monroe did not reply to Paine's plea, perhaps because he had no idea what to say. Contrary to the claims of Conway and other nineteenth-century biographers of Paine, the United States Government had taken no firm stand of any kind on the matter of the author's citizenship. Was he American, British, or French? No one really knew. The new nation, struggling to establish her identity and to stand clear of Europe's complicated rivalries, was more concerned with her own survival than with that of the author who had done so much for her in her days of great need.

Paine waited a week and then wrote Monroe a second letter; again there was no reply. So Paine found another way to communicate with him:

As soon as I was able to write a note legible enough to be read, I found a way to convey one to him by means of the man who lighted the lamps in the prison, and whose unabated friendship to me, from whom he never received any service, and with difficulty accepted any recompense, puts the character of Mr Washington to shame. In a few days I received a message from Mr Monroe, conveyed in a note from an intermediate person, with assurances of his friendship, and expressing the desire that I should rest the case in his hands. After a fortnight or more had passed, and hearing nothing farther, I wrote to a friend, a citizen of Philadelphia, requesting him to inform me what was the true situation of things with respect to me. I was sure that something was the matter; and I began to have hard thoughts of Mr Washington, but I was unwilling to encourage them. In about ten days I received an answer to my letter, in which the writer says: 'Mr Monroe told me he had no order (meaning from the President, Mr Washington) respecting you, but that he (Mr Monroe) will do everything in his power to liberate you, but, from what I learn from the Americans lately arrived in Paris, you are not considered, either by the American government or by individuals, as an American citizen.'

Inasmuch as Gouverneur Morris had not yet left Paris, Paine immediately cast him as the villain. As a matter of fact, the above account indicates a measure of confusion on the author's part. Since he had previously sent two notes to Monroe, why should he have waited until he 'was able to write a note legible enough to be read' before sending the third? Also, since prisoners were permitted to correspond with those on the outside, provided the Luxembourg censors approved of their communications, why should Paine have found it necessary to send this third note via the man who lighted the prison lamps? It is difficult to resist concluding that Paine enjoyed dramatizing his situation somewhat.

Monroe was well aware of Paine's plight, but moved cautiously. The citizenship of the controversial prisoner was in doubt, and the new United States minister had no desire to place his own mission in jeopardy by taking a firm stand that he could not substantiate. At the same time, however, Monroe was a humanitarian and endowed with a sharp memory; he could not forget Paine's contributions to the cause of American independence, so he began to make discreet inquiries. If, for example, he found that various members of the Committee of Public Safety or officials of the Foreign Ministry regarded Paine as an American citizen, it would ease the task of winning his release from prison.

The anxious Paine, who knew nothing of the new minister's attitude and had little idea of what was taking place beyond the walls of the prison, wrote a 10,000-word 'Memorial to Monroe' outlining his position in detail. There was nothing new in these desperate arguments of a desperate man, but he discussed his plight in detail, then dwelled at length on the legal, moral, philosophical, and personal grounds why he should be released without delay. Afraid that he would remain imprisoned until he rotted or was sent without explanation to the guillotine, Paine summoned the last of his intellectual and physical powers in the preparation of the memorial.

On September 18, 1794, Monroe wrote to him for the first time. The minister confessed that the question of Paine's citizenship was confusing but expressed his determination to act on the assumption that the author was a citizen of the United States, adding:

> It is unnecessary for me to tell you how much all your countrymen, I speak of the great mass of the people, are interested in your welfare. They have not forgotten the history of their own revolution, and the difficult scenes through which they passed; nor do they review its several stages without reviving in their bosoms a due sensibility of the merits of those who served them in that great and arduous con-

flict. The crime of ingratitude has not yet stained, and I trust never will stain, our national character. You are considered by them, as not only having rendered important services in our revolution, but as being on a more extensive scale, the friend of human rights, and a distinguished and able advocate in favor of public liberty. To the welfare of Thomas Paine the Americans are not and cannot be indifferent. Of the sense which the President has always entertained of your merits, and of his friendly disposition towards you, you are too well assured to require any declaration of it from me. That I forward his wishes in seeking your safety is what I well know; and this will form an additional obligation on me to perform what I otherwise should consider as a duty.

You are, in my opinion, menaced by no kind of danger. To liberate you will be an object of my endeavors, and as soon as possible. But you must, until that event should be accomplished, face your situation with patience and fortitude; you will likewise have the justice to recollect, that I am placed here upon a difficult theatre, many important objects to attend to, and with few to consult. It becomes me in pursuit of those, to regulate my conduct in respect to each, as to the manner and the time, as will, in my judgment, be best calculated to accomplish the whole.

With great esteem and respect consider me personally your friend . . .

But a full month passed before the unhappy prisoner received the letter. Perhaps it was delayed by the censors or by other prison authorities. Certainly there can be no valid basis for Conway's claim that Gouverneur Morris, who did not leave France until mid-October, was in some way responsible.

The communication itself was a minor diplomatic masterpiece. Promising nothing and reserving the right to act according to the dictates his mission required, Monroe nevertheless flattered the worried prisoner and offered him at least some encouragement. Paine regarded the document as his salvation.

The hopes revived by Monroe's letter subsided again, however, when the weeks passed and he heard nothing more. During the early autumn of 1794 he fell into despair. He had placed his hopes in the new American minister, but Monroe seemed unable to do anything for him. Brooding in his damp cell, suffering from a physical ailment that today we call a bleeding stomach ulcer, and further punishing his body by drinking large quantities of brandy, Paine finally reached the conclusion that George Washington had turned against him. The American minister in Paris could do virtually nothing until he received specific instructions from his government, but the President remained silent, refusing to sign a brief letter that would open the gates of prison for the man he had called his friend.

Paine's notion was entirely the product of his fevered imagination and had no basis in fact. But Washington's seeming perfidy was so real to him then that he could never disabuse himself of the idea that his old friend had played him false.

On November 1, 1794, Monroe finally received the word he had awaited, contained in a letter from Edmund Jennings Randolph, who in December, 1793, had succeeded Jefferson as secretary of state. 'We have heard with regret,' Randolph wrote, 'that several of our citizens have been thrown into prison in France, from a suspicion of criminal attempts against the government. If they are guilty we are extremely sorry for it; if innocent, we must protect them.' Monroe, genuinely eager to help Paine, decided that this letter contained all the authorization he needed to proceed on his own initiative, and on the following day he sent a brief, firmly worded letter to the Committee of General Surety:

> The citizens of the United States cannot look back upon the time of their own revolution without recollecting among the names of their most distinguished patriots that of Thomas Paine; the services he rendered to his country in its struggle for freedom have implanted in the hearts of his countrymen a sense of gratitude never to be effaced as long as they shall deserve the title of a just and generous people.
>
> The above-named citizen is at this moment languishing in prison, affected with a disease growing more intense from his confinement. I beg, therefore, to call your attention to his condition and to request you to hasten the moment when the law shall decide his fate, in case of any accusation against him, and if none, to restore his liberty.
>
> Greetings and fraternity,
> MONROE

Once again the new minister demonstrated his talents as a diplomat. Carefully sidestepping the question of Paine's nationality, Monroe hinted strongly that the people of the United States thought of Paine as a fellow citizen but referred to Paine as 'the above-named citizen'. Whether he was a citizen of the United States or France was left unsaid. He made no mention whatever of the position, if any, taken by the State Department in the matter; this evasion was dictated by necessity, of course, as no specific ruling had yet been made.

Members of the committee appreciated this subtlety and were

grateful for the opportunity to save face. Neither they nor the Convention had been obliged to bow to a curt demand from another nation, particularly the ally whose existence owed so much to France. Those who had disliked Paine, including Robespierre – assuming it was true that he regarded the author as an enemy, a questionable thesis – were no longer alive. Also, the complaints of liberals in the United States and Great Britain to the effect that one of the most distinguished men of the era was being unjustly imprisoned had long been a source of embarrassment to the government of Revolutionary France.

On November 4, 1794, a scant forty-eight hours after receiving Monroe's letter, the Committee of General Surety ordered that 'Citizen Thomas Paine be set at liberty, and the seals taken from his papers'. The decree was not lacking in ironies. One of the eight members of the committee who signed it was Bentabole, the representative who had first moved that Paine be expelled from the Convention. The order removing the seals from the author's papers was meaningless because no seals had ever been placed on them. They had been examined and studied at great length by committees of experts and had been left unsealed, because in the opinion of the philosophers of the French Revolution nothing he had written was antipathetic to that cause.

Monroe reaffirmed his own opinions on the subject of Paine's citizenship in a letter to Secretary Randolph on November 7, in which he passed along the good news that the great propagandist had been set free:

He was actually a citizen of the United States, and of the United States only; for the Revolution which parted us from Great Britain broke the allegiance which was before due to the Crown, of all who took our side. He was, of course, not a British subject; nor was he strictly a citizen of France, for he came by invitation for the temporary purpose of assisting in the formation of their government only, and meant to withdraw to America when that should be completed. And what confirms this is the act of the Convention itself arresting him, by which he is declared a foreigner. Mr Paine pressed my interference. I told him I had hoped getting him enlarged without it; but, if I did interfere, it could only be by requesting that he be tried, in case there was any charge against him, and liberated in case there was not. This was admitted. His correspondence with me is lengthy and interesting, and I may probably be able hereafter to send you a copy of it. After some time had elapsed, without producing any change in his favor, I finally resolved to address the Committee of

Public Surety in his behalf, resting my application on the above principle. My letter was delivered by my Secretary in the Committee to the president, who assured him he would communicate its contents immediately to the Committee of Public Safety, and give me an answer as soon as possible. The conference took place accordingly between the two Committees, and, as I presume, on that night, or on the succeeding day; for on the morning of the day after . . . I was presented by the Secretary of the Committee of General Surety with an order for his enlargement. I forwarded it immediately to the Luxembourg, and had it carried into effect; and have the pleasure now to add that he is not only released to the enjoyment of liberty, but is in good spirits.

Thanks to James Monroe's adroit diplomatic footwork the French government was relieved of a burden that had clouded her relations with well-wishers in the English-speaking countries. And after spending ten months and nine days in prison Thomas Paine was again a free man.

19

The Age of Reason

By the end of January, 1794, Part One of *The Age of Reason* was ready for publication, and Joel Barlow obligingly sent it off to a printer in London. Another copy went to a Parisian friend, François Lanthenas, who painstakingly translated it into French, and that edition appeared in August.

According to Thomas Rickman, Paine immediately went to work on Part Two of the work, laboring on it prior to his illness and returning to the task as soon as possible after his recovery. But the bookseller was mistaken. Paine was too weak to work after his fever, and his emotional depression was so great that he was unable to do any serious writing. Furthermore, he made frequent, detailed references to the Bible in Part Two, and the jailers of the French Revolution did not allow prisoners to keep copies of the Bible in their possession.

Paine used a copy of the King James Version that was the property of his friend James Monroe, who was his host immediately after his release from prison. So it is safe to say categorically that the author did virtually no work on Part Two until he had been released from prison. Most of it was written to refute the charges of his critics.

Although half-forgotten in a more sophisticated time, *The Age of Reason* became the best-known of all of Paine's works in his own lifetime and probably caused the most furor. Some of his contemporaries even said that he was fortunate to have been in prison when it was published, because he might have been lynched by outraged mobs had he been free.

Until Paine's *Age of Reason* appeared few people in Great Britain, France, or the United States were acquainted with deism. Paine's function here, as it had been in the political sphere, was principally that of a propagandist; *The Age of Reason* was read by many hundreds of thousands of persons who had been totally unaware of deist convictions and arguments. In effect, he ripped away the verbose, intellectual rationalizations of the deist philosophers and explained their fundamental beliefs to people who took religion for granted.

Deism originated before the Enlightenment as a philosophical approach to religion grounded in the belief that God exists but does not influence the actions of men. The first deist writer of consequence is generally believed to have been Lord Herbert of Cherbury, who lived from 1583 to 1648. The deist movement, which later became more or less incorporated into the Unitarian Church, reached a high point during the first half of the eighteenth century, when the influence of the Age of Reason was at its peak. Henry St John, Viscount Bolingbroke, was the most important deist writer of the period.

Later in the century deism was introduced into the German states, and its influence was felt in the upper classes in America. Benjamin Franklin was an enthusiastic, articulate deist, and the first three Presidents of the United States – Washington, John Adams, and Jefferson – regarded themselves as deists. Jefferson wrote extensively on the subject; most of his work appeared subsequent to the publication of Paine's pamphlets, but his own thinking was already formed, and it is unlikely that he was influenced by his friend's views.

The deists believed in God but denied that the Almighty took an active part in the affairs of man. God was the Supreme Creator and the Supreme Intelligence, the force that had made the

217

world; thereafter He withdrew allowing man to make his own life by either obeying or defying the laws of nature. The deists offered purely and exclusively rational proofs that God existed. They based these largely on the findings of the English Enlightenment's greatest scientist, Isaac Newton, whose devoutly Christian theological convictions they conveniently ignored. They were opposed to all religious ceremony and believed that man had been confused and misled by the clergy, who were themselves misguided. Most deists did not accept the Christian doctrine that Christ was God, but held him in the same regard as Moses, Buddha, Mohammed, and other spiritual leaders. Good deists viewed miracles as mere superstition, and they rejected whatever was denied by reason and logic.

Paine's reasons for writing *The Age of Reason* were manifold. In both Great Britain and France he had observed that the bulk of the clergy allied themselves with the reactionaries and resisted social and political change of any kind. In his opinion they were conspiring with the monarchists to preserve the *status quo* at the expense of the common man. But now in France there was a new element of concern that stirred him. The excesses of the Revolution were making atheists of the people, and something definitive had to be done to reverse this trend. *The Age of Reason* was not intended primarily as an assault on organized religion. Paine regarded it as the affirmation of his faith and consequently of all true faith, the only faith to which a thinking man could adhere. Part One opens with what he called 'The Author's Profession of Faith'.*

As several of my colleagues, and others of my fellow-citizens of France, have given me the example of making their voluntary and individual profession of faith, I also will make mine; and I do this with all that sincerity and frankness with which the mind of man communicates with itself.

I believe in one God, and no more; and I hope for happiness beyond this life.

I believe in the equality of man and I believe that religious duties consist in doing justice, loving mercy, and endeavoring to make our fellow-creatures happy.

But, lest it should be supposed that I believe many other things in addition to these, I shall, in the progress of this work, declare the things I do not believe, and my reasons for not believing them.

* See Appendix, pages 326-328, for complete text.

The Age of Reason

In the largest sense *The Age of Reason* is a logical sequel to *The Rights of Man*. In the earlier work he was demanding political freedom, while in the later work he was saying that man could not be completely free until he rid himself of the religious superstitions of the past, which bound and gagged him as much as political oppression.

Certainly Paine had no idea that his two deist pamphlets would cause him to be vilified and attacked as never before; but even such fore-knowledge would not have deterred him. As he saw it, the truth was paramount at all times and in all matters relating to man, and he felt obligated to tell it regardless of the consequences. Other deists were less violent in their beliefs and unlike Paine did not see the world in such clearly black-and-white terms. Although Paine believed himself the most reasonable and logical of men, *The Age of Reason* revealed his own prejudices. Apparently it did not occur to him that attacking the religious convictions of others was not the same thing, either in principle or in practice, as assaulting others' political views. The philosophers of deism had been graceful thinkers and writers, men who confined the expression of their opinions to the abstract. Paine, the self-appointed popular champion of deism, with the fury of the born iconoclast smashed the concepts he regarded as idolatrous. Here was the eighteenth-century Don Quixote at his best – or worst. Lacking all compassion for organized religions, refusing to believe in their accomplishments, he flailed at them without mercy or tact.

His worst mistake was his failure to understand that he was decrying what most people in Western civilization held sacred. Reason might move them to change their political opinions, but their faith in God, as they conceived of Him, could not be swayed by mere argument. It is no wonder that he antagonized the overwhelming majority of the many hundreds of thousands who read either portion of *The Age of Reason*.*

Not satisfied with attacking and ridiculing basic Christian tenets, Paine went even farther. The Christian Church, he said, 'have erected their fable, which, for absurdity and extravagance, is not exceeded by any thing that is to be found in the mythology of the ancients'. In fact, he added, most of the base of Christianity is an outgrowth of old Greek and Roman mythology. Having made his point repeatedly, he then drove it home with shocking

* See Appendix, pages 328-330, for excerpts from Part One.

219

bluntness: 'Putting aside everything that might excite laughter by its absurdity, or detestation by its profaneness, and confining ourselves merely to an examination of the parts, it is impossible to conceive a story more derogatory to the Almighty, more inconsistent with His wisdom, more contradictory to His power, than this story is.'

Paine assaulted the Old Testament with equal vigor and scorn. He ridiculed the Creation of the world as the account was given in Genesis, and said that Moses, who 'was not an Israelite', refused to have his name attached to such a story. Occasionally he became vituperative: 'Whenever we read the obscene stories, the voluptuous debaucheries, the cruel and torturous executions, the unrelenting vindictiveness, with which more than half the Bible is filled, it would be more consistent that we called it the word of a demon than the Word of God. It is a history of wickedness that has served to corrupt and brutalize mankind; and, for my part, I sincerely detest it as I detest everything that is cruel.'

Pointing out what he regarded as errors of language in the Bible, Paine emphasized that the meaning of words is constantly changing. In addition, he declared, translators, copyists, and printers make mistakes which, 'together with the possibility of willful alteration, are of themselves evidence that the human language, whether in speech or in print, cannot be the vehicle of the Word of God. The Word of God exists in something else'. That something, he insisted, was not the Bible. In fact, he continued, 'When I see throughout the greater part of this book scarcely anything but a history of the grossest vices, and a collection of the most paltry and contemptible tales, I cannot dishonor my Creator by calling it by His Name.'

The New Testament fared no better at Paine's hands, and he mocked the very name: 'The *New* Testament! that is the *new* will, as if there could be two wills of the Creator.' Had Christ intended to establish a new religion, Paine said, 'he would undoubtedly have written the system himself, or procured it to be written in his lifetime.' But there is no publication extant that is authenticated by his name. All of the books were written after his death. The Gospels, he declared, do not give a history of the life of Jesus, 'but only detached anecdotes of him'. He called Saint Paul, whose authorship of the books bearing his name Paine questioned, 'that manufacturer of quibbles'. He questioned Paul's theological teachings, too, saying that he was a founder of a religion 'interlarded with quibble, subterfuge and pun'. And such a religion, he added, 'has a tendency to instruct its professors in the practise of these arts'. The doctrine of redemption, Paine insisted, 'was originally fabricated on purpose'. The reason seemed obvious to him: The Christian churches of various faiths became wealthy by charging the faithful money for their own redemption.

Using eighteenth-century scientific discoveries to substantiate his arguments he said that both Judaism and Christianity were based on ancient pagan superstitions, and that Christianity was in fact pantheistic. He refused to believe that human life exists only on the planet Earth, and in almost the same breath he decried what he termed the contradictory claims of the many religions practiced on this planet.

Paine reserved some of his more sardonic observations for the stories of miracles in both the Old and New Testaments:

> The story of the whale swallowing Jonah, though a whale is large enough to do it, borders greatly on the marvelous; but it would have approached nearer to the idea of a miracle if Jonah had swallowed the whale. In this, which may serve for all cases of miracles, the matter would decide itself, as before stated, namely, is it more probable that a man should have swallowed a whale or told a lie?
>
> But suppose that Jonah had really swallowed the whale, and gone with it in his belly to Nineveh and, to convince the people that it was true, had cast it up in their sight, of the full length and size of a whale, would they not have believed him to be the devil instead of a prophet? Or, if the whale had carried Jonah to Nineveh, and cast him up in the same public manner, would they not have believed the whale to have been the devil, and Jonah one of his imps?
>
> The most extraordinary of all the things called miracles, related in the New Testament, is that of the devil flying away with Jesus Christ, and carrying him to the top of a high mountain, and to the top of the highest pinnacle in the temple, and showing him and promising to him all the kingdoms of the World. How happened it that he did not discover America, or is it only with *kingdoms* that his sooty highness has any interest?
>
> I have too much respect for the moral character of Christ to believe that he told this whale of a miracle himself; neither is easy to account for what purpose it could have been fabricated, unless it were to impose on the connoiseurs of miracles.

God-fearing Britons and Americans reacted violently to Part One of *The Age of Reason*, and even many of Paine's supporters in both countries were shocked. Jefferson and other deists were privately chagrined, believing that the crude vehemence of his attack on organized religion would do their own cause more harm than good. The author was denounced from hundreds of pulpits, and there were few who defended him. He thought that he lost President Washington's friendship because of the pamphlet.

The reaction of the French is more difficult to judge. The French edition was published in August, 1794. There were no public condemnations of the work, for any citizen of France who was devout in his religious convictions knew that the guillotine awaited him if he expressed his beliefs aloud. When it was called to the attention of members of the Committee of Public Safety, they began to wonder for the first time whether it might be wise to release him from prison.

Much of the criticism directed at Paine in the United States and Great Britain concentrated on his many inaccuracies regarding events related in the Bible. Paine, who was mildly surprised but in no way dismayed by the increase in the ranks of his enemies, replied in the introduction to Part Two that he had written the first pamphlet without recourse to the Bible. He had worked from memory, he said, because no copy of the Scriptures had been available to him at the time. In the preparation of Part Two he kept a copy of the Bible at his elbow as he wrote.

As usual, opposition whetted Paine's appetite for combat, and his assault on Christianity and Judaism, particularly the former, became even more emphatic in Part Two of *The Age of Reason*.

In *The Rights of Man* a wiser Thomas Paine had tolerantly written, 'Every religion is good that teaches man to be good, and I know of none that instructs him to be bad.' He saw no contradiction of that stand in his *Age of Reason* attacks and later tried to counter them by insisting that he had announced his own creed, a belief in God, in the preamble. The argument lacked conviction.

Moses, he said in Part Two, was the supposed author of the Pentateuch, but it had been proved that these Books were written some hundreds of years after his time. The Book of Isaiah made no sense at all. He agreed with Spinoza that the Book of Job, which he liked, had been written by a Greek, not a Hebrew; he based this view on the fact that the astronomical observations were Greek rather than Israelite in origin. Ecclesiastes, he said, consisted of the 'solitary reflections of a worn-out debauchee . . . who, looking back on scenes he can no longer enjoy, cries out, "All is vanity".' He showed contempt for the Book of Ruth, calling it a 'foolish' story about 'a strolling country-girl, creeping slyly to bed with her cousin Boaz'.

He was even more devastating in his attacks on the New Testament and delighted in pointing out contradictions and discrepancies in the Gospels. For example, he said that the genealogies of Christ in Matthew and Luke showed only two names in common. He reserved much of his thunder for the Epistles of Paul, who, he said contemptuously, tried to prove doctrine by argument. He cited the doctrine of the Resurrection as the prime example and contradicted Paul, declaring that the same body, if resurrected, would die again. For himself, he remarked dryly, he would prefer a better body. In any event, he declared, man's continued and continuing existence depended on his consciousness, not his body.

The full weight of his scorn was directed at the influence of Christianity, which he termed pernicious. The faith, he said, rested on 'three pillars: the fire, the sword, and the faggot'. Millions had been faced with the choice of becoming Christians or perishing. Loving one's enemies, he said, was a hypocritical doctrine, and he refused to accept it. He did not advocate returning evil for evil, but saw no reason why one should reward a bad deed by performing a good deed in return. Summarizing his views, he remained firm:

> The opinions I have advanced . . . are the effect of the most clear and long-established conviction that the Bible and the Testament are impositions upon the world, that the fall of man, the account of Jesus Christ being the Son of God, and of his dying to appease the wrath of God, and of salvation by that strange means are all fabulous inventions, dishonorable to the wisdom and power of the Almighty; that the only true religion is Deism, by which I . . . mean the belief of one God, and an imitation of His moral character, or the practice of what are called moral virtues – and that it was upon this only (so far as religion is concerned) that I rested all my hopes of happiness hereafter. So I say now – and so help me God.

Viewed as an expression of philosophy, there is nothing new in *The Age of Reason*; Shaftesbury and Bolingbroke had said the same thing, and so had Voltaire and Diderot. But they had taken their stand on a high and sometimes convoluted intellectual level. What was startling about Paine's two pamphlets was his blunt vituperation, written in plain language that the common man could understand. He was the first author of consequence to state flatly and without equivocation that the Bible was not the Word of God. Moreover, the title effectively summed up his century in a catchphrase that has endured, recognized even today by thousands who have never read the work.

Men of many denominations raced to the defense of the faith; scores of blistering replies to Paine were published in both the United States and Great Britain, some in the form of newspaper letters, others in printed pamphlets. By far the most popular of the latter was *An Apology for the Bible*, written by an Anglican bishop, Richard Watson, and published in 1796. Active members of the Anglican Church saw to it that virtually every literate man and woman in the British Isles received a free copy of the Watson pamphlet.

They erred in their zealousness. Watson made frequent references to *The Age of Reason*, quoting it at length, and there were many who had not previously heard of Paine's work but who consequently became interested in it. The London Corresponding Society, a majority of whose members were deists, persuaded a printer, Thomas Williams, to publish a cheap edition of the Paine pamphlets, and then distributed them all over Great Britain. In 1797 the Crown brought action against Williams, charging that he had published a blasphemous work. By ironic coincidence the prosecutor was Thomas Erskine, the attorney who had defended Paine in his sedition trial. Writing an open letter to him, Paine remarked that 'it is difficult to know when a lawyer is to be believed'. Then, repeating his conviction that the Bible was not the Word of God, he argued that until he was *proved* wrong there could be no legitimate grounds for the charge of blasphemy. The Bible, he asserted, was filled with ambiguities, contradictions, and immoralities, and this proved it could *not* be the Word of God. He added:

What! does not the Creator of the Universe, the Fountain of all Wisdom, the origin of all Science, the Author of all Knowledge, the God of Order and of Harmony, know how to write? When we contemplate the vast economy of the creation, when we behold the unerring regularity of the visible solar system . . . – when we trace the power of a creator, from a mite to an elephant, from an atom to an universe – can we suppose that the mind that could conceive such a design, and the power that executed it with incomparable perfection, cannot write without inconsistence, or that a book so written can be the work of such a power?

Every man's religion should be a private matter between himself and his Creator, Paine told Erskine, and no third party, such as a government or a prosecutor, had a right to interfere. Religious worship was a sacred duty, he insisted, but this should 'not be confounded with Christianity'.

Paine's adamant stand was courageous, but it lacked discretion. Until the publication of *The Age of Reason* Paine had enjoyed universal high regard in America and had been widely admired in Great Britain. Now people began to turn away from him in vast numbers; the publication of Part Two in 1795 marked the beginning of his decline in public favor.

At first glance it appears that either Paine or the times had changed, but this was not the case. His following – in America, in Great Britain, and even in France – had been essentially middle class. The bourgeoisie had been ripe for political change, ready to experiment. Monarchy had failed in the New World and in France, and there were many in Britain who saw the deficiencies of their system of government; so Paine's revolutionary political ideas had found favor. In matters of religion, however, a far different situation existed. The United States and Great Britain were essentially God-fearing countries. The middle class was firm in its devotions to God; people were totally unprepared for a violent attack that contradicted the essence of their most closely held convictions.

In France matters were somewhat more complicated. The Revolution there had officially terminated all ties with the Roman Catholic Church, which had been banned. But a decree declaring that the nation was now atheistic did not make her people less religious. Neither the middle class nor the peasants could worship openly, to be sure, but they clung to their religious convictions in private, and the failure of the Revolution can be traced, at least in part, to the abolition of religion. Similarly Napoleon was able to consolidate his power because, among other reasons, he permitted the return of religious worship.

Thomas Paine's great error was his belief that people would follow him down the radical road in religion as they had in politics. But he had struck a more sensitive chord there, and his followers resisted, then turned away in anger and disgust. Unlike Napoleon he failed to differentiate between politics and religion, and he paid a heavy price for his mistake.

20

A Reputation Restored

Before going to his old lodgings or seeking a new place to live after his release from the Luxembourg Prison, Paine went to the residence of James Monroe to thank the American minister for his intervention, and promptly collapsed on the stoop. His emotional state may have been partly responsible for his condition, but a physician summoned by Mrs Monroe quickly confirmed that the author's health had deteriorated in prison. He had never regained his strength after overcoming his severe bout of fever, and his bleeding ulcer was causing him great distress.

At the insistence of the minister and Mrs Monroe, Paine was put to bed in a guest room located on the top floor of their official residence, and there he stayed for the next month, cared for by his hostess and her two young daughters and pampered as never before in his life. Monroe visited the invalid each day, and the two men gradually formed a close friendship that would last until the end of Paine's life. Of all great Americans who came to know the author well, Monroe seemed to understand him best. Monroe, himself meticulous, could overlook his friend's slovenliness, unfailingly cheered him when he became depressed, and influenced him so much that Paine drank with moderation when in the minister's presence. Monroe, who was thirty-six, had been deeply impressed by *Common Sense* and the *Crisis* pamphlets in his youth, and his open admiration speeded his guest's recovery. Paine's battered ego healed more quickly than did his stomach condition, and he was soon in high spirits again.

He and his host both enjoyed reports that appeared in a number of English newspapers to the effect that Paine had been executed by the French. According to this story he had died on September 1, 1794, and had gone to the guillotine carrying a copy of *The Rights of Man* in his hand. The account even included his supposed last words: 'Ye numerous spectators gathered around, pray give ear to my last words; I am determined to speak the Truth in these my last moments, altho' I have written and spoken nothing but lies all my life. Alas! too late have I discovered the error of my ways. Too late have I learned that those who preach violence and the overturning of the established order must themselves die violently. In these final moments of my life I can but regret any disrespectful hatred toward the Crown, the Church of England and other Churches that I may have been responsible for promulgating. The institutions created by man over many centuries have survived because they are right and just; their destruction creates the tyranny that encompasses France, and the guillotine that will take my life has become the symbol of the worst oppression man can visit upon man. I go to my Maker knowing I was mistaken in all that I believed, and I can but pray that He will forgive my trespasses.'

An enlarged version of this fanciful statement soon appeared in pamphlet form. In it Paine supposedly confessed that he was an archtraitor, and his ghost-writer specifically repudiated many of the major theses he had advocated over a period of two decades. A copy of this curious document came into Paine's possession and became a treasured memento. In the margin he indicated his editorial opinion of the style. 'Flowery,' he said severely, or 'abstruce.' In one section his exasperation overcame his amusement and he wrote in a bold hand, 'Never have I written like this!' He wanted to send letters to the newspapers that published the story of his death and to track down the author and printer of the pamphlet, but Monroe dissuaded him. It would be far better, the minister said, to permit the fact that he was alive speak for itself. Paine agreed but continued to collect accounts of his execution.

When he became convalescent, he wanted to find a place of his own and so relieve the Monroes of the burden imposed on them by his presence under their roof. But his host and hostess insisted that he remain with them until his recovery was complete, and he spent most of the winter of 1794–95 with them.

His political rehabilitation was even more rapid than his physical recovery. Many French friends visited him at the American minister's house, telling him that the Terror was passing, that a new era was dawning in Revolutionary France. Almost without exception they urged him to resume an active role in the affairs of state. Paine was flattered, but the long months he had spent in prison made him cautious, and he refused to commit himself.

His friends took it upon themselves to act on his behalf, and on December 7, 1794, Antoine Clare Thibaudeau, long an admirer of Paine's philosophy, made a brief, impassioned speech on the floor of the Convention, every pause punctuated by heavy applause:

It yet remains for the Convention to perform an act of justice. I reclaim one of the most zealous defenders of liberty – Thomas Paine. My reclamation is for a man who has honored his age by his energy in the defence of the rights of humanity, and who is so gloriously distinguished by his part in the American revolution. A naturalized Frenchman by a decree of the legislative assembly, he was nominated by the people. It was only by an intrigue that he was driven from the Convention, the pretext being a decree excluding foreigners from representing the French people. There were only two foreigners in the Convention; one is dead, and I speak not of him, but of Thomas Paine, who powerfully contributed to establish liberty in a country allied with the French Republic. I demand that he be recalled to the bosom of the Convention!

Standing applause greeted the address, and Paine's seat was restored to him by acclamation. Then, in an attempt to make reparations to a man who had been treated harshly, the Convention voted Paine, a literary pension for the contributions that *Common Sense* and *The Rights of Man* had made to the French Revolution.

Paine's funds had dwindled and the possible sources of his future income were uncertain, but his pride intervened and he refused the pension. On one occasion he remarked to Monroe that the French were more generous than the United States Congress. But the minister convinced him that he still enjoyed an enormous popularity in America.

This picture was not as accurate as Monroe himself may have wished. Many Americans were shocked by *The Age of Reason*. Paine's enumeration of the inconsistencies in the Bible persuaded them that he was an atheist, regardless of his avowal of deist beliefs. Consequently there was a growing aversion to him in the United States, where men of all faiths took their religion seriously. Paine himself had miscalculated when he had thought that *The Age of Reason* would be welcome in his adopted land. He knew how to arouse the support of Americans for a political cause, but he failed to realize that many of the colonies had been founded by religious enthusiasts and that there was no deeper strain in American life than the faith of her people in God.

Monroe, perhaps suspecting that Paine's position in the United States was eroding, made an attempt to bolster his position there. France was planning to send a special envoy to America to arrange for an expansion of the Treaty of Friendship and Commerce between the two countries, and on January 4, 1795, the minister wrote to the Committee of Public Safety urging that the post be given to Paine. He even suggested that the appointment be made in secret so the British would not try to capture the distinguished author when he sailed to New York.

Only the Convention could grant a passport to one of its own members, and that body, meeting behind closed doors, declined to give Paine the appointment or grant him a passport for the purpose. 'The position he holds will not permit him to accept it,' Monroe was told in the official reply. The actual reason was not mentioned, but it appeared that members of the Convention were afraid that Paine would remain in America once he reached its friendly shores. His presence in France was badly needed to bolster the image of a government whose violent excesses had caused many abroad to turn from it in disgust. So, regardless of whether Paine became active in the Convention again, he was required to remain in France.

The Foreign Office was negotiating peace treaties with both Great Britain and Spain, and Paine became interested for the sake of the United States. He sent two letters to the Foreign Ministry in his capacity as a member of the Convention, one urging that a treaty with Britain include guarantees that American commerce would be respected. The other, which was even longer, requested that peace with Spain be made contingent on an iron-clad promise that Spain would grant complete freedom of Shipping to the United States on the Mississippi River.

It was too late for Paine to influence the preparation of the treaty with Britain; negotiations with London had already been concluded. The French envoys did make an effort in the talks with Spain to include a guarantee that the Mississippi River would be kept open, but the representatives of Madrid resisted, and the French, who had nothing to gain themselves by the inclusion of such a clause, let the matter drop.

Paine's physical recovery was hampered by an abscess in his side that failed to drain properly. He found it difficult to make his way to the second-floor dining room for his meals and made no attempt to leave the Monroe house. Virtually cut off from the outside world, he spent much of his time brooding, in spite of the efforts of the Monroe family and his French visitors to cheer him. He was still obsessed with the false notion that President Washington, whom he had regarded as one of his closest and most loyal friends, had abandoned him and was totally indifferent to his fate. Monroe could not clear his guest's mind of this imagined grievance. Washington was a perfidious, treacherous man, he said, and his popularity in the United States was undeserved. Sooner or later the truth would have to be presented to the American people.

Why did the President fail to intervene personally on Paine's behalf? There is no clear answer to the question, but a number of Washington's biographers have indicated that he well may not have known of Paine's situation. Even if he did hear that his one-time colleague had been imprisoned, there was no reason for him to believe that Paine's life was in danger. No one in the United States, even at the highest levels of the new government, realized the extent to which the French Revolution was indulging in excesses.

The problem posed by Paine's citizenship was difficult, too. He had been an American citizen by virtue of his contribution to her Revolution, but now he was a self-proclaimed citizen of another nation, taking an active part in her political life and sitting in her Convention, her supreme legislative body. Even if

Washington had been made aware of Paine's precarious situation, and there is no evidence extant to suggest he knew of it, the President of the United States would have had to proceed with delicacy in such a complex matter, particularly when dealing with a nation that had been America's best friend.

Paine, believing that all who were not aggressively for him were against him, seized on Washington's inactivity on his behalf as 'proof' that the President had become his personal enemy. But this enmity existed only in Paine's mind.

Paine spent several hours each day writing Part Two of *The Age of Reason*. His physical weakness made it impossible for him to write at his customary swift pace, but the work progressed steadily, and by the spring of 1795 it was ready to be sent off to a London printer. Even though the publication of Part One had created a storm of controversy, it apparently had not occurred to the author that Part Two would further offend many who had been his friends and would cause him to lose stature throughout the English-speaking world.

Now in his fifty-eighth year and still convalescing, Paine looked twenty years older and walked with an old man's shuffle. Although he had announced to Thibaudeau after being restored to the Convention that he intended to depart for America in the spring, he postponed sailing, explaining to Monroe that for the present he could do more to foster Franco-American relations if he remained in Paris. He was free now, able to go where he pleased, but a strange lethargy seemed to possess him, and he drifted almost without purpose.

In the spring of 1795 he became strong enough to leave the Monroe house, and for the first time he returned to the Convention. There he sat on a back bench, listening to the debates but taking no active part in them. Although he had not yet learned to speak more than a smattering of French, he had learned enough of the language to make out the import of the discussions. By this time he had lost faith in the future of the French Revolution, and when interest in a new constitution was revived he predicted to Monroe that France would never adopt a truly republican constitution but would always lean toward one incorporating a monarchy. France, he believed, would neither duplicate nor translate into its own terms the successful American experiment in establishing a new type of government.

In fact, his experience in prison had made him even more cynical than he had been. Some years later, when discussing this period of his life he said, 'They first voted me out of the Convention for being a foreigner, then imprisoned me on the ground of being a foreigner, then voted me in again by annulling the vote that had declared me a foreigner.' Certainly he seemed somewhat lost, and lacked a specific objective. He was the professional revolutionist who, for the moment, had no revolution to foster, and had he not been living under Monroe's watchful eye he well might have turned again to liquor.

France at that time was considering the adoption of a new constitution that, as he had predicted, might open the door to an eventual restoration of the monarchy, and Paine was furious. He wrote a new pamphlet to sway public opinion against the proposal and worked so long and arduously that he further damaged his already precarious health. He called this work *A Dissertation on First Principles of Government*, and he repeated many of his now-familiar arguments, using the errors of the French Revolution to prove his points. His attack was forthright:

Had a Constitution been established two years ago, as ought to have been done, the violences that have since desolated France and injured the character of the revolution, would, in my opinion, have been prevented. The nation would have had a bond of union, and every individual would have known the line of conduct he was to follow. But, instead of this, a revolutionary government, a thing without either principle or authority, was substituted in its place; virtue or crime depended upon accident, and that which was patriotism one day, became treason the next. All these things have followed from want of a Constitution; for it is the nature and intention of a Constitution to prevent governing by party, by establishing a common principle that shall limit and control the power and impulse of party, and that says to all parties, Thus far shalt thou go, and no farther. But in the absence of a Constitution men look entirely to party; and instead of principle governing party, party governs principle.

An avidity to punish is always dangerous to liberty. It leads men to stretch, to misinterpret and to misapply even the best of laws. He that would make his own liberty secure, must guard even his enemy from oppression for if he violates this duty, he establishes a precedent that will reach himself.*

Paine's principles remained firm and unyielding; his own experience in prison and his physical suffering had convinced him

* See Appendix, pages 330–331, for further excerpts.

that all would be lost if man abandoned principle for expediency. His belief in a constitutional, republican form of government was almost mystical.

In none of his earlier political pamphlets had Paine been more cogent and lucid. Had the *Dissertation* been published in the United States it would have been monumentally effective, just as it would have created a furor in Great Britain. A French translation, however, had almost no effect on the people, sold poorly, and was virtually ignored. A few moderates – all intellectuals – hailed it and praised the author, but the literate book-buyers of Paris and the provinces merely shrugged.

Paine's great error in dealing with the French was his assumption that all nations were fundamentally similar. This conviction grew out of the almost identical approaches, intellectual and emotional, taken by Britons and Americans. Apparently it did not occur to the busy Paine that the Anglo-Saxons shared the same heritage as the Americans, that the English Bill of Rights was regarded as sacred on both sides of the Atlantic, and that both nations spoke the same political language when they used such words as liberty.

The Gallic heritage was far different. Even that most cynical of iconoclasts Voltaire, who had so daringly espoused the cause of freedom, had been a devoted monarchist, a man who had been flattered by invitations to the courts of Louis XV and Frederick the Great. In brief, the French had no idea of what Paine was talking about, and his logical pleas for equal rights fell on deaf ears. Free for the first time in their history because of the Revolution, the French were groping their way toward the establishment of a government that would grant liberty in a manner suitable to the Gallic temperament – a painful process that still would not be completed almost two centuries afterward.

The failure of the French to heed his words of advice embittered Paine. He was outraged by the terms of the proposed constitution submitted to the Convention at the end of June, 1795. Only those who paid direct taxes or army veterans who had served in one or more campaigns would be granted the franchise. At least half of the potential voters in the country would be denied the ballot. On July 7 Paine broke his long silence, appearing in the Convention to deliver a speech on the subject. He made his way to the podium slowly, leaning heavily on his gold-handled cane; he was so out of breath when he finally climbed the steps that the president urged that he not read his speech, as he had intended, but that they proceed without delay to the clerk's reading of the French translation. Paine, who looked as though he might faint, readily agreed. The effects of a malignant fever contracted in prison had prevented him from attending to his duties in the Convention, he declared, but the matter now before the body was of such magnitude that regardless of his health he could remain silent no longer. He proceeded to defend his own record as a champion of liberty and made it clear that in spite of his persecution and imprisonment by political enemies he bore no grudge against the innocent people of France. Finally, he declared, the proposed constitution would 'subvert the basis of the Revolution' and would 'extinguish the enthusiasm which has hitherto been the life and soul' of the Revolution. He presented all of his familiar arguments in favor of universal enfranchisement of the electorate, and his address was greeted with perfunctory applause.

Neither his correspondence nor that of any of his contemporaries indicates whether Paine realized that nothing he said would have the slightest influence on the decision of the Convention. Perhaps, in his innocence of the intricacies of French politics he actually believed that the members of the Convention might heed his words. In that event he failed to understand that the fundamental nature of the Revolution had changed: that the French people as well as the men who represented them longed for a return to a more orderly, conservative form of government that would nevertheless continue to uphold the principles of liberty, equality, and fraternity, the original goals of the Revolution.

Paine's speech failed to change even a single vote, and the constitution he opposed was adopted by an overwhelming majority. This ended Paine's active political career in France on a dismal note, although he always asserted that he had remained true to his principles, which was accurate if not consoling.

The National Convention itself was disbanded in October, 1795, when the Directory was formed, and Paine retired to private life, never again to hold public office in France, or, for that matter, anywhere else. His friends, James Monroe among them, thought the fifty-eight-year-old Paine was dying; but Paine proved that his recuperative powers were greater than anyone suspected and that his days as an energetic and outspoken advocate of human liberty were far from ended.

21

George Washington, My Enemy

Late in the summer of 1795 Thomas Paine suffered a relapse so severe that his friends were afraid for his life. In September James Monroe wrote that the author could not survive for more than another month or two. Paine himself believed that he would die soon and that no care he might exercise would save him. Anxious to complete his work before he expired, he plunged back into his writing, recklessly ignoring his health.

His principal concern was *The Age of Reason*, which he regarded as his most important work. Dissatisfied with Part Two, he cast aside most of what he had written and began again. In all of his many pamphlets, articles, and essays, he had never before made sweeping revisions of what he had already put on paper. He believed that *The Age of Reason* was his legacy to mankind and was determined to polish it until it 'gleamed like a beacon light for the centuries to come'.

His poor health and the strains that he placed on it made him increasingly morbid, and his state of mind was undoubtedly responsible for his increasing hostility to George Washington. The President's failure to write to him bothered him more and more and by the autumn of 1795 became an obsession. What Paine appeared incapable of realizing was that the first President of the United States was ever conscious of his own position and of any precedents he might create. He believed that it would have been improper for him to intervene directly in the case of a man whose citizenship was questionable and who had been imprisoned by the government of France. Moreover, Washington had no time to spare for personal correspondence, and Paine was not the only friend he was forced to neglect. The demands on the President's energies were enormous, constant, and pressing, and the difficulties he faced during his second term forced him to devote himself exclusively to his duties.

Paine only knew that the man he had considered his good friend was ignoring him, and the author's sense of bitter frustration became intensified. Early in 1795 he wrote a letter to Washington, ostensibly to congratulate him on his sixty-third birthday, but Monroe persuaded him not to send it, chiefly because his attacks on Gouverneur Morris and John Jay, the United States minister to England, had created a new anti-Paine feeling in the United States. The passages of this unmailed letter that chastise the President accurately reflect Paine's attitude toward him:

> As it is always painful to reproach those one would wish to respect, it is not without some difficulty that I have taken the resolution to write you. The danger to which I have been exposed cannot have been unknown to you, and the guarded silence you have observed upon the circumstance, is what I ought not to have expected from you, either as a friend or as a President of the United States.
>
> You knew enough of my character to be assured that I could not have deserved imprisonment in France, and without knowing anything more than this, you had sufficient ground to have taken some interest for my safety. Every motive arising from recollection ought to have suggested to you the consistency of such a measure. But I cannot find that you have so much as directed any enquiry to be made whether I was in prison or at liberty, dead or alive; what the cause of that imprisonment was, or whether there was any service or assistance you could render. Is this what I ought to have expected from America after the part I had acted towards her? Or will it redound to her honor or to your's that I tell the story?

I do not hesitate to say that you have not served America with more fidelity, or greater zeal, or greater disinterestedness, than myself, and perhaps with not better effect. After the revolution of America had been established, you rested at home to partake its advantages, and I ventured into new scenes of difficulty to extend the principles which that revolution had produced. In the progress of events you beheld yourself a president in America and me a prisoner in France; you folded your arms, forgot your friend, and became silent.

As everything I have been doing in Europe was connected with my wishes for the prosperity of America, I ought to be the more surprised at this conduct on the part of her government. It leaves me but one mode of explanation, which is, that everything is not as it ought to be amongst you, and that the presence of a man who might disapprove, and who had credit enough with the country to be heard and believed, was not wished for. This was the operating motive of the despotic faction that imprisoned me in France (though the pretence was, that I was a foreigner); and those that have been silent towards me in America, appear to have acted from the same motive. It is impossible for me to discover any other.

Monroe tried to soften Paine's hostile attitude, but in vain. He realized the author felt badly hurt, but believed that once Paine understood that the men with whom he had been corresponding had been ignorant of his plight, he would no longer hold them responsible. Paine, however, clung to his position. Jefferson, whom he had regarded as a good friend, had been silent, too. So had Samuel Adams and many others. The American leaders were ungrateful, selfish men who had forgotten what the American people could not and would not forget – that Paine's words had rallied them in their time of greatest danger. It did not occur to Paine that almost a decade had passed since he had left the United States, that he had not kept in touch with his friends there, and that their own lives and problems kept them busy. Like all egotists he believed his existence was the center of the universe, and he could not forgive those who failed to act accordingly.

The publication of *The Age of Reason* in the United States ultimately caused many who had been fond of Paine to turn away from him. But in all justice to him, Part One had not yet been printed there, and only a handful of English copies were in circulation. This controversial work was therefore in no way responsible for his American friends' seeming indifference to his fate.

Several times in 1795 Monroe managed to persuade Paine to refrain from writing a letter to President Washington that he might later regret. But by early autumn Paine refused to heed the minister's advice any longer; he was convinced that he was dying and had only a few weeks to live. He wanted to unburden himself, and on September 20 he finally sent a bitter letter to Washington:

Sir, – I had written you a letter by Mr Letombe, French Consul, but at the request of Mr Monroe, I withdrew it, and the letter is still by me. I was the more easily prevailed upon to do this, as it was then my intention to return to America the latter end of this present year; but the illness I now suffer prevents me. In case I had come, I should have applied to you for such parts of your official letters (and your private ones, if you had chosen to give them) as contained any instructions or directions to Mr Monroe, to Mr Morris, or to any other person, respecting me; for after you were informed of my imprisonment in France it was incumbent on you to make some enquiry into the cause, as you might very well conclude that I had not the opportunity of informing you of it. I cannot understand your silence upon this subject upon any other ground, than as a connivance at my imprisonment; and this is the manner in which it is understood here, and will be understood in America, unless you will give me authority for contradicting it. I therefore write you this letter, to propose to you to send me copies of any letters you have written, that I may remove this suspicion. In the Second Part of 'The Age of Reason' I have given a memorandum from the handwriting of Robespierre, in which he proposed a decree of accusation against me "for the interest of America as well as for France.' He could have no cause for putting America in the case, but by interpreting the silence of the American government into connivance and consent. I was imprisoned upon the ground of being born in England; and your silence in not inquiring the cause of that imprisonment and reclaiming me against it, was tacitly giving me up. I ought not to have suspected you of treachery; but whether I recover from the illness I now suffer, or not, I shall continue to think you treacherous, till you give me cause to think otherwise. I am sure you would have found yourself more at your ease had you acted by me as you ought; for whether your desertion of me was intended to gratify the English government, or to let me fall into destruction in France that you might exclaim the louder against the French Revolution; or whether you hoped by my extinction to meet with less opposition in mounting up the American government; either of these will involve you in reproach you will not easily shake off.

THOMAS PAINE

Conway, Paine's principal apologist, tried to claim there was a measure of validity in the author's notion of a conspiracy against him, insisting that Gouverneur Morris was largely responsible for his imprisonment. But there is no substance to this assertion. By the standards of reasonable men Paine's charges were outrageous. He accused the President of the United States of treachery and connivance against him; his letter seethed with hate. Obviously he had talked himself into a dangerous state of mind; his conduct can be explained only on the grounds that his stay in prison, coupled with his illness, had exacerbated his tendency to see enemies everywhere. Only a sick mind could have imagined that Washington had allowed him to remain in prison because the United States was trying to curry favor with Great Britain.

Washington may have been startled by the letter, but his reaction is not known; he retreated into a dignified silence and made no reply. He had far more important matters on his mind than the far-fetched complaints of a former colleague whom he had befriended and supported ten years previously.

In the months that followed Washington must have supposed that Paine was deranged, at least on the subject of the conspiracy against him. Angered anew by the President's silence, the author wrote to him again on December 19, 1795. This time Paine said he understood on good authority that James Monroe had been telling various highly placed French officials that 'he had no doubt but that, if they did what was proper here, he and his friends would turn out Washington'. He offered no explanation of what he meant by 'doing what was proper', he did not identify Monroe's supposed friends, nor did he indicate how he thought they might 'turn out' the President. Again Washington took the only course open to him and maintained an aloof silence.

Paine's hatred became a mania, and he began sending letters attacking the President to other prominent Americans. James Madison, in a letter to Thomas Jefferson dated January 10, 1796, refers to a communication he received from Paine and comments on his 'indelible rancor' against Washington. 'His letter to me is in the style of a dying [man],' Madison observes.

Paine waited several months after writing his letter of September 20 to the President, and then he opened a public campaign. He wrote an open *Letter to George Washington*, which he had printed in Philadelphia at his own expense. It was dated July 30, 1795, but neither the full pamphlet nor excerpts from it appeared until later in the year. This document, written with all of Paine's skill and cunning as a propagandist, caused an uproar in the United States. In order to understand and measure its impact, it is necessary to review certain events that occurred after Paine's release from the Luxembourg Prison.

When the author left prison he learned that John Jay had been sent to London in June, 1794, to negotiate differences that had grown out of the Treaty of 1783. The results of the talks appeared one-sided to many Americans, Paine among them. Jay had granted the British a number of valuable trade concessions, but the advantages that accrued to the United States were less readily apparent. Paine was indignant, and in March, 1795, he wrote an angry letter to Samuel Adams, saying that all Americans would react 'with shame' to Jay's agreement. In his opinion President Washington's administration had sold out to the British.

A few months later, when Rufus King, the new American minister to Great Britain, visited Paris briefly as Monroe's houseguest, Paine gave him an essay, intended for publication in London, that attacked the new treaty. After King reached London he had misgivings, and before following Paine's instructions to have the article printed, he wrote to Monroe asking his advice. Monroe was horrified, and requested King to return the piece to Paine. 'For altho' Mr. Paine's political principles are sound,' he wrote, 'and his comments upon all political subjects may be so likewise, yet I do not think that this is a veritable theater for this publication in regard to our political transactions, *especially when it is considered that he lives in my house*.' King acted accordingly, and the piece attacking Jay's Treaty did not appear in Britain.

Monroe revealed in a letter to Madison on January 20, 1796, that, shortly after Paine's release from prison, he had requested the author to write nothing on any political subject for publication either in the United States or in Europe while he lived under the diplomat's roof. The merits of his views were irrelevant, Madison explained, and his only concern was his own standing and integrity as the representative of the United States in France. Paine had demurred, denying 'the principle, intimating that no one would suppose his writings, which were consistent, were influenced by anyone; that he was accustomed to writing upon publick subjects & upon those of America in particular'. But Monroe had held firm, saying he had to guard his own good

name and character against 'any improper imputation or com-
promittment whatever'. Under the circumstances Paine had been
forced to agree, regardless of his own feelings.

The problem became more acute when Thomas Pinckney
stopped in Paris to visit Monroe while traveling from Spain to
London. Paine chose to ignore his promise, and he gave Pinckney
a new essay dealing with American affairs and asked that they be
given to a London printer. Like King, Pinckney elected instead
to go to Monroe. Alarmed and irritated, Monroe confronted
Paine, who not only admitted that he had given Pinckney the
material, but also revealed that the essay was an extract from a
longer piece he had sent to Frederick Muhlenberg of Philadelphia for publication there. Monroe immediately appealed to
Madison for help, and his friend wrote a reassuring reply, telling
him that Muhlenberg had received no material from Paine and
would refrain from printing it, if and when it arrived.

By October, 1795, about a month after sending his vicious
letter to Washington, Paine's health began to improve. In
November he wrote a new pamphlet, *Agrarian Justice*, in which
he urged both the United States and Great Britain to levy an
inheritance tax of 10 per cent on all real estate holdings and
personal property, with the funds acquired to be used for the
care of the elderly. The idea was regarded as revolutionary on
both sides of the Atlantic. The concept, now being utilized in one
variation or another by many nations, appears to have been
original with Paine. The idea of levying an inheritance tax on the
wealthy was not his, to be sure, and had already been advocated
by Jeremy Bentham, William Godwin, and other English re-
formers. But he seems to have been the first to think of providing
state aid for the aged, and if such an idea had previously been
presented by any other writer, there is no evidence to suggest
that Paine was familiar with his work. Strangely, Paine has never
been given due credit for the proposal, perhaps because few
historians have regarded him as a social economist.

In February, 1796, he started to work on yet another pamphlet, *The Decline and Fall of the English System of Finance*, in
which he predicted that the Bank of England would collapse
within twenty years because of growing inflation caused by
Britain's recent wars. On April 27, 1796, he presented this work
to the people of France. François Lanthenas, who was now a
member of the Council of Five Hundred, enthusiastically called

this work a masterpiece, and the council promptly ordered it printed and disseminated at government expense. The Directory ordered one thousand copies for propaganda purposes, and French envoys abroad were instructed to stress that Britain was tottering. Editions were printed in every major European language, and before the end of the year thirteen different English editions were published. Two replies inspired by the Bank of England also appeared during this time. The Directory called Paine's pamphlet 'the most combustible weapon which France could at this moment employ to overthrow and destroy the English government'. When, the following year, the Bank of England was forced to suspend payments for a short time, Paine immediately claimed full responsibility and thereafter remained convinced that his predictions would always come true.

Meanwhile, in spite of his new successes, the author continued to brood over President Washington's refusal to answer his letter. He began to compose the *Letter to George Washington** and appears to have completed it on July 30. Whether this work was written in James Monroe's house has never been determined.

Paine left Monroe's house sometime between the beginning of 1796 and June of that year. It is not accidental that the precise date is unknown; Monroe went to great lengths to conceal it since he wanted to disassociate himself from Paine's latest work. On May 13 the Directory issued a decree exempting Paine from the law that all former members of the Convention were required to live elsewhere than in Paris. The author spent the summer in Versailles, probably staying for part of that time in the summer home of Fulwar Skipwith, the American consul in Paris. On July 5 Monroe wrote to Madison that Paine ,'having resolved to continue in Europe some time longer and knowing it was inconvenient for me to keep him longer in my family, and wishing also to treat on our politics, which he could not well do in my house, left me some time since'. The minister took care to mention no specific date. 'He thinks the President winks at his imprisonment and wished he might die in gaol, and bears him resentment for it; also he is preparing an attack on him of the most virulent kind. Through a third person (Dr. Enoch Edwards) I have endeavored to divert him from it without effect. It may be said I have instigated him, but the above is the truth.'

In any event, Monroe's friendship for the author was beginning

* See Appendix, pages 333-334, for excerpts.

to cool. Members of the Directory had become reserved toward the minister and were openly skeptical of his reports to them on attitudes and conditions in the United States. Monroe suspected that Paine, resenting his reports that Washington had achieved universal popularity, was somehow responsible for the sudden change. He went to Jean François Reubell of the Directory and inquired whether Paine had contradicted his recent reports. At first the official refused to reply, then gave an evasive answer.

Paine refused to heed Monroe's repeated requests to end his assault on Washington. On July 5 Monroe wrote to Madison that he was deeply embarrassed because he had been so close to Paine, and that, in return for his kindness to the author, he had expected neither ingratitude nor a breach of confidence. On July 21 Dr. Edwards sent the minister a memorandum outlining Paine's recent activities, including his work on the *Washington* pamphlet. Edwards also advised Monroe not to communicate with the author in writing, saying Paine might publish the document as proof of their close friendship. The memorandum also stated that Paine brushed aside all suggestions that he give up his attack on President Washington by replying that he wrote 'for posterity'.

By July 31 Paine sent the completed pamphlet to Franklin's nephew, Benjamin Franklin Bache of Philadelphia, editor of the anti-administration newspaper *Aurora*, who shared his dislike of the President. The paper printed excerpts on October 17 and on several days in November, and in February, 1797, just before Washington left office, the entire pamphlet was published and disseminated. In this extraordinary work Paine flailed at many foes, real and imagined. He accused Gouverneur Morris of conspiring against him and against the best interests of the United States. He regarded John Jay as a virtual traitor because of the terms he had granted Great Britain in Jay's Treaty. And, for no discernible reason, he vigorously assaulted Vice-President John Adams, who was elected to the Presidency in November, 1796:

John Adams has said (and John it is known was always a speller after places and offices, and never thought his little services were highly enough paid) John has said, that as Mr Washington had no child, the Presidency should be made hereditary in the family of Lund Washington. He did not go so far as to say, also, that the Vice-Presidency should be hereditary in the family of John Adams. He prudently left that to stand on the ground that one good turn deserves another.

John Adams is one of those men who never contemplated the origin of government, or comprehended anything of first principles. If he had, he might have seen that the right to set up and establish hereditary government never did, and never can, exist in any generation at any time whatever; that it is of the nature of treason; because it is an attempt to take away the rights of all the minors living at that time, and of all succeeding generations. It is of a degree beyond common treason. It is a sin against nature. The equal right of every generation is a right fixed in the nature of things. It belongs to the son when of age, as it belonged to the father before him.

John Adams would himself deny the right that any former deceased generation could have to decree authoritatively a succession of governors over him, or over his children; and yet he assumes the pretended right, treasonable as it is, of acting himself. His ignorance is his best excuse.

Most of Paine's venom was reserved for President Washington. On page after page he denigrated the character and career of the man generally acknowledged to be the greatest of living Americans. The only phase of Washington's life he missed, and it could only have been an oversight, was the fact that he was a major slave-owner. It is surprising that Paine, whose antislavery sentiments were unwavering, should have omitted this aspect.

Paine held Washington personally responsible for the fact that he was not released from Luxembourg Prison until James Monroe arrived in Paris and clarified the issue of his American citizenship. Washington, he declared, was unprincipled and selfish, both in politics and his personal relations. His 'private conduct' was a match for the 'corruption and mismanagement' of his administration. As all who were well acquainted with him knew, he had no friendships and was incapable of forming any. He could serve or desert a man or a cause with 'constitutional indifference', and it was this 'cold, hermaphrodite faculty' that his enemies as well as his admirers for a time called prudence, moderation, and impartiality. Washington's reputation had been made as commander in chief during the American Revolution, but Paine savagely attacked that reputation. Washington's strategy had been that of 'doing nothing'; his campaigns were distinguished by 'prolonged languor'. He took credit for the great victories won by better generals, among them Horatio Gates, Philip Schuyler, and 'Mad Anthony' Wayne. Above all,

Paine characterized Washington as 'treacherous in private friendship . . . and a hypocrite in public life'. Speaking directly to the President in his closing sentences, Paine said the world 'will be puzzled to decide whether you are an apostate or an impostor; whether you have abandoned good principles or whether you ever had any'.

President Washington offered no explanation, either in public or private, for his failure to come to Paine's assistance, and to anyone who saw the affair in perspective, there was no need for him to speak. In all probability he knew nothing about Paine's incarceration in the Luxembourg Prison until the State Department told him of Monroe's report announcing that he had been successful in winning the author's release. The truth of the matter is that Paine was not the major American figure that he imagined himself to be. He had made valuable contributions to the cause of liberty during the Revolution, but his importance had dwindled year by year for a decade and a half. He had not been forgotten, but his deeds belonged to the past, not the present, and this was something his inflated ego would not allow him to admit. It was inconceivable to him that there could have been anyone in the United States, much less the President, who was not thoroughly familiar with his predicament.

By the time the complete pamphlet was published in February, 1797, Washington's popularity had already declined somewhat, but he was still revered by a vast majority of his countrymen. The viciousness of Paine's attack turned people against the author by the hundreds of thousands. The *Letter to George Washington*, which was read by most Americans, was even more responsible than *The Age of Reason* for Paine's loss of stature. The reasons for his assault were strictly personal, as he himself admitted; the manner in which he chose to vent his spleen aroused universal anger and disgust. Until this time he had shared the standing of a folk hero, along with other Founding Fathers; but the pamphlet destroyed his popularity with the public, and he never recovered from the blow.

The Federalists, who revered Washington, were particularly indignant, and many of the author's acquaintances in New England, New York, and Pennsylvania refused to speak to him after he returned to the United States several years later. Some of Jefferson's followers, the new Republican-Democrats, enjoyed the attack on John Adams, but they, too, were made uneasy by

245

the hysterical nature of Paine's assault on Washington. Apart from a small handful of extremists, there were few who appreciated or agreed with Paine's sentiments.

No American was placed in a more precarious position than Monroe, under whose roof the work that smeared the outgoing and incoming Presidents of the United States may have been written. Regardless of whether Paine actually penned the *Letter to George Washington* while living in Monroe's house, it was no secret that he had turned out his previous communications to Washington while dwelling there. It seems likely that this circumstance was at least in part responsible for Monroe's abrupt recall, without explanation, in August 1797, and his replacement by Charles Cotesworth Pinckney. Many historians say that Monroe lost his post because Alexander Hamilton and other Federalists believed that he had been lax in representing the interests of the United States in France. But Washington, Adams, and their royal supporters would have been less than human had they not suspected that Monroe had plotted with Paine against the best interests of both administrations.

Washington himself is known to have made only one reference to the pamphlet. In a letter to David Stuart written on January 8, 1797, speaking of himself in the third person, he said, 'Although he is soon to become a private citizen, his opinions are to be knocked down, and his character reduced as low as they are capable of sinking it, even by resorting to absolute falsehoods. As an evidence whereof, and of the plan they are pursuing, I send you a letter of Mr. Paine to me, printed in this city [Philadelphia], and disseminated with great industry.'

Paine enjoyed the furor he created. Ignoring the correspondence telling him that he had destroyed his good name in the United States, he managed to convince himself that most Americans shared his sentiments. He had developed an unlimited ability to fool himself, to believe what he wanted to believe.

He was now sixty years old, and although he continued to live for twelve more years, the career on which his renown rests was over. Rum and brandy may well have been symptoms of his deterioration, but it would be an exaggeration to say that liquor was responsible for his decline. It was his tension-laden stay in prison, where he thought each day was his last, coupled with his physical ailment that warped Paine and transformed him into a combative, aggressively unpleasant old man. Until this time he had been mildly eccentric, but now all of his bad habits became more pronounced. He wore soiled linen, neglected his appearance and bathed infrequently. He drank steadily and heavily, although few ever saw him intoxicated. His inflated ego made it impossible for anyone to hold a meaningful conversation with him, and he quarreled with those who dared to oppose his views, more often than not becoming vituperative.

Far more important than the increasing disintegration of his personality was his failure to produce new works of significance. Although Paine himself did not realize it, he no longer had a goal and began to drift. The rule of the Directory, followed by the Consulate of Napoleon Bonaparte, changed the direction of the French Revolution, and not even a man endowed with a limitless capacity for self-delusion could convince himself that France would adopt the American system of government. Still under indictment for treason in Great Britian, Paine could not return to London; he had to content himself with the hope that, in time, his attacks on the monarchy and other national institutions there would be productive. As for the United States, he was living outside the mainstream of her current experience, although he didn't realize it; his work there was done.

It has been said that Paine would have been fortunate had he died before writing his *Letter to George Washington*. A later age would accept *The Age of Reason*, and his reputation would have been secure for all time.

22

Free in Paris

Ever since his release from prison Paine had written and spoken of returning to the United States at the earliest opportunity. There was nothing to prevent his departure in 1797; even Paine himself knew that he was no longer an influence on the French Government. Yet he nevertheless continued to make his home in Paris. He seemed still to be suffering from the lethargy brought about by a slow recovery from his illness. It is difficult, however, to avoid the thought that he remained in France because he was afraid that a cold or hostile reception in America would cause him to lose face. He might pretend to others that he had anticipated the reactions of George Washington's followers to his pamphlet and that they represented a small minority of American opinion. But it is likely that he was surprised by the vehemently negative response to his pamphlet, and it may have occurred to him belatedly that he had seriously miscalculated the thrust of American public opinion.

Inasmuch as he was never callous to anything that directly concerned him, he could not have been indifferent to America's rejection of his attack on Washington. He had gained his stature principally because of the effect his writing had had on the course of the American Revolution, and to be rebuffed now by the people of the United States would have been more than he could have borne. So it may be that he decided to wait until public feeling in America became calmer before he returned there.

Meanwhile, both portions of *The Age of Reason* had been published in a single pamphlet in London in January, 1797. The reaction throughout the English-speaking world was explosive. Other eruptions followed in France, the German states, Holland, and Sweden when the work was translated there. Five Anglican bishops issued a joint statement in London, solemnly branding the author as 'an evil anti-Christ', and clergymen of every denomination thundered against him from their pulpits. This was a battle to Paine's liking. In a reply to the English bishops he said, 'In writing upon this, as upon every other subject, I speak a language plain and intelligible. I deal not in hints and intimations. I have several reasons for this: first, that I may be clearly understood; secondly, that it may be seen I am in earnest; and thirdly, because it is an affront to truth to treat falsehood with complaisance.'

The Anglicans had the last word. The Bishop of Llandaff made a long speech in the House of Lords in which he condemned Paine for his ideas, his denials of Christianity, his assault on the Bible, and even his language. This harangue, which required almost three hours to deliver, subsequently was printed in pamphlet form and was widely distributed throughout Great Britain. Several copies appeared in America; edited versions of the address were printed by Episcopalian presses in New York and Hartford.

During the first six months of 1797 Paine spent most of his time answering letters about *The Age of Reason*, most of them damning, and replying to attacks on the work made in public. His pen was rarely still, and he relished every moment of the experience. Something in his nature made him happy when he was a center of controversy and could lash out in response to his critics.

Not all of his writing was harsh, however. He had formed a close friendship with Sir Robert Smyth, a wealthy banker who lived in Paris, and was delighted to discover that Lady Smyth, long an admirer of his work, had been the anonymous correspondent who had written to him in prison. Not to be outdone, he gallantly wrote a poem and dedicated it to her:

> In the region of clouds, where the whirlwinds arise,
>   My castle of fancy was built;
> The turrets reflected the blue from the skies,
>   And the windows with sunbeams were gilt.
>
> The rainbow sometimes, in its beautiful state,
>   Enamelled the mansion around;
> And the figures that fancy in clouds can create
>   Supplied me with gardens and ground.
>
> I had grottos, and fountains, and orange-tree groves,
>   I had all that enchantment has told;
> I had sweet shady walks for the gods and their loves,
>   I had mountains of coral and gold.
>
> But a storm that I felt not had risen and rolled,
>   While wrapped in a slumber I lay;
> And when I looked out in the morning, behold,
>   My castle was carried away.
>
> It passed over rivers and valleys and groves,
>   The world it was all in my view;
> I thought of my friends, of their fates, of their loves,
>   And often, full often, of you.
>
> At length it came over a beautiful scene,
>   That nature in silence had made;
> The place was but small, but 't was sweetly serene,
>   And chequered with sunshine and shade.
>
> I gazed and I envied with painful good will,
>   And grew tired of my seat in the air;
> When all of a sudden my castle stood still,
>   As if some attraction were there.
>
> Like a lark from the sky it came fluttering down,
>   And placed me exactly in view,
> When whom should I meet in this charming retreat,
>   This corner of calmness, but – you.
>
> Delighted to find you in honour and ease,
>   I felt no more sorrow nor pain;
> But the wind coming fair, I ascended the breeze,
>   And went back with my castle again.

Even a cursory examination of these lines reveals that Paine was not a great poet. But the effort is noteworthy because it reveals a side of Paine that he usually tried to hide from the world. In his prose writing he was blunt and heavy-handed, firing salvo after salvo with his verbal howitzers and cannon. Here, in a few simple lines to a charming lady who treated him with kindness, he lowered his guard and disclosed a delicacy of imagery and touch seldom encountered in his serious works. It might be too much to suggest that had he devoted more time to his poetry, he might have become a passably accomplished writer of light verse. But the poem for Lady Smyth does indicate that he sometimes thought in terms not generally associated with the political, moral, and philosophical themes on which he loved to expound.

Even in his dealings with Lady Smyth, however, he could not play the role of the gallant consistently, and inevitably returned to the themes that preoccupied him, as an except from a letter he sent to her in the spring of 1797 indicates:

To reason against feelings is as vain as to reason against fire; it serves only to torture the torture, by adding reproach to horror. All reasoning with ourselves in such cases acts upon us like the reasoning of another person, which, however kindly done, serves but to insult the misery we suffer. If Reason could remove the pain, Reason would have prevented it. If she could not do the one, how is she to perform the other? In all such cases we must look upon Reason as dispossessed of her empire, by a revolt of the mind. She retires to a distance to weep, and the ebony sceptre of Despair rules alone. All that Reason can do is to suggest, to hint a thought, to signify a wish, to cast now and then a kind of bewailing look, to hold up, when she can catch the eye, the miniature shaded portrait of Hope; and though dethroned, and can dictate no more, to wait upon us in the humble station of a handmaid.

Paine had good reason to be feeling in high spirits in the spring of 1797. If the reaction of America to his *Washington* pamphlet disappointed him, no one knew it, and he was heartened by the enormous response, both favorable and angry, to *The Age of Reason*. His mode of living improved, thanks to the kindness of the Smyths, who remained in their Paris town house and gave him the exclusive use of a villa they owned near Versailles. The place was fully staffed, a brook ran across the property, and the garden was filled with flowering fruit trees. Paine took his ease there, attended by the servants, and spent most of his time outdoors, sitting in the garden even when he wrote letters.

The French Government held his pamphlet *The Decline and*

Fall of the English System of Finance in high regard and saw to it that copies were placed on sale throughout the country. Paine could have used the royalties the work earned him, but he could not resist making a gesture of contempt toward Great Britain. He regarded debtors' prisons as barbaric and gave all of his earnings from the pamphlet for the relief of those who were being held in London's Newgate Prison for debts which they were in no position to pay unless they were released and could earn money. The Directory's interest in the pamphlet led to its translation into every major European language; its resounding success everywhere added to Paine's fame. In Austria, Sweden, and several of the German states he was regarded primarily as an economist; virtually nothing was known of his political writing in those places, and *The Age of Reason*, although published in Stockholm and Vienna, did not circulate freely, largely because of the clergy's adamant opposition to the work.

Paine appears to have given up his active sex life after his imprisonment and illness, and although a major scandal cast a shadow over his final years, he seems to have discontinued his evenings with young harlots. He also drank more moderately, at least during his sojourn at the Smyth villa, and his health improved rapidly. His hair had turned white in prison, but otherwise he appeared younger than in recent years; there was a spring in his step again, his self-confidence returned, and his eyes were clear. There was now no visible sign to indicate that his sufferings had taken a permanent toll.

He came into Paris frequently, often escorting Mrs Joel Barlow to dinner parties while her husband was in North Africa as the representative of the United States to the Barbary States. There can be little doubt that Paine, although lacking political power, enjoyed the full confidence of the French Government at this time. Sir Robert Smyth wanted to make a business trip to Hamburg, but could not obtain a visa that would enable him to leave and re-enter France. So the author applied on his behalf to the minister of foreign affairs, and Smith's passports were delivered to him within twenty-four hours.

For the first time in his life Paine took a genuine interest in food, perhaps because his meals in prison had been so monotonous. France was enjoying a wave of prosperity, Paris was crowded with new restaurants, and the foreigners in the city, including Paine and his friends, visited many of them. Mrs Barlow wrote to her husband that he would scarcely know his old friend: Paine now had long discussions with waiters, in his halting French, on such subjects as the recipes for the superb sauces he was learning to appreciate.

The Age of Reason had made Paine an expert on the subject of religion, at least in the eyes of his friends in Paris, and in January, 1797, he was one of the members of a small group that founded a new church. They called themselves Theophilanthropists, Paine having coined the word, which he defined as 'lovers of God and man, or adorers of God and friends of man'. In the spring of 1797 the group rented quarters at 34, rue Denis, where they held their own worship services, and before summer they rented an adjoining house, which they used as a library. Paine, who was the moving spirit of the organization, defined its aim in a broadside he wrote and had printed for the benefit of all who might be interested:

> The society is at present in its infancy, and its means are small; but I wish to hold in view the subject I allude to, and instead of teaching the philosophical branches of learning as ornamental branches only, as they have hitherto been taught, to teach them in a manner that shall combine theological knowledge with scientific instruction. To do this to the best advantage, some instruments will be necessary for the purpose of explanation, of which the society is not yet possessed. But as the views of the society extend to public good, as well as to that of the individual, and as its principles can have no enemies, means may be devised to procure them. If we unite to the present instruction, a series of lectures on the ground I have mentioned, we shall, in the first place, render theology the most entertaining of all studies. In the next place, we shall give scientific instruction to those who could not otherwise obtain it. The mechanic of every profession will there be taught the mathematic principles necessary to render him proficient in his art. The cultivator will there see developed the principles of his vegetation; while, at the same time, they will be led to see the hand of God in all these things.

This ambitious program was never realized, but the society did flourish, thanks in part to the curiosity of many who were drawn to the meetings because of the author's renown. As many as forty persons attended the services, which were usually held on Sundays.

Late in 1797 the Theophilanthropists published a 214-page manual or handbook, much of it the work of Paine. This document reveals that members read odes in unison and sang what they called 'theistic and humanitarian hymns'. At each meeting there were 'ethical readings' from the Old and New Testaments, from the Koran, and from Hindu, Greek, and Chinese philosophers. The group observed four holidays each year, and it is ironic that one of these, chosen by Paine, was February 22, the birthday of George Washington, in whose honor 'an intellectual festival' was held. The former President's contributions to human liberty, it appeared, outweighed Paine's personal dislike of him. The three remaining holidays honored Rousseau, Saint Vincent de Paul, and Socrates. A small, plain altar stood at the front of the church, and each week was decorated with flowers, symbolizing all races and creeds. Various quotations 'enjoining domestic kindness and public benevolence' were painted on the walls.

As far as is known, the Theophilanthropists made up the first of many ethical-religious societies that sprang up in the United States and Great Britain during the nineteenth century. A number found their inspiration in Paine's group and modeled their services on theirs.

Early in the autumn of 1797 Paine wrote a letter to Camille Jordan, the chairman of a French Government committee, who had just recommended to the Directory that the Church be restored to a place in the life of the nation. The letter illustrates the fundamentals of Paine's approach to religion.

It is a want of feeling to talk of priests and bells whilst so many infants are perishing in the hospitals, and aged and infirm poor in the streets. The abundance that France possesses is sufficient for every want, if rightly applied; but priests and bells, like articles of luxury, ought to be the least articles of consideration.

No man ought to make a living by religion. It is dishonest to do so. Religion is not an act that can be performed by proxy. One person cannot act religion for another. Every person must perform it for himself; and all that a priest can do is to take from him; he wants nothing but his money, and then to riot in the spoil and laugh at his credulity. The only people who, as a professional sect of Christians, provide for the poor of their society, are people known by the name of Quakers. These men have no priests. They assemble quietly in their places of worship, and do not disturb their neighbors with shows and noise of bells. Religion does not unite itself to show and noise. True religion is without either. . . .

Why has the Revolution of France been stained with crimes, while the Revolution of the United States of America was not? Men are physically the same in all countries; it is education that makes them different. Accustom people to believe that priests, or any other class of men, can forgive sins, and you will have sins in abundance.

Religion did not occupy all of Paine's time and attention during this period. His interest in American politics continued to grow, and he did what he could to meddle from a distance. He regarded the recall of James Monroe as a typical blunder of the Washington administration, caused at least in part by his own friendship with the minister. When Charles Cotesworth Pinckney arrived in Paris late in the autumn of 1796, Paine wrote at once to the French Ministry of Foreign Affairs urging that the new envoy not be recognized. As it happened, Pinckney was not allowed to present his credentials, although the reasons for his refusal were in no way related to the author's demand. The Directory was annoyed because Jay's Treaty gave preferences to Great Britain in America's dealings with European nations, and the government established the policy of refusing to recognize the new United States envoy until its grievances were heard and explained. Paine, of course, claimed complete credit for Pinckney's difficulties.

The Monroe family planned to return to the United States early in the spring of 1797. It was Paine's original intention to travel with his friends; he went with them to Le Havre in March, 1797, but changed his mind when they made their travel arrangements there. The ship on which they were to sail was not swift enough to avoid British patrols, and he was afraid the Royal Navy would not hesitate to capture him and return him to London as a traitor. He remained in Le Havre for almost four months and several times booked passage to America, but changed his mind each time. When he received word that the vessel on which the Monroes had sailed had been halted on the high seas and that a thorough search had been made for one Thomas Paine by a boarding party, he made a definite decision not to return to America. It was obvious to him that a British agent in Le Havre had reported his intentions to London and that the Royal Navy was lying in wait for him.

So, in mid-summer, he returned to Paris. His fear of capture was the immediate motive that kept him in France, but there was another that was equally important. It was rumoured that the French were planning a large-scale invasion of England, and Paine was eager to participate in it. He believed that the people of England would respond to such an action by revolting and throwing off the yoke of their masters, and he wanted to take what he regarded as his natural and inevitable place in that uprising.

The French Government had notified Monroe, immediately prior to his departure, that it regarded Franco-American relations broken because the United States accepted the British interpretation of maritime laws, giving the British the right to halt and search neutral vessels on the high seas. The Foreign Ministry told Monroe that France would prefer to regard the United States as an avowed enemy than as a 'treacherous friend'. Paine placed full blame for this development on what he considered President Washington's pro-British bias. Relations between America and her ally could be restored without delay, he believed, if firm steps were taken, and he wrote a number of long letters on the subject to friends across the Atlantic, among them Thomas Jefferson and Samuel Adams. The administration of President John Adams should take a bold diplomatic initiative, he asserted, and should band together with other neutral nations to protect its own rights. No neutral power possessed the strength to stand up alone to the Royal Navy, but by joining forces it would be possible for all to protect their rights. Paine later incorporated this idea into a long pamphlet which he called *Pacte maritime*.

He also originated yet another plan, under which France would retaliate against Britain by halting and seizing the cargoes of all neutral ships bound to and from British ports. Late in the spring he made the suggestion in a letter to Minister Charles Delacroix de Constant, and the idea was received so favorably that in July it was established as a formal French policy. Thereafter the French treated neutral ships 'in the same manner as they suffer the English to treat them', and French warships began to halt American vessels and seize their cargoes. These acts were regarded with such hostility in the United States that war with France was threatened. President Adams responded to the crisis by appointing three commissioners to find a common ground for the restoration of amicable relations between the two nations. The group consisted of John Marshall, Elbridge Gerry, and Pinckney, who had not yet left Paris.

Paine promptly became involved in the controversy. Beginning in August, 1797, he wrote a number of open letters to Secretary of State Timothy Pickering which were published by a liberal Paris newspaper, the *Bien informe*. Its editor, Nicolas de Bonneville, who had been associated with Paine and Condorcet in the earlier days of the French Revolution, was fast becoming one of the author's closest friends and associates. A generation younger than Paine, the editor regarded him as one of the greatest men of the era. His wife, Marguerite Brazier de Bonneville, reputedly one of the most handsome young women in Paris, also became very fond of the author, and he was invited frequently to dine with the couple. When their third son was born, late in 1797, they named the boy Thomas Paine de Bonneville.

In his letters to the newspaper Paine argued that the policies followed by Monroe had been right, and that the United States could quickly restore friendly relations with France by returning to them. He proceeded to develop his idea of forming a league of neutral nations, too, and in September, when all three American commissioners gathered in Paris, he presented his plan to them.

Paine had also written some days earlier to the French foreign minister, Charles Maurice de Talleyrand. A former bishop who had reverted to the laity during the Revolution, Talleyrand went on to display an astonishing ability to survive change. In the course of his long and distinguished career, he became the Emperor Napoleon's principal foreign officer, represented his country at the Congress of Vienna following the fall of Napoleon, and remained active in the formulation of French foreign policy until the mid-1830's. Always quick to grasp and appreciate new ideas, Talleyrand saw the merits of Paine's scheme at a glance, and wrote him a warm letter of appreciation.

The germ of Paine's idea was that the neutral nations, after banding together, would remove all arms from their merchant ships and send only these unarmed vessels on their trade missions. Any nation that halted such a vessel on the high seas, searched her, and confiscated her cargo would be denied the right to use the ports of *all* neutral nations.

The idea was ingenious and, directed primarily against Great Britain, which arrogated to herself the right to halt all shipping anywhere on the high seas, could have been a powerful weapon in the French fight against the British. It is no wonder that Talleyrand was pleased – or that London sent warnings to all neutral governments to the effect that His Majesty's government would regard the adoption of the plan by any neutral nation as an unfriendly act. Paine had devised a formula that, if used in concert by enough nations, would completely disrupt the British blockade of French ports.

The head of the American commission was John Marshall, later to become the most renowned of all chief justices of the United States. Paine wrote him long reports on the internal state of French politics, and a memorandum advising him that the United States would be unwise to offer to cede to France rights which the French believed they had already attained in the Treaty of 1778. Only his own plan would interest the French, Paine warned. These reports were delivered to Marshall at his hotel on the day of his arrival. Aware of Paine's contribution to the cause of liberty during the American Revolution, the Virginian regarded him as an expatriate, at best. Pinckney, who believed that Paine was at least partly responsible for the refusal of the French government to accept his credentials as United States minister, had no reason to be fond of the author. Only Elbridge Gerry, who had known him fairly well during his stay in America, was friendly toward him.

Paine followed up his written communications with a personal visit to Marshall the following day. The head of the American commission and Paine – who still regarded himself as an unofficial American diplomat and an expert on foreign affairs – appear to have disliked each other from the outset. Paine's linen was soiled, he had probably not bathed for several days, and his grim insistence that no scheme but his own would be accepted by France all combined to impress Marshall unfavorably. He sent Paine's proposal to the State Department, indicating that he did not believe it worthy of serious consideration. In his private diary Marshall called the plan 'an insult which ought to be received with that coldness which would forbid the repetition of it'.

Under the best of circumstances Paine was incapable of separating a rejection of one of his ideas from a rejection of his person. In this instance it seemed obvious to him that Marshall disliked him, and he heartily returned the sentiment. For the rest of his life he regarded John Marshall as his enemy, and as an enemy of the American people second in importance only to George Washington.

The commission accomplished nothing in France. A clumsy attempt was made by unauthorized persons to bribe the American representatives, who withdrew angrily, returning home at once. The incident, known as 'the XYZ Affair', caused great repercussions in the United States and contributed to virtually a complete breakdown in the relations between the two nations.

Paine, continuing to express his opinions freely in Bonneville's newspaper, insisted that the American commissioners were at fault; they should have known better, he declared, than to have had dealings with anyone other than official representatives of the French Foreign Ministry. He said, too, that France was to blame for not making known the identities of the men who had offered the Americans the bribes and punishing them for their temerity.

So his own plan was disregarded, and he had displeased both countries with his criticisms. His attempt to act the role of a mediator failed miserably, and damaged his standing in both the United States and France.

23

Bonaparte and Other Complications

When Paine returned to Paris from Le Havre in the summer of 1797 he took up temporary residence in a hotel. In the autumn he accepted an invitation from the Bonnevilles to move into their house at 4, rue du Théâtre Français. He was given a bedchamber adjacent to his host's study, which the hospitable Bonneville vacated for him, presumably for a week or two. But Paine was so comfortable in the home of the engaging couple and the servants pampered him so much that his 'visit' lasted for five full years. Even the location was perfect, and the newcomer could enjoy his walks to nearby newspaper, book, and magazine publishers.

Now in his sixty-first year, Paine was too old to change any of his habits, so the Bonnevilles and their three small sons accommodated themselves to his routines. He slept late, read a stack of English and French newspapers at breakfast, and then expected his host to be on hand afterward for a discussion of the important news of the day. He then retired to his own quarters, wrote for several hours, and emerged in time for dinner. He always took an after-dinner nap before venturing abroad, usually in the late afternoon. Paris now boasted carriages for hire at nominal rates, but Paine preferred to walk, saying he regarded the hiring of a conveyance for purposes of transportation as the worst of all possible extravagances. The cook catered to his taste for plainly prepared food, the children learned never to play in the vicinity when the great man was at work, and Marguerite de Bonneville made it her business to entertain guests whom the visitor found interesting.

The greatest convenience Paine enjoyed was that of living in the house of a publisher who owned his own printing presses. Bonneville was always willing to publish Paine's writings in his newspaper, and the presses were available to Paine when he wanted a pamphlet printed in either French or English. In 1798, for example, he wrote a short piece, *On the Jacobinism of the English at Sea*, and Bonneville obligingly printed copies for dissemination to high French government officials. This work, two shorter pieces, and the *Pacte maritime* were reprinted in a single pamphlet, and late in 1800 the *Compact Maritime* was run off on the Bonneville press in a complete English version. Early in the winter of 1801 Thomas Jefferson, at Paine's request, had the latter work reprinted in Washington, the new capital of the United States. The *Compact Maritime* was one of Paine's favorite works, and he included key portions of it in the seventh of a series of *Letters to the Citizens of the United States* after his return to America.

Bonneville, a dedicated idealist who dreamed of remaking society in a new image, called his press the Cercle Social, which was the name of a club he and a friend had co-founded several years earlier. An active Freemason, he was convinced that the principles and aims of Masonry, if applied to the world's ailments, would bring peace and prosperity to all nations.

Early in September, 1797, some members of the newly-elected Council of Five Hundred engaged in a conspiracy to overthrow the Directory and restore the Bourbon monarchy. The plot was discovered and the members of the Directory acting with the full support of the powerful French Army abolished the Constitution, took all authority into their own hands, and made it illegal to support either the monarchy or the Revolution – thus preparing the way for the dictatorship that Napoleon Bonaparte would establish.

It might be supposed that Paine would join the forces opposed to the Directory, but this was not the case. He sat down without delay and wrote a new pamphlet, *Letter of Thomas Paine to the People of France, and the French Armies, on the Event of the 18th Fructidor, and its Consequences*, published by Bonneville in October. The pamphlet is Paine's strangest work. Much of it is devoted to the subject of Great Britain. Paine insisted that France would never be at peace until the Hanoverian succession was abolished in Britain and a true republic established there. To achieve this end, he believed, France should launch an invasion of England, send the royal family back to Hanover, free all political prisoners, and obtain the right for the British people to prepare a constitution that would guarantee their sacred liberties.

Like most liberals, he accepted the action by the Directory with benumbed complacency. He declared that the great evil – to be dreaded and avoided at all costs – was the Bourbon monarchy, and that the steps taken by the government were justified because they prevented a return to France's miserable past. The Constitution of 1795, he continued, was the best document of its kind ever devised by wise men; its only weakness was the narrow base of suffrage that had been granted. Its abolition had been necessary, however, to prevent a counterrevolution, and Paine expressed the certainty that when the danger of a monarchist coup was successfully avoided, the Constitution would be restored.

The situation in France was not unique, Paine pointed out: At one precarious period of the American Revolution, the Continental Congress had granted dictatorial powers to General Washington, who had elected not to use them, and at another time during the American Revolution the government of Pennsylvania had suspended itself and invoked martial law. Under the present circumstances, Paine concluded, the government of France had done the right thing.

Copies of the pamphlet were sent to all government officials, among them François de Neufchâteau, the executive of the Directory, who replied in a gracious letter, saying that he prized the pamphlet because it had been written and presented to him 'by one of the old friends of liberty'.

The position of France in Europe was changing rapidly, due to the steady rise and increasing influence of the most extraordinary genius in her history, the Corsican-born Napoleon Bonaparte.

An obscure brigadier-general when he had been given command of the French armies in Italy, he displayed a mastery of both strategy and tactics that no other commander could match and, inspiring fanatical devotion in his troops, inflicted a series of humiliating defeats on the proud divisions of imperial Austria. Her self-respect restored by Napoleon's victories, France gradually achieved a return to domestic stability. In spite of all she had suffered, France was still the wealthiest agricultural nation on the Continent, her trade was reviving, and she began to live up to her potential. Few people as yet realized it, but the Revolution was coming to an end, and France stood on the threshold of a new era.

General Bonaparte returned to Paris, loaded with honors after his spectacularly successful military campaign in Italy and the diplomatic triumph over Austria sealed by the Treaty of Campo Formio. Some weeks after his arrival someone showed him a copy of Paine's pamphlet, and early one evening the great general arrived at the Bonneville house unannounced and alone. He chatted with Paine for a time – presumably aided by an interpreter – then invited the author to dine with him, and they went off together to a restaurant for the evening. He questioned Paine closely about his ideas, and in reply Paine showed the general a series of articles he had written for Bonneville's *Bien informé*. England could be defeated, he had argued, by an army transported in a fleet of a thousand gunboats, which would cost 10 million livres to build. The population of France was now more than 25 million, and he believed it would not be necessary to raise taxes to finance the campaign: The fleet could be built with money contributed by patriotic citizens. He himself had already offered 100 livres to start the campaign. He also showed the general an unpublished pamphlet on which he had been working intermittently since living at the home of James Monroe. Called 'Observations on the Construction and Operation of Navies, with a Plan for an Invasion of England and the Final Overthrow of the English Government', it contained a full set of accurate maps of the English Channel.

Bonaparte, who informed his flattered guest that he slept with a copy of *The Rights of Man* under his pillow and that he believed a statue of pure, solid gold should be erected in Paine's honor, was fascinated by the plan, perhaps because it so closely paralleled his own thinking. In fact, he considered it superior to the tentative invasion plans he had drawn up, and therefore decided to adopt Paine's scheme, refining it slightly so that one hundred soldiers would be carried in each of the thousand gunboats. As a grand climax to the evening, General Bonaparte invited the author to accompany the expedition.

Paine readily agreed because, as he wrote to Thomas Jefferson in the spring of 1797, 'the intention of the expedition was to give the people of England an opportunity of forming a government for themselves, and thereby bring about peace'. His meeting with Napoleon had revived his great dream: He imagined a republican Britain that would unite for peace with the Republic of France and the United States of America; soon monarchies throughout Europe would fall, and nation after nation would establish republics, too. Scarcely able to contain his joy, Paine became one of Bonaparte's strongest and most vocal supporters. Long after the Empire was established and Napoleon crowned himself, Paine persisted in praising him. He may have been blind to Napoleon's dictatorship because the Emperor was emphatic in his guarantees of the civil rights of Frenchmen in most spheres – provided they agreed with him. But it was the hope of invading England that was basically responsible for Paine's myopia. Not until 1806 did he abandon this hope, and even then he found it difficult to find fault with Napoleon in any way. A man who would invade England in the name of liberty could not be less than magnificent.

Bonneville, who had first published *The Rights of Man* in France, was in complete agreement with his friend, and thereafter the *Bien informé* gave General Bonaparte its unstinting support. Napoleon well knew how to win liberals to his cause.

He was also a master of military deception, a fact which Paine learned in 1798, to his intense disappointment. The Paris newspapers announced that 250 gunboats had been built for use in the invasion of England. Paine's original contribution to the plan was praised repeatedly in newspapers representing virtually every political group in France, and the author was once again considered one of the most prominent men in the country. Not until later that year did he begin to suspect that the public had been deceived. Britain, warned by the French newspapers' reports of the planned invasion, had prepared herself for attack. In the meantime Bonaparte, outwitting the British fleet, landed a large French army in Egypt hoping to sever Britain's principal trade route to India and the Far East. In his letter to Jefferson, Paine could not help wondering whether he and his plan had been used as decoys to fool the British and give Bonaparte the chance to transport his army to Egypt in safety.

Paine's social life was more active than it had been in years. When Joel Barlow returned to France from Algeria, the Barlows, along with the Smyths, became regular members of the author's circle. Another whom he saw frequently was Robert Fulton, who attained fame in 1807 with the development of a steamboat that successfully navigated the Hudson River from New York to Albany. Fulton, who had come to France from the United States in 1797, was currently working on the steamboat project, as well as on an idea for a steam-propelled submarine that would enable France to dominate the seas of the world.

Paine had never lost his interest in science, and as he had himself first suggested the building of a steamboat in 1778, Barlow and others introduced him to Fulton. The high-strung Fulton had no use for amateurs but quickly realized that Paine easily grasped the ideas he expounded, and the pair became good friends. They dined together often, and Paine freely contributed his own thoughts on steam engines to Fulton, believing that such an engine, when perfected, would help to unify the nations of the world. Other friends took care to absent themselves on the occasions when Paine and Fulton got together; the two men could talk only about engines, and losing all awareness of the proximity of others, happily spent hours drawing sketches and designs on the tablecloth.

Paine also showed Fulton the sketches for a new invention of his own, which he called a 'gunpowder motor'. Gunpowder was still notoriously unstable at the turn of the nineteenth century, principally because manufacturers could not produce grains of uniform size, and the lumpiness of the finished product made the substance very difficult to measure. As a consequence soldiers sometimes blew up their firearms and themselves, and could place little confidence in the powder they were forced to use. Paine's device, which was never fully developed, would have turned out powder of precise uniformity of size at a minimal cost. The inventor, realizing it made no apparent sense for a pacifist to have thought of such a machine, said that the engine would make it so easy for nations to wage war that 'a mutual reign of terror' would 'force all of them to keep the peace, no matter what the cost'.

Rebel!

The opportunity to put his ideas regarding political matters in print as rapidly as he could write them did not serve Paine well in the long run. Bonneville shared his impulsive nature. The editor's lack of judgment, combined with his hero worship for his friend, kept him from providing Paine with any restraining influence to counteract the author's frequent excesses.

In September, 1798, the *Bien informé* printed an unsigned piece, apparently written by Paine as a satire, although it did not bear his signature. It was a detailed plan instructing the French Navy to capture every seaport in the United States, then burn these cities to the ground one by one. On the heels of the publication of the piece relations between the United States and France became still worse, forcing President Adams to contemplate a declaration of war against America's former ally. A copy of the newspaper reached New York, and Paine's enemies promptly published an English translation of the article under a heading, 'Tom Paine's Plan for Revolutionizing America'. The publication of this controversial piece contributed to a fresh decline in Paine's popularity in America. At no time did he ever acknowledge, either openly or privately, that he had been the author of the satiric study, but it was significant that he did not deny it, either.

His renown was still so great, however, that every American who came to Paris wanted to meet him. So did Irish republicans who sought independence from Great Britain, atheists and freethinkers from Holland, philosophers from Belgium and Denmark, and economists from Switzerland. Completely democratic in his tastes, Paine happily chatted with everyone who came to see him, with the inevitable result that he was spending much of his time with these uninvited visitors. His friends regarded this as a frivolous waste of a great man's time and talents, and Marguerite de Bonneville intervened. She screened all visitors, sending away all but those who were prominent in their own right, and although Paine remonstrated with her, his privacy was restored. As it happens, Mme de Bonneville did him no favor, for he might have been better off had he been too busy to write.

The *Bien informé* published the outlines of an ambitious project that would have enabled France and the United States to launch an attack on Ireland from the shores of America, thereby causing a diversion forcing Britain to bring home her troops for the defense of the British Isles. The French Government had good cause to be displeased with this wild proposal: Napoleon was expanding the borders of France to include Italy, Germany, and other European states. The United States was annoyed, too, because the British immediately made their policy of searching American merchant vessels more stringent. Paine continued to promote his plan, and in 1801 another newspaper, the *Citoyen francois*, printed an enlarged, revised version of it.

The scheme's publication in Bonneville's newspaper had increased Paine's contacts with the Irish dissidents who were living in Paris, and he lost no opportunity to urge these men to rebel against the British Government. This meddling cost him the confidence of the French Government. Among those whom Paine saw regularly in 1798 was an Irish priest named Sommers or Somerville. The French Ministry of the Interior suddenly put out a call for Sommers's arrest in December, 1798, but he managed to escape. It was revealed that he had been one of the most clever and successful of British spies in Paris, and Paine's name appeared in a number of letters that Sommers left behind in his quarters. The author was immediately summoned to the headquarters of the Ministry of Interior and interrogated for a week. It was ironic that he should have been suspected of spying for Great Britain, whose government would have hanged him had he come within its jurisdiction; but in spite of the absurdity of the charge the French Government thereafter regarded Paine with suspicion. It may be that Sommers acted with deliberate malice before making his escape. Paine was still a gadfly whose incessant buzzing gave the authorities in London a chronic headache, and if Sommers was responsible for France's loss of confidence in the author, then he did his employers a good turn.

The United States and France were fighting an undeclared war in 1798. The French, like the British, were demanding the right to halt American merchantmen on the high seas, and French captains did not hesitate to confiscate cargoes of raw materials that they believed were being sent to England. The infant United States was caught in the middle of the major powers' tug of war. Paine took it upon himself to intervene with French authorities on behalf of Americans who were in trouble in France, but Conway may have been guilty of exaggeration when he called Paine 'the unofficial American Minister'. It is true, however, that Paine extended himself to help Americans because of his sentimental attachment to the United States. Typical was the case of Captain Rowland Crocker of Cape Cod, the master of a merchantman captured by the French Navy on the high seas. Crocker had resisted the takeover and had been wounded for his pains, taken prisoner, and brought to Paris in chains. Paine immediately protested to the French Foreign Office and was so insistent that Talleyrand quietly arranged for Crocker's release. Paine had him moved to a hotel, paid his bills, and arranged for the services of a physician to treat his injuries. After Crocker recovered his strength, Paine was instrumental in obtaining passage for him on a Swedish ship that would take him safely home. Crocker, who had heard that the author of *The Age of Reason* was a contemptible antichrist, was surprised to find him 'a most gentlemanly man, of sound and orthodox republican principles, of a good heart, a strong intellect, and a fascinating address'.

Bonneville landed in serious trouble with the authorities after publishing in the *Bien conformé* of September 17, 1798, a satiric piece on Sieyès, the former abbé, then a member of the Directory and Bonaparte's closest private collaborator in the French ruling circle. Bonneville attacked him as an incompetent and an impractical dreamer. Sieyès, a very vain man, was proud of the role he had played in preparing the Constitution of 1795. He and his fellow members of the Directory were outraged because he had been treated with such conspicuous lack of dignity. By order of the Directory the publication of the *Bien informé* was suspended indefinitely.

Thomas Paine promptly leaped to his young friend's defense, visiting individual Directors in person and writing a long statement defending the publisher. Bonneville, he wrote, was 'an honest uncorrupted man and as firm a Patriot as any I know'. The author added, 'He is besides a very industrious man – a good husband – a good father – and a good friend.' Paine declared that he was writing of his own accord, and expressed the hope that the ban on the newspaper would be lifted because its subscribers were all patriots, too. Paine was still a man of great stature, and succeeded in influencing the decision of the Directory. Bonneville was forgiven, and was allowed to publish his newspaper again. But the Directory had Bonneville and the other members of his household placed under constant surveillane. Paine found living under such conditions so unpleasant that, at the end of August, 1799, he went to Dieppe to visit a friend and went on to Belgium to spend the winter at the home of his old Luxembourg Prison cellmate, Vanhuele, now the mayor of Bruges.

Shortly after his arrival in Bruges, Paine heard the electrifying news from Paris that Bonaparte with the aid of his brother, Lucien, and of Sieyès, had overthrown the Directory in a bloodless coup, and had established a new government, the Consulate, with himself as First Consul. At first Paine planned to return to Paris almost immediately, but further word gave him pause. Bonneville, in an editorial, had referred to the new chief of state as 'a Cromwell' and was sent to prison for his temerity. Madame Bonneville sent a message to Paine warning him that he was being investigated by the secret police, and that he would be wise to remain beyond the borders of France until the situation became calmer.

Early in the spring of 1800 Paine finally returned to Paris. Bonneville was still in prison, although his release was imminent, and the author again made his home with the editor's family. He quickly discovered that the new master of France was a man with whom it was unwise to meddle. First Consul Bonaparte sent him a notice through the Ministry of Police on April 15, a scant seventy-two hours after he reached Paris, to the effect that 'the police are informed that M. Paine is behaving irregularly, and at the first complaint against him he will be sent back to America, his country'. The new regime evidently did not approve of some of the articles Paine had written for the *Bien informé*, and it was imperative that he exercise care. He heeded the warning, and for the next two years, until a short time before he left France for the United States, he wrote and published literally nothing about the internal affairs of France.

He found it far more difficult to refrain from interfering in the business of the United States. In 1800 President Adams sent a new commission to Paris to work out his country's differences with France; the group was headed by Oliver Ellsworth, a conservative of monumental reserve. The first Americans to call on him were two Jeffersonians, Joel Barlow and the American consul, Skipwith. Ellsworth received them coolly and displayed no interest in the advice they offered him. Paine, who persisted in believing that he played an important, though unofficial, role in the conduct of American diplomacy, waged his own campaign on the new commissioner. In a long letter to Vice-President Jefferson, written on October 1, 1880, after a hiatus of three years, Paine described his activities in the current situation and offered his own advice:

Rebel!

The Commissioners Ellsworth and Co. have been here about eight
months, and three more useless mortals never came upon public
business. Their presence appears to have been rather an injury than a
benefit. They set themselves up for a faction as soon as they arrived.
I was then in Belgia. Upon my return to Paris I learned they had
made a point of not returning the visits of Mr Skipwirth and Barlow,
because, they said, they had not the confidence of the executive.
Every known republican was treated in the same manner. I learned
from Mr Miller of Philadelphia, who had occasion to see them upon
business, that they did not intend to return my visit, if I made one.
This I supposed it was intended I should know, that I might not make
one. It had the contrary effect. I went to see Mr Ellsworth. I told him
I did not come to see him as a commissioner, nor to congratulate him
upon his mission; that I came to see him because I formerly had
known him in Congress. I mean not, said I, to press you with any
questions, or to engage you in any conversation upon the business
you are come upon, but I will nevertheless candidly say that I know
not what expectations the Government or the people of America
may have of your mission, or what expectations you may have your-
selves, but I believe you will find you can do but little. The treaty
with England lies at the threshold of all your business. The American
Government never did two more foolish things than when it signed
that Treaty and recalled Mr Monroe, who was the only man could
do them any service. Mr Ellsworth put on the dull gravity of a Judge,
and was silent. I added, you may perhaps make a treaty like that you
have made with England, which is a surrender of the rights of the
American flag; for the principle that neutral ships make neutral
property must be general or not at all. I then changed the subject, for
I had all the talk to myself upon this topic, and enquired after Sam.
Adams (I asked nothing about John), Mr Jefferson, Mr Monroe,
and others of my friends, and the melancholy case of the yellow
fever – of which he gave me as circumstantial an account as if he had
been summing up a case to a Jury. Here my visit ended, and had Mr
Ellsworth been as cunning as a statesman, or as wise as a Judge, he
would have returned my visit that he might appear insensible of the
intention of mine. . . .

But independently of these matters there appears to be a state of
circumstances rising, which if it goes on, will render all partial
treaties unneccessary. In the first place I doubt if any peace will be
made with England; and in the second place, I should not wonder to
see a coalition formed against her, to compel her to abandon her
insolence on the seas. . . .

In the present state of circumstances, and the prospects arising
from them, it may be proper for America to consider whether it is
worth her while to enter into any treaty at this moment, or to wait the

270

event of those circumstances which, if they go on will render partial treaties useless by deranging them. But if, in the mean time, she enters into any treaty it ought to be with a condition to the following purpose: Reserving to herself the right of joining in an association of Nations for the protection of the Rights of Neutral Commerce and the security of the liberty of the Seas.

Accompanying the letter were the manuscripts of Paine's recent political tracts, such as the *Compact Maritime*. In the letter Paine gave Jefferson a detailed account of their publication and declared, 'I am doing America more service . . . than [her] expensive Commissioners can do, and she has that service from me for nothing.' He concludes the letter by mentioning that Mr Skipwith had called to tell him that the commission would be leaving for Le Havre the following day, October 2. Skipwith's information, however, was not accurate. The commissioners remained in Paris, and on October 4 finally concluded an agreement with the French Government. This treaty, to be sure, did not meet with Paine's approval, and he assaulted it in a whole series of letters to Jefferson. He also indicated that if Jefferson became President, but not otherwise, he would be willing to accept a post from the United States Government in France. 'I am not tired of working for nothing,' he added candidly, 'but I cannot afford it.'

The conclusion of the American treaty with France gave him no additional opportunity to interfere in Franco-American affairs, and he became restless. An idea occurred to him when he received some American newspapers that reprinted an address in defense of democracy made by Vice-President Jefferson in the Senate on the day Congress reconvened. Paine had the speech translated into French, paid for its printing, and distributed it free, telling Henry R. Yorke, a friend, that it was 'by way of contrast with the government of the First Consul'. Bonaparte failed to appreciate the gesture, but the French realized that Jefferson was the leading candidate for President in the forth-coming American elections, and too many complications would have resulted had Paine been expelled from France for having published some of his recent remarks.

Paine also did what might be termed a ghost-writing job for a high-ranking French official in July, 1800, preparing a long memorandum on the subject of such internal improvements as canals, roads, and bridges. He incorporated a scheme for financing these improvements in his report, and he stressed that France, endowed with greater natural resources than Britain, could far outstrip her enemy and become the wealthiest nation in Europe if she increased her manufactures. No known use was ever made of this memorandum, and it is possible it was never seen by anyone other than the unnamed official for whom it was written. Bonaparte did not encourage such initiatives on the part of his subordinates.

Paine was very discouraged whenever he contemplated the work being done by the First Consul. All hope of establishing a republic in France on the American model was dead, and the author now had only one desire – to return at last to the United States as soon as arrangements could be made.

24

The Prodigal Returns

No man could be more outspoken than Thomas Paine when he disliked someone, but his attitude toward Napoleon Bonaparte has always been something of a mystery. He did not write or publish anything critical about the First Consul in France prior to his departure for the United States in 1802, for he had not forgotten the months he had spent in the Luxembourg Prison, and he knew he would be cast into an even less comfortable prison if he launched an attack on Bonaparte. Realizing that the secret police were keeping a close watch on him and suspecting that his mail might be read, he confined himself to brief, bland comments about the First Consul when he wrote to friends in the United States.

Various sources, most of them English, indicate that his spoken comments about the dictator of France, even at social functions, were far less circumspect. Walter Savage Landor, the distinguished author and literary critic, met Paine in 1802 and wrote that Paine's face was 'blotched with the wine he took, and his hand was unsteady'; that he frequently held a glass of brandy in his hand, but his talk was clear, fluent, and incisive. According to Landor, Paine regarded Bonaparte as 'wilful, headstrong, proud, morose, presumptuous. . . . There is not on record one who has committed so many faults and crimes with so little temptation to commit them. . . . Tyrants in general shed blood upon plan or from passion; he seems to have shed it only because he could not be quiet'. Lewis Goldsmith and Henry Redhead Yorke, two young Englishmen, attributed similar sentiments to Paine. Yorke was graphic, too, in his descriptions of Paine's bedchamber and personal appearance: 'The chimney hearth was an heap of dirt; there was not a speck of cleanliness to be seen.' Several shelves were piled high with pasteboard boxes used as filing cabinets, and 'in one corner of the room stood several huge bars of iron, curiously shaped, and two large trunks; opposite the fireplace, a board covered with pamphlets and journals, having more the appearance of a dresser in a scullery than a sideboard'. Paine wore a long, shapeless flannel dressing gown when he greeted his guest, and he looked so old and ravaged that Yorke, who had not seen him in years, was shocked. When the visitor expressed the hope that the republican form of government would prosper in France, Paine became bitter. 'Do you call this a republic? 'he demanded. 'I know of no republic in the world except America.'

These Englishmen, who hated Napoleon Bonaparte passionately, may have put words into Paine's mouth or exaggerated what he said. After Paine's return to the United States, when he could have spoken freely, without fear of reprisal, he wrote nothing critical about Napoleon.

In any event, Paine saw nothing of Napoleon in person during his last year in France, nor did he hold any meetings of consequence with anyone in the ruling circles of the nation during that time. On July 15, 1801, when Napoleon concluded his Concordat with Pope Pius VII, the secret police promptly closed the doors of the Theophilanthropic Society. Ordinarily Paine would have been the first to complain that the principle of freedom of religion was being contravened and abused, but he accepted without a murmur the collapse of the religious organization he had been so instrumental in founding. As has been seen, he never forgave insult or injury, real or imagined, but in this instance, when an institution close to his heart was destroyed on Napoleon's order, he said nothing, and even after his return to America he refrained from discussing the issue.

Paine's early biographers are at loss to understand his strange silence. Some indicate that the Theophilanthropic movement meant less to him than he had indicated, and that he had established it merely to pass the time. *The Age of Reason* proves that the subject was close to his heart. Other biographers hinted that he was growing mellow, but this claim is absurd. Paine remained actively belligerent until the end of his days.

He remained quiet while still in France because it was in his own best interest not to arouse Napoleon's ire. And, after he left France, other matters of greater concern occupied his mind and his time. For these simple reasons, it appears, the passing of the Theophilanthropists remained unmourned by the men who had created the movement.

Only one letter was written by Paine to any French government officer during his final year in France. In a brief communication to the minister of the interior he offered his design for an iron bridge to be used for the building of a new span across the Seine. The minister replied cordially, but nothing ever came of the project.

Late in April, 1801, Congressman John Dawson of Virginia arrived in Paris on a mission, bringing with him a new treaty of friendship signed by Thomas Jefferson, who had just been elected President of the United States, Jefferson did not forget old friends, and Dawson carried a private letter to Thomas Paine, which the new President had written on March 18, 1801, only two weeks after taking office. He assured Paine that the *Compact Maritime* had been sent to the printer in accordance with the author's instructions and reported that anti-French sentiment in the United States had died away. His next paragraph would, by the end of the year, be reprinted by hundreds of newspapers in America, France, Great Britain, and elsewhere. It read:

You expressed a wish to get passage to this country in a public vessel. Mr Dawson is charged with orders to the captain of the *Maryland* to receive and accommodate you back if you can be ready to depart at such short warning. Rob. R. Livingston is appointed minister plenipotentiary to the republic of France, but will not leave this [country] till we receive the ratification of the convention by Mr Dawson. I am in hopes you will find us returned generally to sentiments worthy of former times. In these it will be your glory to have steadily labored, and with as much effect as any man living. That you may long live to continue your useful labors and to reap the reward in the thankfulness of nations, is my sincere prayer. Accept assurances of my high esteem and affectionate attachment.

Paine's pride knew no bounds. The President of the United States had confirmed his own high opinion of himself, and thought enough of his safety to have ordered the *Maryland*, a powerful frigate of forty-two guns, to transport him across the Atlantic to America. Unable to keep the good news to himself, he leaked the story to the *Moniteur*, and when a reporter visited him for confirmation, he allowed the paragraph to be copied. A month later the story was reprinted by the Washington *Intelligencer*.

Jefferson's enemies, including the New England Federalists who had not forgotten Paine's attack on George Washington, saw an opportunity to make political capital at the President's expense. They charged that Paine – the antichrist, the atheist, the man who had sullied the name of Washington – had dared to demand that a ship of the United States Navy be sent to fetch him home from France at public expense, and that the craven President had agreed. In their accounts they did not mention that the *Maryland* would be bringing back Congressman Dawson with the ratified treaty so that Livingston, the new minister to France, could depart and take up his duties.

As it happened, the French were slow in ratifying the treaty so that the *Maryland* was still riding at anchor when summer came, and the arrival of a merchantman carrying American newspapers brought the full story to the Americans in Paris. The editorials in the Federalist press, indicating that Jefferson shared his friend's wildly radical views, charged that the President wanted to transform the country into an atheistic, immoral land. Paine was aghast: Jefferson was being attacked unfairly because of friendship for him. Complicating the situation still further was a letter Paine received, in mid-September, 1801, from Dr. William Eustis, a Jeffersonian congressman, who enclosed a clipping from the Washington *Intelligencer*. The President himself, Eustis intimated, was responsible for an editorial on the subject. It read, in part:

We imagined that it was possible for an individual of one set of religious principles to feel charity for the misfortunes of a fellow mortal of another set, or of no religious opinions whatever; we imagined that virtue was not exclusively confined to one kind of political sentiments; and we imagined that a country might feel grateful for the distinguished services of a man, rendered in a period of difficulty and danger, though such a man might afterwards avow opinions which some might think good, others might think bad.

Paine was deeply hurt by the implied reference to charity. It was true that his assets had dwindled and that he was short of cash, but he was by no means a public charge, and he hated being portrayed as a pauper. But he refused to accept Eustis's hint that Thomas Jefferson was responsible for the defensive, semi-apologetic tone of the *Intelligencer* editorial. The President was his good friend and had found a way to do him a favor; that was the situation, no matter how much the Federalists twisted the truth. Conway refutes the claim, made by Paine's earlier biographers, that the offended author felt Jefferson had deserted him, and in this instance Conway appears to be right. At no time either in correspondence or conversation, did he indicate annoyance with the President. In fact, he continued to bombard Jefferson with friendly letters and thanked him repeatedly for his generous offer. At the same time, however, a sense of loyalty to Jefferson may have made him anxious to silence the Federalist barrage of criticism. That, coupled with his sense of pride, impelled him to seek another means of returning home.

An opportunity for Paine to leave arose when Napoleon unexpectedly concluded a tenuous peace agreement with Great Britain. The basic issues in the power struggle had not been resolved; it was obvious that the war would be resumed after both sides had rested and regrouped their forces. For the immediate present, however, Europe was at peace and the British naval blockade off the coast of France was discontinued; if Thomas Paine sailed to the United States on a merchant ship he would run no risk of being picked up at sea by a Royal Navy warship and returned to England as a traitor.

Paine happily elected to decline President Jefferson's offer, and made his own travel arrangements. Sailings could be scheduled in advance now that brigs were no longer menaced by men-of-war, and in July he booked passage on an American merchantman that was due to put into Le Havre from the Baltic in time to cross the Atlantic in September. He was still short of cash, but two English friends, Sir Francis Burdett and William Bosville, who came to Paris to visit him, made him a gift of 500 louis d'or (equivalent to $5,000 today) 'in appreciation' of *The Rights of Man*. So Paine had more than enough money to settle his debts in France and pay for his passage.

The prospect of leaving the Bonnevilles was painful, and Paine saw an opportunity to return the hospitality they had extended to him over the past five years. Bonneville had been released from prison, but, no longer allowed to publish the *Bien informé*, he earned a precarious living only by printing non-political pamphlets, broadsides, and the like. Paine offered to share his home in America with the family and to help them start life again in the New World. Bonneville, still a patriot even though he had lost favor with Napoleon's regime, was somewhat dubious and hesitated in making a decision; but Marguerite was eager to see the United States and wanted to accept. Paine, who had been living a bachelor existence for so long, said he had no other family and made his offer more attractive by promising to leave the bulk of his estate to the Bonnevilles if they came to America. It should be noted that he kept his word.

Madame Bonneville followed Paine to the United States accompanied by her children, but her husband, in spite of his assurances that he would come at some later time, remained in France. She had become estranged from her husband while he had been imprisoned, and her departure represented their final separation.

Thomas Paine was sixty-five years old at the time of his return to America and, as nearly as can be determined, no longer led an active sex life. Marguerite de Bonneville had not yet turned thirty, and although she demonstrated a healthy interest in members of the opposite sex in the United States, Paine was not one of those men. Friends who had an opportunity to observe them together, and who at first may have been somewhat dubious about the propriety of the relationship, said that they behaved like uncle and niece. There was a trace of formality in their approach to each other, and Marguerite was obviously in awe of the author, regarding him as one of the truly great men of his era. The barrier between them that prevented intimacy in France was not lowered in America. Only a few of the letters they exchanged have survived, but these documents indicate that they were never casual with each other. One of the Bonneville sons, who became an American citizen and enjoyed a distinguished career in the United States, subsequently indicated his firm belief that the association between his mother and Paine had never been an intimate one.

Arrangements for the Bonneville family to follow Paine were more or less completed in August. The last week of that month Clio Rickman came to Paris to spend a few days with his old friend and, like Yorke and others, was shocked by Paine's appearance. On August 29 they went to Le Havre together, and on September 1 Paine finally set sail across the Atlantic, speeded on his voyage by Rickman's sentimental lines of farewell:

> Thus smooth be thy waves, and thus gentle the breeze,
>   As thou bearest my Paine far away;
> O! waft him to comfort and regions of ease,
>   Each blessing of freedom and friendship to seize,
> And bright be his setting sun's ray.

Paine had not achieved his goals in either Great Britain or France, and although *The Rights of Man* had enhanced his reputation, *The Age of Reason*, which he regarded as his major work, had been rejected with scorn by a shocked public. What emotions he may have felt as the brig carried him home to America can only be conjectured. He kept no diary on board ship, and later, in his correspondence, he made only fleeting references to the voyage. Most of his thoughts appear to have been concentrated on his future. He wanted to earn his living as an engineer and was bringing his model bridges with him, as well as models of wheels he had devised. He hoped that Jefferson would use his influence to persuade Congress to build over major American rivers a number of the bridges he had designed.

The United States to which Paine returned was far different from the country he had left a decade and a half before. The American experiment was considered a success. The new Constitution had given the federal government the strength and flexibility to administer the nation's affairs effectively. Immigrants were arriving at a rate of more than 10,000 per year, many of them from England, Scotland, and Ireland, and those who did not settle in such major centers as New York, Philadelphia, and Boston were moving out to the ever expanding western frontier. Within a few months of Paine's arrival the purchase of the Louisiana Territory transformed the United States from a seaboard nation into one that spanned half a continent and overnight gave her the potential of becoming a major world power.

The Industrial Revolution had spread to America, too, to the distress of President Jefferson, who believed that her economy should be based on her agricultural produce. She became less dependent on Great Britain as she turned more and more to local industries for her manufactured goods. Approximately one hundred new factories were being built each year along the seaboard, with the bulk of unskilled labor provided by immigrants. Large fortunes were being accumulated by manufacturers, merchants, traders, and bankers, but there was still relatively little poverty in the land. The poor were migrating to Kentucky, Tennessee, and the fertile Ohio Valley, where land was free, and established their homesteads there.

Perhaps the most significant change, as it touched Paine, was that the spirit of the Revolution had vanished. Two decades had passed since the war had ended. A new generation had grown to manhood and, with the exception of Jefferson and a few other senior leaders, most of the posts in the executive, legislative, and judicial branches of the government were held by men who had been junior officers during the war. The veterans of the Continental Line exerted little influence, and men did not look back. Instead they were concerned with the current problems of their rapidly growing nation and expanding economy. The principles that Thomas Paine held dear were no longer argued about; they had been incorporated into the American system and were taken for granted. The nation was at peace, and her citizens were more concerned about prosperity than they were with the rights that had become part of their heritage.

The American press had been heralding Paine's arrival, and when his ship put into Baltimore, on October 31 or November 1, 1802, a large, noisy crowd was on hand to greet him. In addition to a score of Jeffersonian Republican-Democrats, a number of Maryland's Federalist leaders appeared, too, and were very cordial to him. Paine took advantage of the presence of reporters by showing them his model bridges.

He was conducted to an inn, where he intended to spend the night before going on to Washington. There, less than two hours after his arrival, he was placed under arrest on a charge of indebtedness. A man named O'Maly or O'Malley claimed that he had advanced fifty guineas to Paine when the author had been confined in the Luxembourg Prison, and that in spite of repeated attempts he had not been able to recover the sum. The Federalist press happily reported the incident, and Paine was obliged to remain in Baltimore until the matter was settled.

On November 13 in an interview in the *American Patriot*, Baltimore's leading newspaper, Paine denied that he owed O'Maly any money and insisted that he had never even heard of the man. On the following day, in reply, O'Maly stated that he had obtained a judgment against the author in a Paris court, but had not been able to collect. On November 16 the case came to trial, and it transpired that O'Maly had merely been acting as the commercial agent for an old friend of Paine's, a man named M'Coy. Paine had borrowed the money from M'Coy before leaving the United States, and M'Coy had sold the debt to O'-Maly. The indignant Paine offered to repay M'Coy at once, with interest, but would have nothing to do with O'Maly, charging that the man had tried to embarrass him for political reasons. On this one occasion his suspicions appear to have been right. The Federalists were losing no chance to harass President Jefferson, who had sent Paine a dinner invitation, and the Federalist press was screaming that an atheist soon would be entertained in the President's house. O'Maly's attack had centered on Paine's finances, but he could be made to appear even less attractive on religious grounds, so the anti-Jefferson Federalists were quick to take advantage.

On Monday, November 17, Paine set off for Washington after settling the debt. That night he went to the President's house, where he dined in private with Jefferson, now a widower. There were no other guests, and the two men spent the evening reminiscing. Before Paine returned to his hotel they went out for a stroll together, and as the Federalist newspapers reported, 'Washington City last night was treated to the spectacle of seeing our President walk arm-in-arm with a confessed atheist!'

Soon every newspaper in the country was reporting Paine's return. The Federalists attacked him mercilessly, and a number of editorials stated flatly that 'the people cannot but wish that Mr Paine had remained in Europe'. Paine himself took notice of all the publicity and wrote to Rickman that he was being greeted everywhere with either praise or abuse. The praise was relatively faint. Many of the Republican-Democrats felt that Paine was a liability to President Jefferson, and their newspapers reflected their concern. Members of Congress were timid, afraid their constituents would disapprove, and a number of them became alarmed when the newcomer took up residence at a boarding-house called Lovell's Hotel.

Washington was at that time a raw boomtown, where only a few government buildings had been completed. The sound of hammers and saws could be heard daily; the streets were rutted dirt roads and a plan to pave Pennsylvania Avenue was called visionary. High-ranking members of the administration owned or rented homes, where they lived with their families, but there were no similar facilities available for senators and congressmen. When Congress was in session, its members lodged in boarding-houses where, since there were only two public inns in the town, they also took their meals.

There were sixteen senators and congressmen living at Lovell's Hotel, nine of them Republican-Democrats, and without exception they treated Thomas Paine like a leper. They avoided sitting next to him at meals and spoke to him only when necessary. Most of them, however, did not shun him for personal reasons. Although neither they nor their constituents had read *The Age of Reason*, they had been informed, particularly by the Federalist press, that it was an atheistic document. They could not forget, either, that Paine was the man who had savagely attacked George Washington. As a result it was not politically healthy for a senator or congressman to become friendly with such a controversial figure.

Thomas Jefferson did not share the concern of Congress. He considered Paine an old comrade-in-arms, a friend who had shared the most difficult of times with him, and he insisted on treating the visitor accordingly, Paine dined at least twice each week at the President's house, and other visitors reported that he was very much at home there, on terms of easy familiarity with the First Citizen.

There were others as well who rallied to Paine's side. Mrs Albert Gallatin, the former Hannah Nicholson, now the wife of the secretary of the treasury, had known Paine sixteen years earlier. She was genuinely delighted to see him, and Paine dined frequently at the Gallatin house. The secretary of war, Major General Henry Dearborn, had been friendly with Paine during and after the American Revolution; he, too, refused to snub an old friend, and Paine was a welcome guest at the Dearborn house. Senator Bradley, the President *pro tem* of the Senate, was yet another who opened his door to Paine, and who emphasized his hospitality by announcing that he would admit no Federalist under his roof.

Paine, who enjoyed being the center of attention, was favored by enough persons in high places to be content, and appeared not to mind the snubs of the Federalists and of the timid Republican-Democrats. Certainly his mind was as active as ever, and on December 24, 1802, he wrote a remarkable letter to Jefferson. The Louisiana Territory had been ceded to France by Spain, and on November 26 the French had closed the port of New Orleans to all foreign shipping, including that of the United States. All American traffic on the Mississippi River was endangered, and the Federalists agitated for firm action, demanding that the President take an uncompromising stand and, if necessary, go to war against Napoleon.

Paine's letter, which bore the heading 'Of Louisiana', demonstrates that he was still able to think in bold strategic terms:

Spain has ceded Louisiana to france, and france has excluded the Americans from N. Orleans and the navigation of the Mississippi; the people of the Western Territory have complained of it to their Government, and the governt. is of consequence involved and interested in the affair. The question then is – What is the best step to be taken?

The one is to begin by memorial and remonstrance against an infraction of a right. The other is by accommodation, still keeping the right in view, but not making it a groundwork.

Suppose then the Government begin by making a proposal to france to repurchase the cession, made to her by Spain, of Louisiana, provided it be with the consent of the people of Louisiana or a majority thereof.

By beginning on this ground, any thing can be said without carrying the appearance of a threat, – the growing power of the western territory can be stated as a matter of information, and also the impossibility of restraining them from seizing upon New Orleans, and the equal impossibility of france to prevent it.

Suppose the proposal attended to, the sum to be given comes next on the carpet. This, on the part of America, will be estimated between the value of the Commerce, and the quantity of revenue that Louisiana will produce.

The french treasury is not only empty, but the government has consumed by anticipation a great part of the next year's revenue. A monied proposal will, I believe, be attended to; if it should, the claims upon france can be stipulated as part of the payment, and that sum can be paid here to the claimants.

Rebel!

I congratulate you on the birthday of the New Sun, now called christmas-day; and I make you a present of a thought on Louisiana.

Paine dined with the President on Christmas afternoon, and was astonished to learn that Jefferson, too, had thought of buying the Louisiana Territory. In fact, Minister Robert Livingston was under instructions to sound out the French Government on the subject, and Talleyrand had displayed some interest. Therefore James Monroe, who was being sent to London as minister to Great Britain, would stop first in Paris under a commission as minister extraordinary, and would assist Livingston in the negotiations.

Paine was particularly pleased when the President went out of his way to extend his own thanks and those of the United States for submitting the suggestion as an original idea. All Paine needed to know to make him happy was the realization that he could still be of service to America and that his efforts were appreciated.

25

A Disillusioned Hero

The Federalists continued their unremitting attack on Paine, calling him an atheist and insisting that he was unfit to consort with God-fearing Americans. A number of prominent Republican-Democrats, among them Levi Lincoln and William Duane, knew that Paine wanted to launch a counterattack, but urged him to refrain for the President's sake. At the same time they tried to reassure Jefferson that his political foes had already done all they could to harm him through Paine, and that henceforth they could not exploit the relationship further.

In mid-December Paine received a letter, written on November 30, from his old friend Samuel Adams, now the retired governor of Massachusetts. Adams, who did not have much longer to live, was deeply disturbed by what he had read of Paine's beliefs, as well as by the potential harm to the President that could be caused by his relationship with Paine. He had heard that this good and true friend 'had turned his mind to a defence of infidelity'.

Paine attempted several replies before arriving at a version that pleased him. On January 1, 1803, he wrote to Adams, quoting his creed from *The Age of Reason* and asking, 'My good friend, do you call believing in God infidelity?' He added:

We cannot serve the Deity in the manner we serve those who cannot do without that service. He needs no service from us. We can add nothing to eternity. But it is in our power to render a service acceptable to him, and that is, not by praying, but by endeavoring to make his creatures happy. A man does not serve God by praying, for it is himself he is trying to serve; and as to hiring or paying men to pray, as if the Deity needed instructions, it is in my opinion an abomination. I have been exposed to and preserved through many dangers, but instead of buffeting the Deity with prayers, as if I distrusted him, or must dictate to him, I reposed myself on his protection; and you, my friend, will find even in your last moments, more consolation in the silence of resignation than in the murmuring wish of a prayer.

Paine was Jefferson's houseguest when the President's daughter, Maria Jefferson Eppes, whom the author had first known in Paris, came to see her father early in 1803. The Federalist barrage was beginning to get on Paine's nerves, but he gave no sign of it until February 23, when he was told of a toast at a Federalist dinner, 'May they never know pleasure who love Paine'. This jibe was too much for him, and he wanted to reply in kind, but was dissuaded by Senator William Plumer of New Hampshire, who convinced him, at least for the moment, that the Federalist assault would be meaningless if it was ignored. Paine nevertheless felt the need to relieve his feelings on paper, and writing a reply in doggerel, presented it to Jefferson. It read:

> I send you, Sir, a tale about some Feds,
> Who, in their wisdom, got to loggerheads.
> The case was this, they felt so flat and sunk,
> They took a glass together and got drunk.
> Such things, you know, are neither new nor rare,
> For some will hary themselves when in despair.
> It was the natal day of Washington,
> And that they thought a famous day for fun;
> For with the learned world it is agreed,
> The better day the better deed.
> They talked away, and as the glass went round
> They grew, in point of wisdom, more profound;
> For at the bottom of the bottle lies
> That kind of sense we overlook when wise.

A Disillusioned Hero

Come, here's a toast, cried one, with roar immense,
May none know pleasure who know Common Sense.
Bravo! cried some – no, no, some others cried,
But left it to the waiter to decide.
I think, said he, the case would be more plain,
To leave out Common Sense, and put in Paine.
On this a mighty noise among
This drunken, bawling, senseless throng.
Some said that Common Sense was all a curse,
That making people wiser made them worse;
It learned them to be careful of their purse,
And not be laid about like babes at nurse,
Nor yet believe in stories upon trust,
Which all mankind, to be well governed must;
And that the toast was better at the first,
And he that didn't think so might be cursed.
So on they went, till such a fray arose
As all who know what Feds are may suppose.

The alleviation of Paine's ruffled feelings afforded by this effort
was only temporary. The Federalists kept up their barrage, and
by the beginning of March, 1803, after tolerating their abuse for
four months, he ignored the advice of his Democratic-Republican
friends and countered with thunderbolts of his own.

He wrote a series of letters, *To the Citizens of the United States*,
over a period of many years. These communications were first
published in the Washington *Intelligencer*, and subsequently
were reprinted by more than fifty other newspapers sympathetic
to Paine and the causes he represented. The first, which appeared
early in March, was written shortly before he left Washington;
those that followed were prepared in Philadelphia, New York,
and Bordentown.

The first two letters were direct attacks on the fundamental
concepts of the Federalists, who, he charged, considered
'government as a profitable monopoly, and the people as hereditary property'. During the first days of the Republic, Paine said,
the term Federalist had been an honorable designation for those
who had recognized the absolute necessity for the establishment
of a common representative government in whose administration
all the states participated. Gradually the significance of the name
had changed, having been adopted by unscrupulous politicians
who had been trying to destroy the very principles of representative government. During the Presidency of John Adams, in

fact, they had tried to transform the United States into a hereditary monarchy. They had hoped to attain this end by the establishment of a large standing army and the creation of enormous
government revenues, trying to frighten the people into submission with cries of internal treason and the threat of a French
invasion. The talk of traitors had been unfounded, Paine asserted,
and as he himself had been living in France, where he had been
well acquainted with leading members of the government, he
was in a position to know that at no time had France even
contemplated an invasion of the United States.

In his third letter Paine finally replied to his critics on the
subject of his religious convictions. He reaffirmed his belief in
deism, but he appealed to his present readers through an account
of his personal experiences rather than the abstract concepts he
had discussed in *The Age of Reason*. He told in detail how he had
almost been captured by the British when leaving England, how
he had escaped the guillotine when held in the Luxembourg
Prison and how he had come within a hair's breadth of being
taken by a British frigate. Either good luck or Divine Providence
had looked after him, he declared, and he preferred to think it
was the latter. In fact, Providence had provided him with special
protection, and inasmuch as Providence could not be accused of
patronizing infidelity, his own religious opinions were therefore
both pious and rational.

In his fourth letter Paine found further confirmation of the
support of Divine Providence in his present happy condition.
Thanks to Providence his business affairs were in good shape,
he was enjoying every material comfort, his health was excellent,
and his frame of mind was serene.

The Republican-Democrats tried in vain to silence him as each
of his letters caused another Federalist outburst. On neither side
was the conduct of the feud rational. John Adams, the titular
head of the Federalist party, was a member of the Unitarian
Church, and his religious beliefs were in fact remarkably similar
to those of Paine and Jefferson. But everyone concerned was too
busily engaged in the game of name-calling and mud-slinging to
examine the substance of their supposed differences.

In his sixth letter Paine tried to halt the exaggerated attacks on
Jefferson by publishing the full text of the President's letter
inviting Paine to return to the United states on the American
warship *Maryland*. He made it clear that they had sailed to

France on a diplomatic mission unconnected with him and his problems, and that it would have cost the taxpayers nothing had he come home on the ship. But, as he discovered, he was merely adding more kindling to the fire; the Federalists merely stepped up their attacks.

Soon after writing the first of these letters Paine made up his mind to leave Washington. He was eager to return to his cottage in Bordentown and did not want to be the cause of any further embarrassment to the President. Baltimore was his first stop, in February, 1803, and there he revealed that the fight with the Federalists had not harmed his sense of humor. A preacher named Hargrove accosted him, informing him that the key to the Scriptures had been found after being lost for four thousand years. Paine regarded him in unblinking silence for a moment, and said, 'Then it must be very rusty'.

Paine spent a week in Philadelphia, where he arranged for an exhibit of his model bridges at Peale's Museum. (Jefferson had supported him so staunchly that he had refrained from asking the President to perform another favor by presenting the models to Congress.) During his stay some of his old Philadelphia friends were conspicuous by their failure to call on him or otherwise acknowledge his presence in the city. Among them was Dr Benjamin Rush, who later wrote, 'His principles avowed in his "Age of Reason" were so offensive to me that I did not wish to renew my intercourse with him'. Among the old friends he did see there was George Clymer.

When Paine arrived in Bordentown, he found his cottage as he had left it, thanks to the care and devotion of friends. Colonel Kirkbridge gave him a riotous welcome, and John Hall, who had helped him with previous inventions, wrote, 'I never saw him jollier'. Paine, he said, was full of 'mechanical schemes and whims' which they made plans to develop together.

Even in rural Bordentown Paine kept up with events of the day. On March 12, soon after his arrival, he wrote a blistering attack on the Federalists for suggesting that New Orleans be taken by force. In April he wrote three letters for publication, all of them in defense of Jefferson's policies, and also drafted a reply to an attack on the President. In May he found a little time for his own concerns, and wrote several enthusiastic letters about his hope of constructing his iron arch bridges over the Delaware and Schuylkill rivers.

Late in the spring of 1803 the country was stunned by the news of the Louisiana Purchase. Napoleon, who realized the difficulty of defending his New World possessions and who wanted to concentrate his resources on his war with the British, made the United States what was tantamount to a gift: For the sum of $15 million he sold the United States a tract of 828 million acres, increasing the territory of the United States by 140 per cent. Thirteen new states were ultimately carved out of these holdings and the nation became a first-rate power. In spite of the lip service that Paine paid to the cause of democracy and the right of a people to any form of government or religion they chose, he betrayed his own skepticism in a revealing letter he sent to President Jefferson from Bordentown on August 2. He wrote on the subject of Louisiana:

I take it for granted that the present inhabitants know little or nothing of election and representation as constituting government. They are therefore not in an immediate condition to exercise these powers, and besides this they are perhaps too much under the influence of their priests to be sufficiently free.

I should suppose that a Government *provisoire* formed by Congress for three, five, or seven years would be the best mode of beginning. In the mean time they may be initiated into the practice by electing their Municipal government, and after some experience they will be in train to elect their State government. I think it not only would be good policy but right to say that the people shall have the right of electing their Church Ministers, otherwise their Ministers will hold by authority from the Pope. I do not make it a compulsive article, but to put it in their power to use it when they please. It will serve to hold the priests in a stile of good behavior, and also to give the people an idea of elective rights. Anything, they say, will do to learn upon, and therefore they may as well begin upon priests.

Paine also made it his business in the late spring and early summer to write to various Republican-Democrats in the Senate. He appears to have been afraid, needlessly, that the Federalists would try to block the treaty with France that would make the Louisiana Purchase legal. He freely gave the senators his advice on their treaty-making powers under the Constitution and urged them not to falter in the pursuit of their duty.

In another age his advice to the President and to the senators would have been regarded as officious meddling, but Paine did not see his counseling activities in such a light, nor did his ocrrespondents. As an old colleague of Jefferson he thought of himself as the President's equal; no matter what opinions the Federalist held of Paine, he considered himself one of America's elder statesmen, a leader who had earned his right to speak his mind.

He also enjoyed playing the natural role of village sage in Bordentown. During his daily walks he usually dropped in at the Washington House, a tavern owned by one Debora Applegate, and later in the day he had his regular table there. He sat for several hours, a drink of brandy in his hand, and happily conversed on topics of the day with anyone who wanted to speak with him.

Paine found himself in the unusual position of having no financial worries, due to the care exercised by his friends on his behalf during his long absence from America. His property was now worth slightly in excess of £6,000 and brought him a return of £400 per year, or about $1,800, enough to enable him to live comfortably, if not in great style.

But life was not serene for Bordentown's most illustrious citizen. The clergymen of the neighborhood thundered against him in their sermons, and one day in mid-summer the entire town was mysteriously inundated with copies of a cartoon depicting Satan carrying Paine off to Hell. The object of these ineffectual assaults could smile complacently, and remained convinced that *The Age of Reason* was persuading uncounted thousands to think as he did.

One series of incidents, however, gave him pause for sober reflection. Late in the winter he made a trip to New York to see James Monroe off to Europe, and was accompanied on the journey by Colonel Kirkbride. The proprietors of the two stagecoach companies in Trenton refused to sell transportation to Paine on the grounds that he was 'an infidel,' so he decided to go by private chaise. A large, jeering crowd surrounded the carriage and tried to frighten the horses, but the driver pushed forward through the mob and the author and his companion escaped with nothing worse than a bad fright. Paine accepted the rebuffs with philosophical equanimity, remarking to his friend that under the American system of government the people had the right to express any opinions they wished.

In a typical gesture after he reached New York, he gave Monroe a long, detailed memorandum, telling the minister which officials in the French Foreign Office would be most receptive to an American offer to purchase Louisiana. Before he returned to Bordentown the Republican-Democrats of New York held a banquet in his honor, and, Paine noted, 'more than two hundred leading persons in this city' attended the affair.

Louisiana remained very much on his mind. In August he wrote a letter of more than 4,000 words to Senator John C. Breckenridge of Kentucky, who had been designated by the Republican-Democrats to lead the floor fight for ratification of the Louisiana Purchase Treaty. Paine laid out a precise blueprint, assuring Breckenridge that if he followed it to the letter the Senate would be unable to reject the agreement.

Late in the summer Paine returned to New York, but an epidemic of yellow fever in the city drove him away. He went instead to Stonington, Connecticut, to visit an old friend from France, Captain Nathan Hayley, and lived for several months as Hayley's guest. Inevitably, he became interested in Connecticut politics, particularly as Oliver Ellsworth, the leader of the state's Federalists, was anathema to him, and Ellsworth despised him in return. Paine held a number of discussions with prominent local Republican-Democrats, advising them of ways to deprive Ellsworth of his influence. On October 10 he wrote a fiery letter to the Hartford *American Mercury*, charging that Ellsworth was a monarchist who was trying to sabotage the Constitution and establish a hereditary form of government in the United States. He offered no specifics in his diatribe, but cleverly tried to separate Ellsworth from the Federalist rank and file, claiming that the latter were patriotic Americans who failed to realize that men like Ellsworth were trying to lead them up the path of treason.

A large group of Republican-Democrats from New London paid a call on Paine in Stonington, and the leader of the delegation, Nicolli Fosdick, later wrote that the great man was 'sociable and civil in conversation, until he had made too free with ardent spirits'. On this occasion Paine read aloud, at length, excerpts of a letter President Jefferson had written to him on the subject of Louisiana. Fosdick thought it improper for any man to quote from a private letter penned by the President, and wrote to Jefferson to warn him that Paine became careless after consuming too much brandy and rum.

In September Paine was tempted to return to France. The Anglo-French war had been resumed, and reports reaching America indicated that Napoleon intended to launch a major attack on England. Paine wrote to Jefferson that if the invasion was successful he might cross the Atlantic again 'to assist in forming a constitution for England'.

New responsibilities made it difficult for Paine to contemplate joining Napoleon for the forthcoming invasion of England. While he was still in Stonington he received word that Marguerite de Bonneville and her three sons, Benjamin, Louis, and Thomas, had arrived in New York. Having offered them his unstinting hospitality, he hurried to meet them and then faced a perplexing problem. The cottage in Bordentown was too small to accommodate him and four members of the Bonneville family; his house in New Rochelle had burned down during his stay in Europe and only a tiny dwelling had been erected in its place. But the New Rochelle property was far more extensive than the tiny Bordentown plot, so he hastily made arrangements to have the house there made larger, a task that would take the builders some months to complete. In the meantime Madame de Bonneville and her two elder sons lived in the Bordentown cottage. According to some accounts she supported herself and her children by giving French lessons; other versions indicate that she became a governess.

Paine took the youngest boy, Thomas Paine de Bonneville, back to Stonington with him and placed him in the home of the Reverend John Foster of the Universalist Church, who had a congregation there. Assuming full responsibility for the child's support, Paine returned to New Rochelle to 'exhort, encourage & assist' his house builders. He took a room in a nearby lodging-house, much to the distress of local Federalists, who pointed him out to their children as the devil's disciple. But there were far more Republican-Democrats than Federalists in Westchester County, and when a fete was held in Paine's honor in nearby White Plains, more than a thousand persons attended.

Paine went to New York for the winter of 1803 – 4, taking a small suite of rooms for himself in a lodginghouse in Greenwich Village, which was rapidly becoming the most fashionable part of the city. James Wilburn, a prominent Republican-Democrat, was his host. Another lodger there was John Fellows, a veteran of the Continental Line and a graduate of Yale College, and one of Paine's oldest and best friends in America. Fellows had published an edition of *The Age of Reason* in 1795, and had secured the American copyright for the work on Paine's behalf.

Later, when Paine moved into his New Rochelle house, Fellows acted as his literary agent in New York.

The English-born William Carver was one of Paine's close associates during this period, and they remained friendly for about two years, until Paine discovered that the other man was trying to cheat him. Perhaps the author's best friend in the city was the distinguished Elihu Palmer, a Dartmouth College graduate and former clergyman who, after losing his eyesight due to a bout with yellow fever, became the leader of the deist movement in New York. He edited and published a bi-weekly deist magazine, *The Prospect, or View of the Moral World,* and in 1804 Paine contributed fourteen essays, all of which were, in essence, taken from *The Age of Reason.* No one praised *The Age of Reason* more than Palmer, and it was natural that Paine should regard him with great affection. Mrs Palmer was another of Paine's admirers, and years later after her husband's death, she nursed Paine when he was in the throes of his own terminal illness.

In the winter of 1804, the sixty-seven-year-old Paine was incapacitated by an attack of gout and confined to his bed for a month. The first time he ventured outdoors again he slipped on the ice and suffered such a bad fall that he had to return to bed for several more weeks. It was late March by the time he recovered sufficiently to take an active interest in the affairs of the world.

Thomas Jefferson, he discovered, was in masterful control of the Republican-Democrats and of the United States. The Federalists had been reduced to a harmless if noisy minority, Congress was working in close harmony with the President, and no problems of consequence were troubling the electorate. Paine found tranquility boring, as usual, so he wrote a long letter 'To the People of England on the Invasion of England', which the *Aurora* published in full. In this document Paine assumed that Napoleon still intended to launch his invasion of England. Ingenuously outlining in detail the invasion plan he had himself devised, Paine modestly refrained from taking credit for it, but did state that he intended to accompany the invaders 'to give the people of England an opportunity of forming a government for themselves'. The present government of Great Britain, he declared in his customary incisive manner, lacked the arms, the spirit, and the moral leadership to drive William the Conqueror's successor into the sea. So the time would soon be at hand when the people of the British Isles would be given the chance, unprecedented in their history, to create a government of their own making. If they were wise, Paine told them, they would follow the example of the American Revolution and establish a government on the American model. If they hesitated or became confused, they ran the danger of falling into chaos and repeating the mistakes of the French Revolution.

The article would serve no useful purpose, Paine felt, unless it could be called to the attention of the English, the Scots, and the Irish, so he sent copies to various friends and acquaintances in London, Edinburgh, and Dublin.

It was fortunate for Paine that circumstances made it impossible for him to carry out his scheme. Thomas Barclay, the British consul general in New York, had learned of the author's intentions, and made arrangements to have a Royal Navy frigate intercept Paine's merchant ship at sea. Great Britian had not forgotten the man she still regarded as a traitor, and had Paine been captured he would have been returned to London for trial. When the article was brought to the attention of the authorities by loyal British subjects, and the attorney general grimly announced that the policy of His Majesty's government had not changed: Paine would be arrested and prosecuted the moment he set foot on British soil. American newspapers reprinted the comment, and members of the older generation, who had lived through the Revolution, were inclined to regard Paine with greater tolerance. Anyone who could twist the tail of the British lion and make him roar couldn't be as degenerate as he was made out to be.

26

Forty-five Minutes from Broadway

In the late spring or early summer of 1804 Paine's house in New Rochelle was ready for occupancy. Several small rooms had been added, but by no stretch of even the most vivid early nineteenth-century imagination was it true, as the Federalists charged, that he had built a 'mansion'. The property itself was a working farm, with one hundred acres devoted to orchards, more than two hundred acres to grains and vegetables, and another two hundred or more to grazing pasture for livestock. Portions of the property were still heavily wooded, and in places the thick forest was almost impenetrable. The house itself was so modestly furnished that the overall effect was spartan. No room contained more furniture than it needed, and virtually everything in the house – chairs, tables, lamps, beds, rugs, and linens – had been made by local craftsmen.

Shortly before Paine left New York, Marguerite de Bonneville appeared with all three of her sons in tow and demanded lodging for the family. Some of the other boarders misinterpreted Paine's relationship with her, but he was obliged to engage quarters for her and the boys. He was relieved a few days later when Louis de Bonneville, the eldest of the sons, announced that he did not like living in America and that his place was in France, at the side of his hard-pressed father. Madame de Bonneville gave her consent, and Paine purchased transportation for the youth.

Marguerite made it clear that she had no intention of returning to rural Bordentown. Colonel Kirkbridge had died during the early part of the winter, and most of the neighbors refused to associate with her; besides, a rustic life did not appeal to a lively young woman accustomed to the excitement of Paris. So Paine agreed to take Benjamin and Thomas with him to New Rochelle and to be responsible for their expenses and education, if Marguerite would remain in the city and work there as a governess. But she had no desire to be parted from her sons; she decided that Benjamin should stay in New York with her. Paine firmly announced that he would take both boys or neither. Madame de Bonneville capitulated, but at the last moment she weakened again and decided that she too would go to New Rochelle.

Mother and sons moved in with Paine, but the experiment was not successful. Marguerite had been attended by servants from earliest childhood, and she was bewildered by the egalitarian existence on Paine's farm. There were no serving maids or grooms, and it appeared that she was even expected to wait on the handyman-farmer, Christopher Derrick, who had a room in the house. Paine was disappointed in the woman who had been such a charming hostess in Paris, and said of her, 'She would not do anything, not even make an apple-dumpling for her own children.'

After a short time Marguerite returned to New York. The boys stayed with Paine, who bought new furniture and wallpaper for their rooms. Their mother came to visit on weekends, and a few months later Benjamin went back with her to live in New York, but Thomas stayed on at the farm, where he enjoyed the simple life. Paine spent most of his time writing at his desk and left the chores of farming to Derrick. The author prepared most of the household's meals, consisting principally of milk, tea, fruit pies, plain dumplings, and on occasion, as a special treat, beef or lamb.

Rebel!

The arrangement with Derrick did not last long. The handyman borrowed extensively from Paine, and his drinking made him so unreliable that late in 1805 he was discharged, but agreed to stay on long enough to work out his debt. On Christmas Eve he drank to excess, obtained a gun and, while Paine was reading, shot at him through the living-room window. Fortunately the bullet went astray and lodged in the wall some feet from the target, and no harm was done. Derrick was arrested but Paine refused to press charges, and that was the end of the matter. The Federalist press picked up the story, however, and by the time the London and Paris newspapers printed their own exaggerated versions, it was being intimated that Paine was not safe anywhere in the United States. He was so thoroughly despised, declared the *London Post*, that he was in constant danger of losing his life.

Actually, Paine busied himself with a number of causes while living in New Rochelle. He was fascinated by the fact that the state, having contented itself with readopting the original charter granted to it as a colony by King Charles II, had no constitution of its own. In Paine's opinion this was a serious deficiency, and he wrote about it at length to Elisha Babcock, publisher of the Hartford *American Mercury* and former partner of Joel Barlow. Babcock printed excerpts from the letter on August 2, 1804, and Paine promptly wrote a much longer communication, 'To the People of Connecticut, on the Subject of a Constitution,' in which he urged the calling of a constitutional convention. The second letter was published in full on September 6, and the Republican-Democrats soon picked up the cry.

In 1804 former Secretary of the Treasury Alexander Hamilton, the head of the Federalist party, was killed in a duel by Vice-President Aaron Burr, a wily opportunist who for the moment had been calling himself a Republican-Democrat. The Federalist newspapers eulogized the party's tragically fallen leader, and even the Republican-Democratic press mourned his loss. Thomas Paine, however, took a daring stand on the subject in two letters printed by the *Aurora*. He made no direct attack on Hamilton, to be sure, since not even he had the courage to defy custom and denounce a dead man; instead he attacked the eulogies that portrayed Hamilton as the greatest of American leaders. Paine had known Hamilton as an officer on George Washington's staff during the Revolution, and their relationship had been friendly but casual. Paine bore Hamilton no grudge, but his ire was aroused when the principal funeral oration was delivered by the man whom he regarded as his archenemy, Gouverneur Morris. Paine still believed that Morris had been negligent in trying to obtain his release from the Luxembourg Prison. Never, not even in his assault on George Washington, had Paine been so vitriolic. He declared that Morris was a 'babe' in business and a 'visionary' in politics, and that 'the older he grows the more foolish he becomes'. By his reckless, intemperate language, Paine succeeded in making such a laughingstock of Morris that the Pennsylvanian lost much of his influence within the Federalist ranks.

In the summer of 1804 Paine wrote one of the more powerful and effective documents of his latter years. The French-speaking inhabitants of Louisiana sent a petition to Congress demanding immediate statehood and the right to continue importing slaves. The extension of slavery to newly acquired territories was already becoming an issue, and Paine wrote an indignant answer in the form of a pamphlet, thousands of copies of which were distributed in New Orleans and the Louisiana hinterlands. He forcefully reminded the petitioners of 'the mischief caused in France by the possession of power before they understood principles'. It would be necessary for the people of Louisiana to learn the basics of the American system of government and the American interpretation of freedom before they could achieve statehood. Obviously, he said indignantly, they were ignorant of human rights if they believed that among these was the right to enslave others. 'Dare you put up a petition to Heaven for such a power, without fearing to be struck from the earth by its justice?' he demanded. 'Why, then, do you ask it of man against man?'

Life in New Rochelle began to improve for Paine when he sold a parcel of 61 acres for $4,000, and used some of the money to make improvements at home. He hired a cook, Rachel Gidney, much to the relief of young Thomas de Bonneville, and hired the woman's husband, Robert Gidney, to work on the farm.

On December 5, 1804, Thomas Jefferson was reelected for a second term, winning 162 out of 176 votes in the Electoral College, and Paine rejoiced for his friend. A few weeks later, on New Year's Day, 1805, the author again assumed the role of an expert and wrote at length to the President about the situation on the island of Hispaniola in the West Indies, where, a year earlier, former slaves had set up the Republic of Haiti. France was blockading the island, hoping to cut off the rebels from outside help and starve them into submission. The United States, Paine wrote, was in an unpleasant position. If American merchantmen tried to break the blockade there would be clashes with the French Navy, and relations between the two nations would deteriorate again. On the other hand, if American ships respected the blockade the Haitian rebels would become so desperate they would turn pirate and raid American shipping in the Caribbean. The best solution, Paine advised Jefferson, would be for the United States to offer her services to both parties as a mediator. If the offer were accepted, he believed, France would withdraw her military and naval forces, permitting the Haitians to set up their own independent government. In return Haiti would consent to grant French interests a commercial monopoly on the island for a number of years. In this way the honor of both sides would be satisfied, and the United States would win the good will of everyone concerned.

Paine wanted to go to Washington to attend Jefferson's inauguration, but an attack of gout made it impossible for him to travel. Instead he sent the President a continuous stream of letters on many subjects, ranging from the Louisiana slave trade to specific plans for settling Scotch-Irish immigrants in the new territory. He worried about Spain's inefficient administration of her largest North American colony, Mexico, and he was deeply concerned about the impressment of American merchant seamen by Britain's undermanned Royal Navy. Nothing in American life was too insignificant to capture his attention, and any thoughts of consequence on any subject were forwarded to Jefferson.

It is untrue that, as several of Paine's earliest biographers claimed, President Jefferson paid no attention to his letter and merely humored an old friend in his responses. On the contrary Jefferson was one of the few who realized that in spite of his advancing years, Paine was still endowed with sharp insights and could express coolly calculated opinions on many subjects. So the President kept up his end of the correspondence and repeatedly solicited his old friend's views, even though his busy schedule forced him to write relatively short letters. Part of Jefferson's genius was his ability to make use of the ideas of many men, yet always remembering the peculiarities and character deficiencies of those who advised him.

In 1805 or thereabouts Paine's consumption of liquor began to ebb perceptibly. No longer robust, he was afflicted with painful attacks of gout, but he discovered that his health improved if he drank less. Stories to the effect that he became a hopeless alcoholic in his last years have no basis in fact. Enough has been learned about the disease of alcoholism since Paine's day for modern authorities to know that no alcoholic is capable of cutting down on the amount of liquor he consumes. The true alcoholic must either stop drinking completely or drink himself into oblivion. Paine did neither; he was able to make drastic cuts in his consumption of alcoholic beverages voluntarily and seemingly without difficulty. By 1806 he was drinking nothing stronger than a glass or two of diluted wine with his meals.

He began to find that he had insufficient energy to work on the projects that he had formerly accomplished with vigor. It was an effort now to write; he became tired after spending a few hours at his desk. He began the Herculean task of collecting everything he had ever written and wrote to Jefferson that he anticipated the publication of his works in a set of approximately five volumes, each of 400 pages. They would sell 'at two dollars per volume, to be paid on delivery'. The plan eventually foundered because he lacked the time and strength to carry it to completion.

But he did not stop writing. On the contrary, he maintained a pace astonishing for a man of his age and infirmities. In the spring of 1805, working at a leisurely pace, Paine wrote the last of his political pamphlets, *Thomas Paine to the Citizens of Pennsylvania, on the Proposal for Calling a Convention*. It was published by Duane of Philadelphia, and opened in a reminiscent vein: 'Removed as I now am from the place [Philadelphia], and detached from everything of personal party, I address this token to you on the ground of principle, and in remembrance of former times and friendships.' In essence it was a restatement of his political philosophy. On June 7, 1805, he published the last letter in his series *To the Citizens of the United States*. It was the only one in this series he had written in two years, and at the time of its publication he regarded it as the most important. It was an attack on the Federalists, again accusing them of conspiring to destroy the Republic and establish a monarchy. But unlike his other anti-Federalist papers, his language was temperate, his manner was dignified, and he hurled no epithets at his foes. In the past he had claimed that he wrote for posterity; now he seemed to realize that the end was drawing closer.

He was always conscious of a sense of responsibility for the two

Bonneville boys, as a letter to Fellows written in April, 1805, indicates. 'I am now their only dependance,' he said, and he urged Fellows to tell them that 'the better they behaved the better it would be for them'.

The eclecticism of Paine's interests is illustrated by an essay dated June 27, 1805, which he called, 'The cause of the Yellow Fever, and the means of preventing it in places not yet infected with it. Addressed to the Board of Health in America.' The epidemic which struck New York every year, he observed, had been unknown to the Indians. It always began in the waterfront district, but never reached the higher portions of the city. Unlike many of his contemporaries, he rejected the thesis that the disease was imported from the West Indies, and as proof he offered the observation that it did not travel from New York to other places. It was indigenous to New York and the West Indian ports because, he felt, the wharves were filthy and in some way bred the disease. Yellow fever might become a scourge of the past if the wharves were built on stone or iron arches, which would permit the tides to clean the shore and carry away the slime that accumulated on the docks.

One day earlier, June 26, the *American Citizen* published a letter by Paine that referred once again to a proposed constitution for Connecticut. Most of the old constitutions were weak and defective, he said, because they were modeled on the English system of government. At about this same time he also wrote an untitled essay on the subject of Freemasonry, tracing the history and development of the organization's principles from earliest times. This work was not published in his lifetime, but Marguerite de Bonneville printed an expurgated version after his death. Always protective of his reputation, she appears to have believed that some of his views were too strong to win public approval.

In two letters published in the *American Citizen* on July 23 and 24 he vented considerable spleen on a Virginia Federalist named Thomas Turner. Turner had dared to attack President Jefferson in intemperate language, and Paine was furious. Instead of signing his own name or 'Common Sense', as he usually did, he defended his friend under a new pen name: 'A Spark from the Altar of '76.' He was not trying to conceal his identity – he was certain that many readers would recognize his style – but he felt the subject deserved a special pseudonym that would remind every reader of Jefferson's contribution to the authorship of the Declaration of Independence.

Paine occasionally went into New York for a day or two, and the people he saw there were all new friends. Henry Adams observed that those 'who had once courted him as the greatest literary genius of his day' now went out of their way to avoid him. Among those who shunned him were people he had considered intimate friends, none closer than Kitty Nicholson Few, to whom he had written at such length from London. She and her husband had moved from Georgia to New York, and on at least two occasions while driving in her carriage, she passed Paine without speaking to him. *The Age of Reason* and his attack on Washington had cost him many friendships.

Paine never mentioned such snubs to anyone, but he hesitated before moving permanently to New York in the autumn of 1805. The logic of the idea, however, overcame his misgivings: The Bonneville boys were attending boarding school in New Rochelle, Gidney took care of the farm, and the rapidly aging Paine was isolated most of the time; so, ignoring the rebuffs of former intimates, he took up residence in the city. He spent a few months in one small hotel or lodginghouse, then moved to another when fellow boarders began to interfere with the privacy that the habits of a lifetime had made essential to his well-being.

During this period Paine became increasingly friendly with Elihu Palmer; he wrote frequently for Palmer's magazine, *Prospect*, and became involved in the activities of a deist organization whose members called themselves the 'Columbian Illuminati'. He associated principally with members of this group but also received occasional visits from Robert Fulton, who had returned to the United States from France and was now living in New York. It is significant that Paine saw virtually nothing of old friends who had been his comrades in the American Revolution a quarter of a century earlier.

Certainly the articles he wrote for *Prospect* did not encourage such relationships. Paine had no need to express his thoughts on religion, having been sufficiently explicit in *The Age of Reason*, but he was eager to help Palmer's publication achieve a large circulation. His name still guaranteed a brisk sale, and his articles, although they undoubtedly expressed his convictions, were deliberately shocking and controversial to further stimulate sales of the magazine. An excerpt from his first piece illustrates his approach. Published in February, 1805, it was called 'Modern Infidelity', and was designed as a reply to a sermon by a New York clergyman attacking deist beliefs.

> Is it a fact that Jesus Christ died for the sins of the world, and how is it proved? If a God he could not die, and as a man he could not redeem: how then is this redemption proved to be fact? It is said that Adam ate of the forbidden fruit, commonly called an apple, and thereby subjected himself and all his posterity forever to eternal damnation. This is worse than visiting the sins of the fathers upon the children unto the third and fourth generations. But how was the death of Jesus Christ to affect or alter the case? Did God thirst for blood? If so, would it not have been better to have crucified Adam upon the forbidden tree, and made a new man?...
>
> Why do not the Christians, to be consistent, make Saints of Judas and Pontius Pilate, for they were the persons who accomplished the act of salvation. The merit of a sacrifice, if there can be any merit in it, was never in the thing sacrificed, but in the persons offering up the sacrifice – and therefore Judas and Pilate ought to stand first in the calendar of Saints.

His subsequent essays published in *Prospect* were similarly provocative. He quickly succeeded in increasing the magazine's circulation to more than 100,000 per issue. In the process, to be sure, Paine offended a great many people who had not read *The Age of Reason* and were stunned by his candid iconoclasm.*

Many of Paine's important ideas on religion were contained in an unpublished work, 'My private thoughts of a Future State.' This document belongs to his last years, but was not dated, and it was withheld from publication by Madame de Bonneville, to whom he left most of his estate. Under his influence during his lifetime, she became a devout Christian after his death, and thereafter she refused to allow any of his unpublished writings on religion to be printed. Two brief excerpts from this essay are significant because they were written at a time when Paine realized that his days were numbered:

> I have said in the first part of *The Age of Reason* that 'I hope for happiness after this life'. This hope is comfortable to me, and I presume not to go beyond the comfortable idea of hope, with respect to a future state. I consider myself in the hands of my Creator, and that he will dispose of me after this life, consistently with his justice and goodness. I leave all these matters to him as my Creator and

* See Appendix, pages 334-336, for excerpts from these essays.

friend, and I hold it to be presumption in man to make an article of faith as to what the Creator will do with us hereafter. I do not believe, because a man and a woman make a child, that it imposes on the Creator the unavoidable obligation of keeping the being so made in eternal existence hereafter. It is in his power to do so, or not to do so, and it is not in our power to decide which he will do. . . .

The moral world, like the physical world, is composed of numerous degrees of character, running imperceptibly one into the other, in such a manner that no fixed point can be found in either. That point is nowhere, or is everywhere. The whole world might be divided into two parts numerically, but not as to moral character; and therefore the metaphor of dividing them, as sheep and goats can be divided, whose difference is marked by their external figure, is absurd. All sheep are still sheep; all goats are still goats; it is their physical nature to be so. But one part of the world are not all good alike, nor the other part all wicked alike. There are some exceedingly good, others exceedingly wicked. There is another description of men who cannot be ranked with either the one or the other – they belong neither to the sheep nor the goats. And there is still another description of them who are so very insignificant, both in character and conduct, as not to be worth the trouble of damning or saving, or of raising from the dead. My own opinion is, that those whose lives have been spent in doing good, and endeavoring to make their fellow mortals happy, for this is the only way in which we can serve God, will be happy hereafter; and that the very wicked will meet with some punishment. But those who are neither good nor bad, or are too insignificant for notice, will be dropt entirely. This is my opinion. It is consistent with my idea of God's justice, and with the reason that God has given me, and I gratefully know that he has given me a large share of that divine gift.

Matters other than theology also continued to occupy Paine's attention, and he maintained this ever alert watch on the activities of the government. In the winter of 1806, Paine sent a long letter to the President. Napoleon, he said, was in the process of determining whether there would be war or peace in Europe. A war against England would best suit the purposes of the United States, Paine argued, and he was better equipped than anyone currently in the employ of the United States to present the merits of such a campaign to Napoleon. Therefore he proposed that he be sent to France as a special envoy. A lesser man than Jefferson might have been annoyed, but the President displayed both patience and discretion. Again writing in a friendly vein, he thanked his old friend for the offer of service, but gently pointed out that the United States was already well represented in Paris by competent diplomats.

In an essay in the *Public Advertiser* of October 10, 1807, shortly after Chief Justice John Marshall finished presiding over the trial of Aaron Burr, Paine attacked what he regarded as an oversight in the Constitution: No provision had been made for the tenure of Supreme Court justices, who could serve for life if they wished. His approach to the subject undoubtedly was tempered by his memory of Marshall, who in 1797 had rejected the author's plan for a league of neutral nations. Paine seized on the Constitution's stipulation that the judges of the Supreme Court and of inferior courts shall 'hold their offices during good behavior'. He argued that 'there must be a power somewhere to judge of that good behavior or of the breach of it, but of this the Constitution is silent, and herein lies its defect'. The task of organizing the judicial branch of the government at the Constitutional Convention of 1797 had been given to attorneys, he declared, and these men – all of them potential judges – had made the removal of federal judges from office as difficult as they could.

Immediately after the trial of Aaron Burr had ended and Burr had been discharged on technical grounds, Paine wrote a proposed amendment to the Constitution and sent it to Senator Samuel L. Mitchill, a New York Republican-Democrat, who elected not to submit it formally to his colleagues. So Paine's idea is of interest principally as a historical curiosity. He proposed that the wording of the Constitution be changed to read: 'The judges both of the Supreme and inferior courts, shall hold their offices during good behavior, but for reasonable cause, which shall not be sufficient cause for impeachment, the President may remove any of them, on the address of a majority of the houses of Congress.' The weakness of this plan, which was published in 1810, was attacked by men of every political persuasion, who argued that it would be all too easy to remove an unpopular judge on purely political grounds. By that time Paine, no longer living, was beyond the reach of criticism.

27

The Man with Thin Skin

By the spring of 1806 Thomas Paine's wallet was considerably lighter, partly because of his support of the two Bonneville boys and his generosity to their mother, who found it easy to live beyond her own means. Belt-tightening was in order, a process with which Paine long had been familiar, so he moved back to his property in New Rochelle.

He enjoyed writing about his farm in his correspondence, and he made frequent, optimistic references to the crops he would produce, the firewood he would sell, and the cattle he would raise. But he knew nothing about agriculture, and the hired man who worked on the property grew only enough food for his own family's use. As a result the farm brought Paine no income, and he made a valiant but unsuccessful effort to trim his expenses. To his credit, he continued to pay for the schooling and subsistence of the Bonneville boys and still gave money to their mother whenever she asked for it. But he found life on the farm

Rebel!

far too quiet now, and after a short stay there he moved back to the city again, intending to remain there permanently.

A new bill had been introduced into the Virginia legislature awarding him a large parcel of land, and he planned to sell at least a portion of that property to obtain ready cash. But no action was taken on the measure, as was the way of legislatures, so he sent a letter to the President asking him to use his influence to expedite the bill. Jefferson, who was very busy then, found no opportunity to reply to the request. Paine felt slighted, and he wrote again to the President, demonstrating the lack of tact that had injured his relations with so many others over the years. 'Thomas Paine's compliments to Mr. Jefferson, and he desires to be informed if he received a letter from him beginning as follows, "I wrote you this letter entirely on my own account, and I begin it without ceremony." ' Jefferson was upset, and sent a warm, candid reply. He had little influence with either the Virginia legislature or the federal Congress, he said, but he was sincerely devoted to Paine's interests and would do everything possible for him. True to his word, the President forwarded to a member of the legislature his friend's original letter asking that an effort be made to bring the bill to the floor. But Paine's cause in Virginia was hopeless. His attitude on religion had offended many citizens of that predominantly Episcopalian state, and the legislators hadn't forgotten his attack on Virginia's most renowned statesman, George Washington, The measure never reached the floor and died in committee.

Immediately before returning to New York Paine suffered a severe blow to his pride. He went to the polls to vote in a New Rochelle election, but the supervisor refused to allow him to cast his ballot. 'Mr Paine,' said Elisha Ward, who gained a small measure of immortality by virtue of his ruling, 'was disenfranchised and did not regain his citizenship, both Minister Morris and President Washington refusing to reclaim him.' There was no appeal, and Paine had to suffer the mortification of returning home without voting.

In the spring of 1807 Paine could no longer contain his anger at Elisha Ward for having disenfranchised him. He wrote letters to everyone he knew in a position of authority, hoping to obtain a higher ruling in his own favor. He sent a long letter to President Jefferson and another to Vice-President George Clinton. He wrote to Secretary of State James Madison, to his old friends

308

James Monroe and Joel Barlow. All replied sympathetically, but admitted they were helpless to reverse the decision of the New Rochelle supervisor of elections. Paine never again had an opportunity to cast a ballot in an American election.

One of the reasons Paine cut short his stay in New Rochelle was a visit from his friend William Carver, who urged him to return to New York and offered him a room in the Carver house at 36 Cedar Street. Apparently there was a misunderstanding on the matter: Paine had assumed that he would live there as his friend's guest while Carver believed that Paine would pay for his room. Later they exchanged a series of acrimonious letters in which both men haggled at length over the sums that Paine supposedly owed his host. Carver did him no service by making the correspondence public. There were so many eager to believe the worst about the author that a rumour that he had gone bankrupt soon gained credence throughout the country and was believed everywhere after his death.

Rarely had Paine been as thin-skinned as he was during this period just before his health began to fail. And never had he been so jealous of his reputation, as he demonstrated in a letter to Mayor John Inskeep of Philadelphia, which was published in February, 1806, by the Philadelphia *Commercial Advertiser*:

I saw in the *Aurora* of January the 30th a piece addressed to you and signed Isaac Hall. It contains a statement of your malevolent conduct in refusing to let him have Vine-st. Wharf after he had offered fifty dollars more rent for it than another person had offered, and had been unanimously approved of by the Commissioners appointed by law for that purpose. Among the reasons given by you for this refusal, one was, that '*Mr Hall was one of Paine's disciples.*' If those whom you may chuse to call my disciples follow my example in doing good to mankind, they will pass the confines of this world with a happy mind, while the hope of the hypocrite shall perish and delusion sink into despair.

I do not know who Mr Inskeep is, for I do not remember the name of Inskeep at Philadelphia in '*the time that tried men's souls.*' He must be some mushroom of modern growth that has started up on the soil which the generous services of Thomas Paine contributed to bless with freedom; neither do I know what profession of religion he is of, nor do I care, for if he is a man malevolent and unjust, it signifies not to what class or sectary he may hypocritically belong.

As I set too much value on my time to waste it on a man of so little consequence as yourself, I will close this short address with a declaration that puts hypocrisy and malevolence to defiance. Here it is: my motive and object in all my political works, beginning with Common Sense, the first work I ever published, have been to rescue man from tyranny and false systems and false principles of government, and enable him to be free, and establish government for himself; and I have borne my share of danger in Europe and in America in every attempt I have made for this purpose. And my motive and object in all my publications on religious subjects, beginning with the first part of the Age of Reason, have been to bring man to a right reason that God has given him; to impress on him the great principles of divine morality, justice, mercy, and a benevolent disposition to all men and to all creatures; and to excite in him a spirit of trust, confidence and consolation in his creator, unshackled by the fable and fiction of books, by whatever invented name they may be called. I am happy in the continual contemplation of what I have done, and I thank God that he gave me talents for the purpose and fortitude to do it. It will make the continual consolation of my departing hours, whenever they finally arrive.

This communication sounds remarkably like an epitaph, and it may be that Paine had had a premonition of death. But his health was better throughout most of 1806 than it had been in several years. In the summer he wrote an 'Essay on Dreams', in which he repeated some of the arguments he had presented in *The Age of Reason*. It was published in May, 1807, in pamphlet form, and is generally regarded as his last work of consequence. He also finished a project on which he had been working intermittently for years, his reply to the Bishop of Llandaff, which he had intended to publish as Part Three of *The Age of Reason*. In its final form it was far shorter than he had anticipated, however, and lacked the bulk to be presented to the public as a separate work. So he incorporated it into *The Age of Reason*, which thereafter has always been published with this material added. Inasmuch as he was answering specific theological points made by the bishop, the new writing made little sense on its own. It was inferior to the early portions, added nothing new to the thoughts Paine had already expressed, and well could have been omitted without harm to the logic of his arguments.

Late in July or early in August, 1806, Paine suffered a fit of apoplexy on the stairway in Carver's house and tumbled down more than twenty steps. He was rendered unconscious and temporarily paralyzed, and the friends who found him thought that he had died. He was so severely injured that although he recovered from the apoplexy, he was unable to leave his bed for three months and a neighbor, Mrs. Palmer, nursed him for the entire period. Paine's physician said that if he continued to climb stairs regularly it would kill him, and he urged Paine to find another place to live. Late in October Paine made the necessary arrangements with John Wesley Jarvis, a prominent portrait painter of the era. He moved into Jarvis's house at 85 Church Street at the beginning of November and remained there until the following April. The seventy-year-old Paine enjoyed his stay at the house of Jarvis, who was in his thirties. Both were Republican-Democrats, and they sat up very late most evenings discussing Paine's many theories. An audience always made Paine happy, and his stay with the painter left little to be desired.

Jarvis, who had a reputation as a wit, teased his guest one day, telling him he should publish his 'Recantation', keep all the profits for himself and thereby spend his old age in great wealth. Paine, who took the suggestion seriously, replied, 'I do not know what I may do when infested by disease and pain. I may become a second child; and designing people may entrap me into saying anything. Or they may put into my mouth what I never said.' He added that he didn't believe 'what the priests reported of Voltaire's confession on his death bed'. He was himself in sound mind, Paine said, and he felt no inclination to change, correct or reverse any of the opinions he had already expressed in writing.

That winter Carver began to write letters to Paine demanding payment of the $150 that he claimed Paine owed him and in the course of his correspondence became increasingly abusive. In one letter Carver insinuated that Marguerite de Bonneville was Paine's mistress and that the two Bonneville boys who were in America were Paine's illegitimate sons. Carver turned over the entire correspondence to his friend James Cheetham, an opportunistic writer. English by birth and a hatter by trade. Cheetham turned out a cheap, sensationalized biography of Paine which carefully included this misinformation in it. This work was first published in the spring of 1807, and Paine promptly sued for libel. But the case dragged on until after his death, and the matter was pressed to a conclusion by Marguerite de Bonneville. The court was unable to find any shred of evidence that justified Carver's claims; Carver and Cheetham were fined token sums and were ordered to remove all false allegations from later editions of the so-called biography.

Carver, a thoroughly unpleasant man, wrote an apology to Paine shortly before the author's death but received no reply. In later years he claimed to have been present at Paine's deathbed and for the rest of his own life tried to convince the world that he was Paine's ardent disciple and closest friend. Anyone who had known Thomas Paine realized that Carver was a liar, but he persuaded the gullible to accept the myth.

Many of Paine's letters to the press appeared in the *American Citizen*, edited by Cheetham, whose friendship with the author does not appear to have been impaired by the publication of the first edition of his unauthorized *Life of Thomas Paine*. After the author's recovery from his attack of apoplexy he began writing letters once again to the *American Citizen*, often using new pseudonyms unknown to anyone except himself and the editor. One of his principal targets was Stephen Carpenter, a Federalist writer and editor of the *People's Friend and Daily Advertiser*, a leading Federalist newspaper. Paine not only satirized him but attacked him savagely, accusing him of being a traitor and a British spy and revealing unsavory details of his past. Paine was so merciless that in August, 1807, Carpenter retired from the newspaper world and was said to have gone to the Western frontier to start a new life. Paine's assaults on him are worthy of mention chiefly because the once great propagandist was reduced to mud-slinging, and his prose reads like a caricature of his earlier work. Perhaps, as he thought, he was still in possession of his faculties, but the anti-Carpenter letters indicate that his mind was beginning to slip.

In the spring of 1807, after he moved from Jarvis's house to a small lodginghouse on Broome Street, he suddenly came to the conclusion that gunboats would be the future salvation of the United States Navy; men-of-war, frigates, and other large vessels were like whales and could be rendred harmless as easily as a whale could be harpooned. Letter after letter appeared in the *Public Advertiser* in the subject. Paine called on his scientific skills, too, and in September, 1807, he sent to President Jefferson a design for a new double cannon to be used in the prow of a gunboat. Jefferson forwarded the communication to the Department of the Navy for consideration. Secretary Robert Smith ultimately reported to the President that although the gun had merit, the Navy was not planning to build a large fleet of gunboats and so had no use for Paine's design.

When attacking his old foe, Great Britain, Paine demonstrated that he had lost little of his skill in spite of his general mental deterioration. By 1807 the Royal Navy was causing so much harm to American merchant shipping that even the Federalists were becoming Francophiles. In a long letter to the *Public Advertiser* dated June 1, 1807, Paine ridiculed England, presenting a burlesque version of her history and predicting that Napoleon would take London after successfully crossing the English Channel. Subsequent letters, the last of which was dated December 18, 1807, insisted that Britain would continue to impress American seamen, no matter how much the United States Government protested. There was only one way to reply to the Royal Navy, Paine declared: Every American merchant vessel should be armed, and when attempts were made to halt an American ship on the high seas, she should blow her antagonist out of the water.

Life was quiet for Paine after he moved to Broome Street, but he was content. The *American Citizen* and the *Public Advertiser* provided him with outlets in print for his many thoughts. His funds were limited, to be sure, so he dined simply when he wasn't invited to the homes of friends. On weekends he sometimes dined with Marguerite de Bonneville, and once each month her sons came to New York from New Rochelle and dutifully visited him. He walked for at least an hour each day and, boasting that his eyesight was still perfect, continued to read books, magazines, and newspapers in quantity. His evening meal consisted of bread, butter, and tea, and he retired almost immediately after supper. He arose at daybreak to write his letters to the press before eating a simple breakfast.

In March, 1807, when the editor of the *American Citizen* chose not to publish one of Paine's letters, the author abruptly terminated his relationship with Cheetham. Thereafter Cheetham attacked Paine frequently in print, questioning his record as a soldier during the American Revolution, quoting him as saying he had never read a single word written by John Locke, hinting broadly that he never drew a sober breath, and otherwise ridiculing him. Paine replied in the pages of the *Public Advertiser*, at first defending himself with vigor. Late in the summer of 1807 he suddenly launched a counter-offensive of his own, claiming that Cheetham was secretly engaging in a Federalist conspiracy with Carpenter. Further, Paine charged that the *American*

Citizen pretended to be a Republican-Democratic newpaper that supported President Jefferson but in actuality was a reactionary, Tory publication that tried in devious ways to undermine the President and his administration. In one letter, published on September 26, 1807, Paine expressed outrage that the English-born Cheetham had dared to express anti-French sentiments in an editorial. As an adopted American citizen he was meddling in affairs that were none of his business, Paine declared, and in a typically vitriolic passage he added, 'As a John Bull it is impertinence in him to come here to spew out his venom against France. But Cheetham cannot live without quarreling, nor write without abuse. He is a disgrace to the Republicans, whose principle is to live in peace and friendship with all nations and not to interfere in the domestic concerns of any.' The following day Cheetham demanded a public apology from Jacob Frank, the publisher of the *Public Advertiser*. Paine not only said to Frank, 'Tell Cheetham that I am the author of that piece, and if he has any thing to say, he must say it to me,' but he also took pains to make certain that the public knew of his part in the quarrel. He sent a letter revealing his authorship to William Coleman, editor of the Federalist *Evening Post*, who immediately published it.

A few days later Paine inadvertently caused President Jefferson fresh embarrassment. Coleman called on him to discuss the feud with Cheetham, and during a long, rambling conversation Paine blurted out that the President, in a recent letter, had confided that he was afraid of a possible war with Great Britain. When Coleman expressed polite disbelief, Paine foolishly read aloud from the letter: 'In the mean time all the little circumstances coming to our knowledge are unfavourable to our wishes for peace.' The editor committed the quotation to memory, and wrote it down as soon as he returned to his office. Several days later the line appeared in the *United States Gazette* of Philadelphia, another Federalist newspaper. The Federalists immediately began to protest, claiming – justifiably – that the President had been unwise to place his trust in Paine. The Republican-Democrats declared that the story had been invented out of whole cloth by the President's political foes. Paine's friends said that even if the story was true, they saw no harm done to anyone. Thomas Jefferson, mortified, remained silent and waited for the new storm to subside.

In February, 1808, shortly before falling ill, Paine moved from

Broome Street to 63 Partition Street, later Fulton Street. He took a tiny suite of rooms at the rear of a tavern, where he ate all of his meals. Soon after moving Paine suffered an attack of the ague, which later generations called influenza, and thereafter his health declined steadily. He wrote nothing (a sure sign that he was ill) until the summer, when he resumed his letter-writing to the press and launched fresh assaults on Cheetham and the Federalists. The most damning thing he could say about them was that their attitudes were anti-French; in the main he repeated his old arguments.

Worried about the financial security of the Bonneville family and realizing that his health was declining, he arranged for the sale of his New Rochelle farm for $10,000. But the man who agreed to buy the property died very suddenly, and his widow canceled the arrangement. So Paine sent off a sheaf of letters to various members of Congress urgently requesting payment for various services he had performed for the country. He cited, in particular, the inadequate compensation he had received for his first trip to France. His claims were rejected because he sent no documentary evidence proving they were valid. Paine was bitterly disappointed, but Marguerite de Bonneville later wrote that the rejection had been inevitable and that had his mind not been muddled he would have realized it.

By the summer of 1808 it was becoming increasingly difficult for Paine to take care of himself, so he went to board with a family named Ryder on Herring Street, later 293 Bleecker Street. His decline became more pronounced, and by the early winter of 1809 he was confined to his bed. He suffered little discomfort, but his eyesight began to fail and he had to have the newspapers read to him. On January 18, 1809, he picked up a quill pen for the last time to write his last will and testament, in which he left the bulk of his estate to Marguerite de Bonneville and her sons. By early March it was necessary for someone to be in attendance at all times, and Marguerite spent all of her free time with him.

In March he told a friend, Willet Hicks, that he wanted to be buried in a Quaker cemetery, but the request was rejected by the members of Hicks's church. Paine commented that he could not allow himself to be buried as an Episcopalian, 'because they are so arrogant', or as a Presbyterian, 'because they are so hypocritical'. Marguerite comforted him, and told him that his friends would arrange a burying place that would never be sold.

315

On May 4, 1809, Paine moved for the last time. He was so lonely in the Ryder establishment that he asked Marguerite to take him into her own home at 59 Grove Street. She agreed, but he was so weak he could not walk and had to be carried the short distance. On June 5 it was obvious that the seventy-two-year-old man was about to die, and a physician, Dr James R. Manly, asked him if he was willing to accept Jesus Christ as the Son of God. Firm to the end, Paine replied, 'I have no wish to believe on that subject.' His last words were anticlimactic. Early on the morning of June 8 Marguerite, aware that the end was approaching, asked him if he was satisfied with the treatment he had received. 'Oh, yes,' Paine said, and dozed off. He died in his sleep at eight o'clock in the morning.

Marguerite and Benjamin de Bonneville and a small group of friends accompanied the body to New Rochelle for burial the following day, and a grave was prepared on the Paine farm. Years later she described the occasion:

> Contemplating who it was, what man it was, that we were committing to an obscure grave on an open and disregarded bit of land, I could not help feeling most acutely. Before the earth was thrown down upon the coffin, I, placing myself at the east end of the grave, said to my son Benjamin, 'Stand you there, at the other end, as a witness for grateful America.' Looking round me, and beholding the small group of spectators, I exclaimed as the earth was tumbled into the grave, 'Oh! Mr Paine! My son stands here as testimony of the gratitude of America, and I, for France!'

During his last days Paine had told Marguerite that he was afraid his 'enemies' would not let him rest in peace. Four months after he was buried his remains were disturbed, although not as he had supposed. William Cobbett, a one-time foe who had become an ardent disciple, was an English newspaperman temporarily residing in the United States. One night in October, 1809, accompanied by at least two accomplices, he opened the grave and stole the coffin. The sheriff of New Rochelle, according to his own subsequent testimony, pursued the robbers but they escaped. This tale is probably nonsense; men driving a mule cart would have found it difficult to run away from a party of armed horsemen. A later version of the story is more likely to be true. According to this account the sheriff did not learn of the attempt until the following day, and was able to trace the villains only as far as Yonkers, where the trail vanished.

Cobbett, however he managed to accomplish the feat, succeeded in shipping the coffin to England. He had convinced himself that a public display of Paine's remains would cause huge crowds to gather, and that the sentiment thus engendered among the people would force the reformation of both the British Government and the Church of England. Cobbett's daydreams never materialized, of course, and nothing of the kind happened. The British public ignored the exhibition of Paine's remains; no crowds gathered and the event attracted no attention. On both sides of the Atlantic schoolboys soon were chanting a disrespectful jingle:

> Poor Tom Paine! Here he lies,
> Nobody laughs and nobody cries;
> Where he's gone and how he fares,
> Nobody knows and nobody cares.

The limerick was prophetic. Cobbett, who died in 1835, willed Paine's bones to his son. The son subsequently went into bankruptcy, and the Lord Chancellor, in a final insult to Paine, ruled that his bones were not an asset. The author's remains vanished and were never recovered.

Marguerite Bonneville, who dropped the 'de' from her name, inherited more than $10,000 in property and cash from her benefactor. She never rejoined her husband in France and stayed in the United States for the rest of her life, becoming deeply religious in her later years. Thomas Paine Bonneville lived quietly, making a successful career as a businessman. His older brother, Benjamin, entered the United States Army, rose to the rank of brigadier general, and became sufficiently distinguished to become the subject of several biographies.

The Age of Reason continued to plague Thomas Paine's memory, and on both sides of the Atlantic, for more than a century after his death, he was falsely regarded as an immoral atheist. His own estimation of his importance has ultimately been vindicated, and today his works have become both his epitaph and the measure of his worth. If his hope was realized of having been provided a place in the hereafter by his Creator, the knowledge that the world finally has come to give him the approbation he felt he deserved in his own day undoubtedly provides Paine with a satisfaction greater than any he knew in his life-time.

Appendix

I do not believe that the people of England have ever been fairly and candidly dealt by. They have been imposed upon by parties, and by men assuming the character of leaders. It is time that the nation should rise above these trifles. It is time to dismiss that inattention which has so long been the encouraging cause of stretching taxation to excess. It is time to dismiss all those songs and toasts which are calculated to enslave, and operate to suffocate reflection.

On all such subjects men have only to think, and they will neither act wrong nor be misled. To say that any people are not fit for freedom, is to make poverty their choice, and to say they had rather be loaded with taxes than not. If such a case could be proved, it would equally prove, that those who govern are not fit to govern them, for they are part of the same national mass.

I do not believe that monarchy and aristocracy will continue seven years longer in any of the enlightened countries in Europe. If better reasons can be shown for them than against them, they will stand; if the contrary, they will not. Mankind are not now to be told they shall not think, or they shall not read; and publications that go no farther than to investigate principles of government, to invite men to reason and to reflect, and to show the errors and excellencies of different systems, have a right to appear. If they do not excite attention, they are not worth the trouble of prosecution; and if they do, the prosecution will amount to nothing, since it cannot amount to a prohibition of reading. This would be a sentence of the public, instead of the author, and would also be the most effectual mode of making or hastening revolutions.

●

What is the history of all monarchical governments, but a disgustful picture of human wretchedness, and the accidental respite of a few years' repose? Wearied with war, and tired with human butchery, they sat down to rest, and called it peace. This certainly is not the condition that heaven intended for man; and if this be monarchy, well might monarchy be reckoned among the sins of the Jews.

The revolutions which formerly took place in the world, had nothing in them that interested the bulk of mankind. They extended only to a change of persons and measures, but not of principles, and rose or fell among the common transactions of the moment. What we now behold, may not improperly be called a counter-revolution.

Conquest and tyranny, at some early period, dispossessed man of his rights, and he is now recovering them. And as the tide of all human affairs has its ebb and flow in directions contrary to each other, so also is it in this. Government founded on a moral theory, on a system of universal peace, on the indefeasible, hereditary rights of man, is now revolving from West to East, by a stronger impulse than the government of the sword revolved from East to West. It interests not particular individuals, but nations, in its progress, and promises a new era to the human race.

Excerpts from Part Two of The Rights of Man

The origin of the government of England, so far as relates to what is called its line of monarchy, being one of the latest, is perhaps the best recorded. The hatred which the Norman invasion and tyranny begat, must have been deeply rooted in the nation, to have outlived the contrivance to obliterate it. Though not a courtier will talk of the curfew-bell, not a village has forgotten it.

Those bands of robbers having parcelled out the world and divided it into dominions, began, as is naturally the case, to quarrel with each other. What at first was obtained by violence, was considered by others as lawful to be taken, and a second plunderer succeeded the first. They alternately invaded the dominions which each had assigned to himself, and the brutality with which they treated each other explains the original character of monarchy. It was ruffian torturing ruffian.

The conquerer considered the conquered, not as his prisoner, but as his property. He led him in triumph, rattling in chains, and doomed him, at pleasure, to slavery or death. As time obliterated the history of their beginning, their successors assumed new appearances, to cut off the entail of their disgrace, but their principles and objects remained the same. What at first was plunder, assumed the softer name of revenue; and the power originally usurped, they affected to inherit.

From such beginning of governments, what could be expected but a continual system of war and extortion? It has established itself into a trade. The vice is not peculiar to one more than to another, but is the common principle of all. There does not exist within such government sufficient stamina whereon to ingraft reformation; and the shortest, easiest, and most effectual remedy is to begin anew.

●

Hereditary succession is a burlesque upon monarchy. It puts in the most ridiculous light, by presenting it as an office, which any child or idiot may fill. It requires some talents to be a common mechanic; but to be a king, requires only the animal figure of a man – a sort of breathing automaton. This sort of superstition may last a few years more, but it cannot long resist the awakened reason and interest of man.

Hereditary succession requires the same obedience to ignorance, as to wisdom; and when once the mind can bring itself to pay this indiscriminate reverence, it descends below the stature of mental manhood. It is fit to be great only in little things. It acts a treachery upon itself, and suffocates the sensations that urge to detection.

●

We must shut our eyes against reason, we must basely degrade our understanding, not to see the folly of what is called monarchy. Nature is orderly in all her works; but this is a mode of government that counteracts nature. It turns the progress of the human faculties upside down. It subjects age to be governed by children, and wisdom by folly. On the contrary, the representative system is always parallel with the order and immutable laws of nature, and meets the reason of man in every part.

●

A constitution is the property of a nation, and not of those who exercise the government. All the constitutions of America are declared to be established on the authority of the people. In France, the word nation is used instead of the people; but in both cases, a constitution is a thing antecedant to the government, and always distinct therefrom.

In England, it is not difficult to perceive that every thing has a constitution, except the nation. Every society and association that is established, first agreed upon a number of original articles, digested into form, which are its constitution. It then appointed its officers, whose powers and authorities are described in that constitution, and the government of that society then commenced. Those officers, by whatever name they are called, have no authority to add to, alter, or abridge the original articles. It is only to the constituting power that this right belongs.

From the want of understanding the differences between a constitution and a government, Dr Johnson, and all the writers of his description, have always bewildered themselves. They could not but perceive, that there must necessarily be a controlling power existing somewhere, and they placed this power in the discretion of the persons exercising the government, instead of placing it in a constitution formed by the nation.

The act, called the Bill of Rights, comes here into view. What is but a bargain, which the parts of government made with each other to divide powers, profits and privileges? You shall have so much, and I will have the rest; and with respect to the nation, it said, for your share, you shall have the right of petitioning.

This being the case, the Bill of Rights is more properly a bill of wrongs, and of insult. As to what is called the Convention-parliament, it was a thing that made itself, and then made the authority by which it acted. A few persons got together, and called themselves by that name. Several of them had never been elected, and none of them for that purpose.

From the time of William, a species of government arose, issuing out of this coalition Bill of Rights, and more so, since the corruption introduced at the Hanover succession, by the agency of Walpole: that can be described by no other name than a despotic legislation. Though the parts may embarrass each other, the whole has no bounds; and the only right it acknowledges out of itself, is the right of petitioning. Where then is the constitution that either gives or restrains power?

It is not because a part of the government is elective, that makes it less a despotism, if the persons so elected, possess afterwards, as a parliament, unlimited powers. Election, in this instance, becomes separated from representation, and the candidates are candidates for despotism.

I cannot believe that any nation, reasoning on its own rights, would have thought of calling those things a constitution, if the cry of constitution had not been set up by the Government. It has got into circulation like the words *bore* and *quoz*, by being chalked up in the speeches of Parliament, as those words were on the window-shutters and door-posts; but whatever the Constitution may be in other respects, it has undoubtedly been the most productive machine for taxation that was ever invented.

●

From the want of a Constitution in England to restrain and regulate the wild impulse of power, many of the laws are irrational and tyrannical, and the administration of them vague and problematical.

The attention of the Government of England (for I rather choose to call it by this name, rather than the English Government) appears, since its political connection with Germany, to have been so completely engrossed and absorbed by foreign affairs, and the means of raising taxes, that it seems to exist for no other purposes. Domestic concerns are neglected; and with respect to regular law, there is scarcely such a thing.

Almost every case must now be determined by some precedent, be that precedent good or bad, or whether it properly applies or not; and the practise has become so general, as to suggest a suspicion, that it proceeds from a deeper policy than at first appears.

Since the Revolution of America, and more so since that of France, this preaching up the doctrine of precedents, drawn from times and circumstances antecedant to those events, has been the studied practise of the English Government. The generality of those precedents are founded on principles and opinions, the reverse of what they ought to be; and the greater distance of time they are drawn from, the more they are to be suspected.

But by associating those precedents with a superstitious reverence for ancient things, as monks show relics and call them holy, the generality of mankind are deceived into the design. Governments now act as if they were afraid to awaken a single reflection in man. They are softly leading him to the sepulchre of precedents, to deaden his faculties and call his attention from the scene of revolutions.

They feel that he is arriving at knowledge faster than they wish, and their policy of precedents is the barometer of their fears. This political popery, like the ecclesiastical popery of old, has had its day, and is hastening to its exit. The ragged relic and the antiquated precedent, the monk and the monarch, will moulder together.

●

In whatever manner the separate parts of a constitution may be arranged, there is one general principle that distinguishes freedom from slavery, which is, that all hereditary government over a people is to them a species of slavery, and representative government is freedom.

●

Government ought to be as much open to improvement as anything which appertains to man, instead of which it has been monopolized, from age to age, by the most ignorant and vicious of the human race. Need we any other proof of their wretched management, than the excess of debt and taxes with which every nation groans, and the quarrels into which they have precipitated the world?

Just emerging from such a barbarous condition, it is too soon to determine to what extent of improvement government may yet be carried. For what we can foresee, all Europe may form but one great republic, and man be free of the whole.

●

From a small spark kindled in America, a flame has arisen not to be extinguished. Without consuming, like the *Ultima Ratio Regum*, it winds its progress from nation to nation, and conquers by a silent operation. Man finds himself changed, he scarcely perceives how. He acquires a knowledge of his rights by attending justly to his interest, and discovers in the event that the strength and powers of despotism consist wholly in the fear of resisting it, and that in order to be free, it is sufficient that he wills it.

●

Never did so great an opportunity offer itself to England, and to all Europe, as is produced by the two revolutions of America and France. By the former, freedom has a national champion in the Western world; and by the latter, in Europe. When another nation shall join France, despotism and bad government will scarcely dare to appear. To use a trite expression, the iron is becoming hot all over Europe. The insulted German and the enslaved Spaniard, the Russ and the Pole are beginning to think. The present age will hereafter merit to be called the Age of Reason, and the present generation will appear to the future as the Adam of a new world.

A POEM WRITTEN BY PAINE IN 1806, SOON AFTER PITT'S DEATH

Reader! with eye indignant view this bier;
The foe of all the human race lies here,
With talents small, and those directed, too,
Virtue and truth and wisdom to subdue,
He lived to every noble motive blind,
And died, the execration of mankind.

Millions were butchered by his damned plan
To violate each sacred right of man;
Exulting he o'er earth each misery hurled,
And joyed to drench in tears and blood, the world.

Myriads of beings wretched he has made
By desolating war, his favorite trade,
Who, robbed of friends and dearest ties, are left
Of every hope and happiness bereft.

In private life made up of fuss and pride,
Not e'en his vices leaned to virtue's side;
Unsound, corrupt, and rotten at the core,
His cold and scoundrel heart was black all o'er;
Nor did one passion ever move his mind
That bent towards the tender, warm, and kind.

Tyrant, and friend to war! we hail the day
When Death, to bless mankind, made thee his prey,
And rid the earth of all could earth disgrace, –
The foulest, bloodiest scourge of man's oppressed race.

'THE AUTHOR'S PROFESSION OF FAITH' FROM *The Age of Reason*

It has been my intention, for several years past, to publish my
thoughts upon religion. I am well aware of the difficulties that
attend the subject, and from that consideration, had reserved it to
a more advanced period of my life. I intended it to be the last
offering I should make to my fellow-citizens of all nations, and
that at a time when the purity of the motive that induced me to it
could not admit of a question, even by those who might disapprove the work. The circumstance that has now taken place in
France of the total abolition of the whole national order of
priesthood, and of everything appertaining to compulsive systems
of religion, and compulsive articles of faith, has not only precipitated my intention, but rendered a work of this kind exceedingly
necessary, lest in the general wreck of superstition, of false
systems of government and false theology, we lose sight of
morality, of humanity and of the theology that is true.

As several of my colleagues, and others of my fellow-citizens of
France, have given me the example of making their voluntary and
individual profession of faith, I also will make mine; and I do this

with all that sincerity and frankness with which the mind of man communicates with itself.

I believe in one God, and no more; and I hope for happiness beyond this life.

I believe in the equality of man; and I believe that religious duties consist in doing justice, loving mercy, and endeavoring to make our fellow-creatures happy.

But, lest it should be supposed that I believe many other things in addition to these, I shall, in the progress of this work, declare the things I do not believe, and my reasons for not believing them.

I do not believe in the creed professed by the Jewish Church, by the Roman Church, by the Greek Church, by the Turkish Church, by the Protestant Church, nor by any church that I know of. My own mind is my own church.

All national institutions of churches, whether Jewish, Christian, or Turkish, appear to me no other than human inventions, set up to terrify and enslave mankind, and monopolize power and profit.

I do not mean by this declaration to condemn those who believe otherwise; they have the same right to their belief as I have to mine. But it is necessary to the happiness of man that he be mentally faithful to himself. Infidelity does not consist in believing, or in disbelieving; it consists in professing to believe what he does not believe.

It is impossible to calculate the moral mischief, if I may so express it, that mental lying has produced in society. When a man has so far corrupted and prostituted the chastity of his mind as to subscribe his professional belief to things he does not believe he has prepared himself for the commission of every other crime.

He takes up the trade of a priest for the sake of gain, and in order to qualify himself for that trade he begins with a perjury. Can we conceive any thing more destructive to morality than this?

Soon after I had published the pamphlet, 'Common Sense', in America, I saw the exceeding probability that a revolution in the system of government would be followed by a revolution in the system of religion. The adulterous connection of church and state, wherever it has taken place, whether Jewish, Christian or Turkish, has so effectually prohibited by pains and penalities every discussion upon established creeds, and upon first principles of religion, that until the system of government should be changed, those subjects could not be brought fairly and openly before the

327

world; but that whenever this should be done, a revolution in the system of religion would follow. Human inventions and priest craft would be detected; and man would return to the pure, unmixed and unadulterated belief in one God, and no more.

Excerpts from Part One of *The Age of Reason*

Every national church or religion has established itself by pretending some special mission from God, communicated to certain individuals. The Jews have their Moses; the Christians their Jesus Christ, apostles and saints; and the Turks their Mahomet, as if the way to God was not open to every man alike.

Each of those churches show certain books, which they call *revelation*, or the Word of God. The Jews say their Word of God was given by God to Moses, face to face; the Christians say that their Word of God came by divine inspiration; and the Turks say that their Word of God (the Koran) was brought by an angel from heaven. Each of those churches charges the others of unbelief; and for my own part, I disbelieve them all.

•

When . . . I am told that a woman called the Virgin Mary said, or gave out, that she was with child without any cohabitation with a man, and that her betrothed husband, Joseph, said that an angel told him so, I have a right to believe them or not; such a circumstance required a much stronger evidence than their bare word for it but we have not even this – for neither Joseph nor Mary wrote any such matter themselves; it is only reported by others that *they said so* – it is hearsay upon hearsay, and I do not choose to rest my belief on such evidence.

It is, however, not difficult to account for the credit that was given to the story of Jesus Christ being the Son of God. He was born at a time when the heathen mythology had still some fashion and repute in the world, and that mythology had prepared the people for the belief of such a story. Almost all the extraordinary men that lived under the heathen mythology were reputed to be the sons of some of their gods. It was not a new thing, at that time, to believe a man to have been celestially begotten; the intercourse of gods with women was then a matter of familiar opinion.

Excerpts from Part One of The Age of Reason

Nothing that is here said can apply, even with the most distant disrespect, to the real character of Jesus Christ. He was a virtuous and an amiable man. The morality that he preached and practised was of the most benevolent kind; and though similar systems of morality had been preached by Confucious, and by some of the Greek philosophers, many, many years before; by the Quakers since; and by many good men in all ages, it has not been exceeded by any.

Jesus Christ wrote no account of himself, of his birth, parentage, or anything else; not a line of what is called the New Testament is of his own writing. The history of him is altogether the work of other people; and as to the account given of his resurrection and ascension, it was the necessary counterpart to the story of his birth. His historians, having brought him into the world in a supernatural manner, were obliged to take him out again in the same manner, or the first part of the story must have fallen to the ground.

The wretched contrivance with which this latter part is told exceeds every thing that went before it. The first part, that of the miraculous conception, was not a thing that admitted of publicity; and therefore the tellers of this part of the story had this advantage, that though they might not be credited, they could not be detected. They could not be expected to prove it, because it was not one of those things that admitted of proof, and it was impossible that the person of whom it was told could prove it himself.

But the resurrection of a dead person from the grave, and his ascension through the air, is a thing very different as to the evidence it admits of, to the invisible conception of a child in the womb. The resurrection and ascension, supposing them to have taken place, admitted of public and ocular demonstration, like that of the ascension of a balloon or the sun at noon-day, to all Jerusalem at least.

A thing which everybody is required to believe requires that the proof and evidence of it should be equal to all, and universal; and as the public visibility of this last related act was the only evidence that could give sanction to the former part, the whole of it falls to the ground, because that evidence never was given. Instead of this, a small number of persons, not more than eight or nine, are introduced as proxies for the whole world to say they saw it, and all the rest of the world are called upon to believe it.

But it appears that Thomas did not believe the resurrection, and, as they say, would not believe without having ocular and manual demonstration himself. So *neither will I*, and the reason is equally as good for me, and for every other person, as for Thomas.

It is in vain to attempt to palliate or disguise this matter. The story, so far as relates to the supernatural part, has every mark of fraud and imposition stamped upon the face of it. Who were the authors of it is as impossible for us now to know, as it is for us to be assured that the books in which the account is related were written by the persons whose names they bear; the best surviving evidence we now have respecting this affair is the Jews. They are regularly descended from the people who lived in the times this resurrection is said to have happened, and they say, *it is not true*. It has long appeared to me a strange inconsistency to cite the Jews as proof of the truth of the story. It is just the same as if a man were to say, I will prove the truth of what I have told you by producing the people who say it is false.

That such a person as Jesus Christ existed, and that he was crucified, which was the mode of execution of that day, are historical relations strictly within the limits of probability. He preached most excellent morality and the equality of man; but he preached also against the corruption and avarice of the Jewish priests, and this brought upon him the hatred and vengeance of the whole order of priesthood.

The accusation which those priests brought against him was that of sedition and conspiracy against the Roman government, to which the Jews were then subject and tributary; and it is not improbable that the Roman government might have some secret apprehensions of the effects of his doctrine, as well as the Jewish priests; neither is it improbable that Jesus Christ had in contemplation the delivery of the Jewish nation from the bondage of the Romans. Between the two, however, this virtuous reformer and revolutionist lost his life.

FURTHER EXCERPTS FROM *A Dissertation on First Principles of Government*

A nation, though continually existing, is continually in a state of renewal and succession. It is never stationary. Every day produces new births, carries minors forward to maturity, and old persons from the stage. In this ever running flood of generations there is no part superior in authority to another. Could we conceive an idea of superiority in any, at what point of time, or in what century of the world, are we to fix it? To what cause are we to ascribe it? By what evidence are we to prove it? By what criterion are we to know it?

A single reflection will teach us that our ancestors, like ourselves, were but tenants for life in the great freehold of rights. The fee-absolute was not in them, it is not in us, it belongs to the whole family of man through all ages. If we think otherwise than this we think either as slaves or as tyrants. As slaves, if we think that any former generation had a right to bind us; as tyrants, if we think that we have authority to bind the generations that are to follow.

•

Personal rights, of which the right of voting for representatives is one, are a species of property of the most sacred kind: and he that would employ his pecuniary property, or presume upon the influence it gives him, to rob or dispossess another of his property or rights, uses that pecuniary property as he would use fire-arms, and merits to have it taken from him.

Inequality of rights is created by a combination in one part of the community to exclude another part from its rights. Whenever it be made an article of a constitution, or a law, that the right of voting, or of electing and being elected, shall appertain exclusively to persons possessing a certain quantity of property, be it little or much, it is a combination of the persons possessing that quantity to exclude those who do not possess the same quantity. It is investing themselves with powers as a self-created part of society, to the exclusion of the rest.

It is always to be taken for granted, that those who oppose an equality of rights never mean the exclusion should take place on themselves; and in this view of the case, pardoning the vanity of the thing, aristocracy is a subject of laughter. This self-soothing vanity is encouraged by another idea not less selfish, which is that the opposers conceive they are playing a safe game, in which there is a chance to gain and nothing to lose; that at any rate the doctrine of equality includes *them,* and that if they cannot get more rights than those whom they oppose and would exclude, they shall not have less.

When we speak of right we ought always to unite with it the idea of duties; rights become duties by reciprocity. The right which I enjoy becomes my duty to guarantee it to another, and he to me; and those who violate the duty justly incur a forfeiture of the right.

In a political view of the case, the strength and permanent security of government is in proportion to the number of people interested in supporting it. The true policy therefore is to interest the whole by an equality of rights, for the danger arises from exclusions. It is possible to exclude men from the right of voting, but it is impossible to exclude them from the right of rebelling against that exclusion; and when all other rights are taken away the right of rebellion is made perfect.

While men could be persuaded they had no rights, or that rights appertained only to a certain class of men, or that government was a thing existing in right of itself, it was not difficult to govern them authoritatively. The ignorance in which they were held, and the superstition in which they were instructed, furnished the means of doing it.

But when the ignorance is gone, and the superstition with it; when they perceive the imposition that has been acted upon them; when they reflect that the cultivator and the manufacturer are the primary means of all the wealth that exists in the world, beyond what nature spontaneously produces; when they begin to feel their consequences by their usefulness, and their right as members of society, it is then no longer possible to govern them as before. The fraud once detected cannot be re-acted. To attempt is to provoke derision, or invite destruction.

●

A declaration of rights is not a creation of them, nor a donation of them. It is a manifest of the principle by which they exist, followed by a detail of what the rights are; for every civil right has a natural right for its foundation, and it includes the principle of a reciprocal guarantee of those rights from man to man. As, therefore, it is impossible to discover any origin of rights otherwise than in the origin of man, it consequently follows that rights appertain to man in right of his existence only, and must therefore be equal to every man.

The principle of an equality of rights is clear and simple. Every man can understand it, and it is by understanding his rights that he learns his duties; for where the rights of men are equal, every man must finally see the necessity of protecting the rights of others as the most effectual security for his own.

But if, in the formation of a constitution, we depart from the principle of equal rights, or attempt any modification of it, we plunge into a labyrinth of difficulties from which there is no way out but by retreating. Where are we to stop? Or by what princ ple are we to find out the point to stop at, that shall discriminate between men of the same country, part of whom shall we free, and the rest not?

EXCERPTS FROM *A Letter to George Washington*

The character which Mr Washington has attempted to act in the world is a sort of nondesdribable, chameleon-colored thing called *prudence*. It is, in many cases, a substitute for principle, and is so nearly allied to hypocrisy that it easily slides into it. His genius for prudence furnished him in this instance with an expedient that served, as is the natural and general character of all expedients, to diminish the embarrassments of the moment and multiply them afterwards.

●

The Washington Administration shows great desire that the treaty between France and the United States be preserved. Nobody can doubt their sincerity upon this matter. There is not a British minister, a British merchant, or a British agent or a sailor in America, that does not anxiously wish the same thing. The treaty with France serves now as a passport to supply England with naval stores and other articles of American produce, while the same articles, when coming to France, are made contraband or seizable by Jay's Treaty with England. The treaty with France says that neutral ships are neutral property, and thereby gives protection to English property on board American ships; and Jay's Treaty delivers up French property on board American ships to be seized by the English. It is too paltry to talk of faith, of national honor, and of the preservation of treaties, while such a barefaced treachery as this stares the world in the face.

In what a fraudulent light must Mr Washington's character appear in the world, when his declarations and his conduct are compared together!

●

It is laughable to hear Mr Washington talk of his *sympathetic feelings*, who has always been remarked, even among his friends, for not having any. He has, however, given no proofs of any to me. As to the pompous encomiums he so liberally pays to himself on the score of the American Revolution, the reality of them may be questioned; and since he has forced them so much into notice, it is fair to examine his pretensions.

A stranger might be led to suppose, from the egotism with which Mr Washington speaks, that himself, and himself only, had generated, conducted, completed, and established the Revolution: in fine, that it was all his own doing.

In the first place, as to the political part, he had no share in it; and, therefore the whole of *that* is out of the question with respect to him. There remains, then, only the military part; and it would have been prudent in Mr Washington not to have awakened inquiry upon that subject. Fame then was cheap; he enjoyed it cheaply; and nobody was disposed to take away the laurels that, whether they were acquired or not, had been given.

Mr Washington's merit consisted in constancy. But constancy was the common virtue of the Revolution. Who was there that was constant? I know but of one military defection, that of Arnold; and I know of no political defection among those who made themselves eminent when the Revolution was formed by the Declaration of Independence. Even Silas Deane, though he attempted to defraud, did not betray.

But when we speak of military character, something more is to be understood than constancy; and something more *ought* to be understood than the Fabian system of *doing nothing*. The nothing part can be done by anybody. Old Mrs Thompson, the housekeeper of headquarters (who threatened to make the sun and the wind shine through Rivington of New York), could not have done it as well as Mr Washington.

EXCERPTS FROM ESSAYS BY PAINE PUBLISHED IN *Prospect*

Those who most believe the Bible are those who know least about it.

God has not given us reason for the purpose of confounding us.

●

Jesus never speaks of Adam, of the Garden of Eden, nor of what is called the fall of man.

●

The Bible has been received by Protestants on the authority of the Church of Rome.

●

Do Christians not see that their own religion is founded on a human sacrifice? Many thousands of human sacrifices have since been offered on the altar of the Christian Religion.

●

The Cain and Abel of Genesis appear to be no other than the ancient Egyptian story of Typhon and Osiris, the darkness and the light, which answered very well as allegory without being believed as fact.

●

Another observation upon the story of Babel is, the inconsistence of it with respect to the opinion that the Bible is the word of God given for the information of mankind; for nothing could so effectually prevent such a word being known by mankind as confounding their language.

●

We admire the wisdom of the ancients, yet they had no bibles, nor books, called revelation. They cultivated the reason that God gave them, studied him in his works, and rose to eminence.

●

The remark of the Emperor Julian is worth observing. 'If,' said he, 'there ever had been or could be a Tree of Knowledge, instead of God forbidding man to eat thereof, it would be that of which he would order him to eat the most.'

For several centuries past the dispute has been about doctrines. It is now about fact.

•

The same degree of hearsay evidence, and that at third and fourth hand, would not, in a court of justice, give a man title to a cottage, and yet the priests of this profession presumptuously promise their deluded followers the kingdom of Heaven.

•

The Book of Job belongs either to the ancient Persians, the Chaldeans, or the Egyptians; because the structure of it is consistent with the dogma they held, that of a good and evil spirit, called in Job God and Satan, existing as distinct and separate beings, and it is not consistent with any dogma of the Jews. . . . The God of the Jews was the God of everything. All good and evil came from him. According to Exodus it was God, and not the Devil, that hardened Pharaoh's heart. According to the Book of Samuel, it was an evil spirit from God that troubled Saul. And Ezekiel makes God say, in speaking of the Jews, 'I gave them statutes that were not good, and judgments by which they should not live.' . . . As to the precepts, principles, and maxims in the Book of Job, they show that the people abusively called the heathen, in the books of the Jews, had the most sublime ideas of the Creator, and the most exalted devotional morality. It was the Jews who dishonored God. It was the Gentiles who glorified him.

Bibliography

ADAMS, CHARLES FRANCIS. *The Works of John Adams, with Life.* 8 vols. Boston, 1850 – 56.

ADAMS, HENRY. *History of the United States, 1801 – 17.* 9 vols. New York, 1889 – 91.

———. *Life of Albert Gallatin.* New York, 1879.

ADAMS, JAMES TRUSLOW. *The Living Jefferson.* New York, 1936.

ADAMS, JOHN. *The Diary and Autobiography of John Adams.* Boston, 1961.

ADAMS, RANDOLPH G. *History of the Foreign Policy of the United States.* New York, 1924.

ALDRIDGE, ALFRED OWEN. *Man of Reason: The Life of Thomas Paine.* London, 1959.

AVERY, ELROY. *History of the United States.* 7 vols. Cleveland, 1907 – 10.

BANCROFT, GEORGE. *History of the United States.* 6 vols. New York, 1883 – 85.

337

Appendix

BEARD, CHARLES A. AND MARY R. *The Rise of American Civilization.* 3 vols. New York, 1933 – 39.

BECKER, CARL L. *The Declaration of Independence.* New York, 1922.

BEMIS, SAMUEL FLAGG. *The Diplomacy of the American Revolution.* New York, 1935.

——. *Jay's Treaty.* New York, 1923.

BEVERIDGE, ALBERT J. *The Life of John Marshall.* 4 vols. Boston, 1916.

BIDDLE, CHARLES. *The Autobiography of Charles Biddle.* Philadelphia, 1883.

BISSET, EDWARD. *The Life of Edmund Burke.* London, 1798.

BOGART, ERNEST L. *An Economic History of the American People.* New York, 1930.

BOWERS, CLAUDE G. *Jefferson and Hamilton.* Boston, 1925.

BRANT, IRVING. *James Madison.* 6 vols. New York, 1941 – 61.

BROADLEY, A. M. *Napoleon and the Invasion of England.* 2 vols. London, 1908.

BURNETT, E. C. *The Continental Congress.* New York, 1941.

BYRNE, PATRICK. *Lord Edward Fitzgerald.* Dublin, 1955.

CARLILE, RICHARD. *The Life of Thomas Paine.* London, 1819 – 20.

CHALMERS, GEORGE [Francis Oldys]. *The Life of Thomas Paine.* London, 1791.

CHANNING, EDWARD. *History of the United States.* 6 vols. New York, 1905 – 25.

CHEETHAM, JAMES. *The Life of Thomas Paine.* New York, 1807, 1809.

CLARKE, H. H. *Thomas Paine: Representative Selections.* New York, 1961.

COBBAN, A. *A History of Modern France.* 2 vols. New York, 1960.

COMMAGER, HENRY STEELE. *Documents of American History.* New York, 1934.

CONNEL, J. M. *At the Sign of the Bull, Lewes, with an Account of Thomas Paine's Residence in Lewes.* London, 1924.

CONWAY, MONCURE D. *The Life of Thomas Paine.* 2 vols. New York, 1892.

——. *The Writings of Thomas Paine.* 2 vols. New York, 1894 – 96.

CORWIN, EDWARD SAMUEL. *French Policy and the American Alliance.* Princeton, 1916.

CRAGG, G. R. *The Church and the Age of Reason.* London, 1961.

CRANE, VERNER W. *Benjamin Franklin and a Rising People.* New York, 1954.

CRESSON, WILLIAM PENN. *James Monroe.* New York, 1946.

CROLY, GEORGE. *Memoirs of the Political Life.* London, 1840.

CUNNINGHAM, N. N. JR., *The Jeffersonian Republicans.* New York 1958.

DICKSON, HAROLD E. *John Wesley Jarvis.* New York, 1949.

DORCHESTER, DANIEL. *Christianity in the United States.* New York, 1895.

DOS PASSOS, JOHN. *The Head and Heart of Thomas Jefferson.* New York, 1954.

DUMONT, ETIENNE. *Souvenirs sur Mirabeau.* Paris, 1951.

DUVAL, GEORGE. *Histoire de la littérature révolutionnaire.* Paris, 1879.

EAST, ROBERT A. *Business Enterprise in the American Revolutionary Era.* New York, 1938.

EGERTON, HUGH EDWARD. *Causes and Character of the American Revolution.* Oxford, 1923.

FAULKNER, HAROLD U. *American Economic History.* New York, 1924.

FAY, B. *The Revolutionary Spirit in France and America.* London, 1927.

FISH, CARL R. *American Diplomacy.* New York, 1937.

FISHER, H. A. L. *Napoleon.* London, 1913.

FORD, PAUL L. *The True George Washington.* New York, 1896.

FOX BOURNE, H. R. *The Life of John Locke.* 2 vols. London, 1876.

FRANKLIN, BENJAMIN. *Works.* ed. A. H. SMYTH. 10 vols. New York, 1907 – 10.

FREEMAN, DOUGLAS SOUTHALL. *George Washington.* 6 vols. New York, 1948 – 54.

GAGNON, P. A. *France Since 1789.* New York, 1964.

GIMBEL, RICHARD. *Bibliographic Check List of* Common Sense. New Haven, 1956.

GOLDSMITH, LEWIS. *Secret History of the Cabinet of Napoleon.* London, 1810.

GORDY, JOHN P. *Political History of the United States.* 2 vols. New York, 1902.

GOTTSCHALK, LOUIS. *The Era of the Revolution.* New York, 1929.

GUEDELLA, PHILIP. *Fathers of the Revolution.* New York, 1926.

GUERARD, A. *France, a Modern History.* Ann Arbor, 1959.

Appendix

HAMILTON, J. C. *History of the Republic of the United States.* 7 vols. New York, 1857 – 64.

HENDRICK, BURTON J. *The Lees of Virginia.* Boston, 1935.

HOCKETT, HOMER CARY. *Political and Social Growth of the American People.* New York, 1941.

JAMESON, JOHN F. *The American Revolution Considered as a Social Movement.* Princeton, 1926.

JAY, WILLIAM. *Life of John Jay.* 2 vols. New York, 1833.

JEFFERSON, THOMAS. *Works.* ed. P. L. FORD. 12 vols. New York, 1904 – 5.

JOHNSON, WILLIS F. *America's Foreign Relations.* 2 vols. New York, 1916.

KERR, W. B. *The Reign of Terror.* New York, 1927.

KING, CHARLES R. *Life and Correspondence of Rufus King.* 2 vols. New York, 1895.

KIRCHEISEN, E. *Napoleon.* 9 vols. London, 1932.

KOCH, ADRIENNE. *Jefferson and Madison.* New York, 1950.

LANDOR, WALTER SAVAGE. *Complete Works.* ed. T. E. WELBY. 12 vols. London, 1927.

LASKI, H. J. *Political Thought in England from Locke to Bentham.* London, 1920.

LECKY, WILLIAM E. H. *The American Revolution, 1763 – 83.* New York, 1898.

LEFEBVRE, G. *The French Revolution.* 2 vols. London, 1963 – 64.
——. *The Thermidorians and the Directory.* London, 1964.

LEWIS, PAUL. *The Grand Incendiary: The Life of Samuel Adams.* New York, 1973.

LOCKE, JOHN. *Collected Works.* 9 vols. London, 1824.

MADISON, JAMES. *Writings.* ed. GAILLARD HUNT. 9 vols. New York, 1900 – 10.

MAHAN, A. T. *The Influence of Sea Power upon the French Revolution and Empire.* 2 vols. New York, 1893.

MAITLAND, FREDERIC W. *Constitutional History of England.* Cambridge, 1908.

MALONE, DUMAS. *Jefferson and His Time.* 3 vols. New York, 1948 – 54.

MARKHAM, F. M. *Napoleon.* New York, 1964.

MERRIAM, CHARLES E. *History of American Political Theories.* New York, 1903.

MONROE, JAMES. *The Autobiography of James Monroe.* eds. STUART G. BROWN and DONALD G. BAKER. New York, 1959.

MORTON, J. B. *The Bastille Falls*. New York, 1936.

NAMIER, L. B. *England in the Age of the American Revolution*. London, 1930.

NEVINS, ALLAN. *The American States During and After the Revolution, 1775 – 89*. New York, 1925.

NOYES, A. *Voltaire*. London, 1936.

PAINE, THOMAS. *Complete Writings*. ed. PHILIP S. FONER. New York, 1945.

PALMER, R. R., and COLTON, JOEL. *A History of the Modern World*. New York, 1965.

POLLARD, ALBERT F. *The Evolution of Parliament*, London, 1920.

REED, WILLIAM R. *The Life and Correspondence of Joseph Reed*. 2 vols. Philadelphia, 1847.

RICKMAN, CLIO. *Memoirs of the Life of Thomas Paine*. London, 1819.

ROBERTSON, C. H. *England Under the Hanoverians*. London, 1948.

ROBINSON, HOWARD. *Development of the British Empire*. Boston, 1936.

ROUSTAN, M. *The Pioneers of the French Revolution*. London, 1926.

RUSH, BENJAMIN. *A Memorial*. Philadelphia, 1905.

SAINT-GEORGES, DAVID DE. *Achille*. Paris, 1896.

SCHACHNER, NATHAN. *Thomas Jefferson*, 2 vols. New York, 1951.

SCHAPIRO, J. S. *Condorcet and the Rise of Liberalism*. London, 1934.

SEELEY, SIR JOHN R. *Growth of British Policy*. 2 vols. Cambridge, 1895.

SHERWIN, THOMAS. *Memoirs of the Life of Thomas Paine*. London, 1819.

SMELLIE, K. B. *Great Britain Since 1688*. Ann Arbor, 1962.

SMITH, PAGE. *John Adams*. 2 vols. New York, 1962.

SPARKS, JARED. *Diplomatic Correspondence*. 12 vols. Boston, 1829 – 30.

——. *Life of Gouverneur Morris*. 3 vols. Boston, 1832.

SPEARS, J. R. *The Story of the American Merchant Marine*. New York, 1918.

STEPHEN, L. *History of English Thought in the Eighteenth Century*. London, 1876.

STYRON, ARTHUR. *The Last of the Cocked Hats: James Monroe and the Virginia Dynasty*. New York, 1945.

THOMPSON, J. M. *The French Revolution*. New York, 1943.

——. *Napoleon Bonaparte.* New York, 1952.

——. *Robespierre.* 2 vols. New York, 1935.

TREVELYAN, SIR OTTO GEORGE. *The American Revolution.* 3 vols. London, 1905.

VAN DOREN, CARL. *Benjamin Franklin.* New York, 1938.

WATSON, J. S. *The Reign of George III, 1760 – 1815.* London, 1960.

WHARTON, FRANCIS, ed., *Revolutionary Diplomatic Correspondence.* 6 vols. Washington, 1889.

WILLARD, M. W. *Letters on the American Revolution.* Boston, 1925.

WINSOR, JUSTIN. *The Narrative and Critical History of America.* 8 vols. Boston, 1884 – 89.

YOUNG, NORWOOD. *George Washington.* New York, 1932.

Index